Chicago Christmas

Chicago Christmas

One Hundred Years of Christmas Memories

JIM BENES

Cornerstone Press Chicago

Chicago, Illinois

Published by Cornerstone Press Chicago
939 W. Wilson Ave.
Chicago, IL 60640
www.cornerstonepress.com
cspress@jpusa.org

Cover color enhancement by Terry Wheeler
Cover and book design by Hugo Thysse
Cover photo from the Chicago Historical Society. ICHI 16279. Used with permission.

Printed in the United States of America

Decade photo credits:

1900 Caroling around the piano from the collection of Terry Wheeler. Used with permission.
1910 Santa will come from the collection of David R. Phillips. Used with permission.
1920 Children looking in store window. Same as cover photo. Used with permission.
1930 Boy looking up chimney. University of Illinois at Chicago, the University Library, Jane Addams Memorial Collection, Wallace Kirkland Papers. JAMC neg 2268. Used with permission.
1940 Family snapshot from the collection of Terry Wheeler. Used with permission.
1950 Hull House party. University of Illinois at Chicago, the University Library, Jane Addams Memorial Collection, Wallace Kirkland Papers. JAMC neg 2269. Used with permission.
1960 Little girl on Santa's lap from the private collection of Jim Benes. Used with permission.
1970 Used Christmas cards being collected, 1973. Archdiocese of Chicago's Joseph Cardinal Bernardin Archives & Records Center. Used with permission.
1980 Cambodian refugee first Christmas, 1981. From the private collection of Stephen and Phannary Mayer. Used with permission.
1990 Costumed girl in front of tree from the private collection of Mike and Karen Warne. Used with permission.

Library of Congress Cataloging-in-Publication Data

Benes, Jim.
  Chicago Christmas : one hundred years of Christmas memories / Jim Benes.
      p. cm.
  Includes bibliographical references.
  ISBN 0-940895-45-5
    1. Christmas--Illinois--Chicago--History--20th century. 2. Chicago (Ill.)--Social life
and customs. I. Title

GT4986.A2 I34 2000
394.2663'0977311--dc21

                                                        00-059626

For my wife Andi and our little boy Jamie,
who make every Christmas so wonderful. . .

C O N T E N T S

Christmas Snapshots

In our family, Christmas has always been a time to notice the changes in our lives. At first these changes were recorded for posterity with a box camera. Later we used a brownie, then a Polaroid, then home movies, and, finally, videotape. Once we even used a wire recorder to record the sounds of our family at Christmastime. And later, a tape recorder served the same purpose.

We didn't think, at the time, that these snapshots of our family celebrating the holiday would become a visual history of our brood. Indeed, we never even considered that fact. But, as the years passed, we realized that the photos, films, videos, and audio recordings actually provided a signpost, a way to measure ourselves over the years.

Our first family Christmas party was in 1939, the year my parents moved from an apartment and bought a home in the northwest edge of the city of Chicago. They paid, I think, $3,400 for that five-room bungalow.

My folks were the first on my mother's side of the family to own a home, and so it seemed natural and logical to have a family party on Christmas Eve. Everyone came. My mother's father (my grandfather), and her brothers and sisters (my uncles and aunts). And, of course, my mom and dad and my baby brother. Not many spouses and not many cousins, because most of my aunts and uncles had not yet married. One of my uncles appeared in costume as Santa Claus and carried presents for and from everyone. I remember getting a small Lionel electric train with a set of tracks. My uncles helped me open the gift, then took the train and tracks into a bedroom to set it up for me. The bedroom was small and after they got in there, there was no room for me. I had to wait until the next day to play with my train.

As the years passed, the family snapshots at Christmas reflected relatives driving up to my parents' home with a car filled with gifts. They not only show the different automobiles they drove over the years, but tell us what kind of weather we were having. Sometimes there was lots of snow; sometimes no snow at all. Sometimes we could see how cold it was by how bundled up we were. Other times we knew it was a rather warm

Christmas Eve because my aunts and uncles weren't wearing scarves or gloves and their coats were open.

These Christmastime snapshots reflected the marriages of aunts and uncles, the additions of cousins, the absence of a couple of uncles during the World War II years (including the one who posed as Santa), and their return, thankfully, following the end of the war.

In one picture there is an upright, floor-model radio in the corner of the living room, next to the Christmas tree. Years later there appeared a television set in the place where the radio once stood. The once-proud brown mohair davenport gave way to a more modern sectional sofa. A 1930s floor lamp became a 1950s pole lamp. Much later we see a videotape recorder on top of the television set, and more recent snapshots show some of the kids of the cousins at a computer.

Over the years our snapshots show the family expanding, kids growing up, and relatives maturing. Cousins got married, had their own children, and, as often happens, could come only every other year because they were attending Christmas parties given by their spouse's families. And, of course, taking another set of snapshots.

As we look back at these images, we find much happiness at seeing the family together at the end of each year. And, too often, we are saddened to note the absence of a family member who has died.

Family snapshots are a treasured and valuable history. They record not only the changes that occur within the family, but outside of the family as well. They enable us to look back at times that are both sweet and bittersweet.

My friend Jim Benes tells, in this treasured book, the story of a city and its people over the past one hundred years. It is, of course, the snapshot of a family, the citizens of Chicago and its suburbs, told in a marvelous collection of Christmastime events from the last century.

—Chuck Schaden
Radio Historian/Broadcaster

ACKNOWLEDGMENTS

It has taken many good friends and co-workers to make this project the modest success it's been since *Christmas Past* first aired in December of 1980 (anything that's been on the radio for twenty years can be classified as a success of some degree). It has also taken friends and co-workers to turn the program into this book, and thanks are owed to all. At WBBM radio, "Doctor" Lenny Kaye played an invaluable role in scoring the early radio programs. Denise Longley Hines and Anita Guerrero helped out in the production. Al Rosen and Mario Aceto provided technical expertise. Alan Bickley, that man of so many voices, was my partner for many years, narrating excerpts from newspapers and fully utilizing his immense talent for oral interpretation. Also fulfilling that role have been Don Mellema, David Roe, Craig Dellimore, Julie Mann and once, long ago, business editor Len Walter was part of the team.

Thanks do not stop there. So many people in the WBBM newsroom have been supportive of *Christmas Past*. They have been fans, and they have offered their support through the years. Among them are former assistant news director Deidra White, who is perhaps the biggest fan of *Christmas Past*, and the late reporter Ted Hampson, who once told me he thought *Christmas Past* was the best program we had on the air. Thanks, too, go to Rich King, Bernie Tafoya, Kris Kridel, Regine Schlesinger and Felicia Middlebrooks for their valuable opinions, and to former news director Chris Berry, who urged that this all be turned into the book you are reading. Thanks, too to current operations director Georgeann Herbert, who has carried on with the tradition.

Most of the research for the radio/book project was carried out at the Hinsdale Public Library, where Dotty Elmendorf was the first person who took an active interest in helping locate the needed materials. In recent years, all of the people in the reference department have come to know me and to help out with valuable suggestions. Thanks, then, to Susan McNeil-Marshall, Laura Jensen, Ravi Shenoy, Cathy Tuttrup, Janet Widdel, Dianne Brooks, Anne-Marie Suidzinski, Debra Somchay, Rose Cook, Tom Bell and Chris Keefe. A great big *thank you*, as well, to Jack Hurwitz, the well-respected director of the library.

Thanks go to my wife, Andrea Wiley, who has served as editor of first resort for the radio series and the book, as consultant and as patient companion through it all. Thanks, too, go to Linda Jones, the head of the Journalism Department at Roosevelt University, for her help and encouragement. And a most special *thank you* to Jane Hertenstein, my editor at Cornerstone Press Chicago, who enthusiastically embraced this project and spent long, diligent hours seeing it through. Without her and the able assistance of Sally Watkins and Tara Anderson, this book wouldn't have happened.

As the book project took shape and grew, so too did the number of people who provided valuable assistance with editorial and photo research. Thanks, then to the helpful people in the library and in the photo reproduction lab at the Chicago Historical Society; to Dave Phillips for allowing us to use selections from the wonderful collection at the Chicago Architectural Society; to Suzanne Burris at the archives of the Burlington Northern & Santa Fe Railroad; to Julie Satzik at the Archdiocese of Chicago's Archives & Records Center; to Steffani Francis of the Chicago Coalition for the Homeless; to Pat Bukunas of the University of Illinois at Chicago's Special Collections; to Marshall Field's and assistant manager and archive specialist Tony Jahn, who helped in the research on Christmas at Chicago's premier department store; to Bert Gazmen of Lyon & Healy for permission to use the ad for that 1930s piece of furniture I think most of us would love to have in our living rooms, the Philco radio-bar; to the staff at the National Vietnam Veterans Art Museum in Chicago, Illinois; to Mark Busch at Press Republican Newspapers; and especially to Terry Wheeler and Hugo Thysse for their work in scanning and reproducing the photos herein.

A debt of gratitude is owed to all the reporters who ever worked during the Christmas season or covered Christmas, some of whose work you'll see in these pages, and to the people at Chicago's newspapers who helped us gather it and gave permission to use it. Thanks, then, to Sandy Spikes and Associate Editor Joe Leonard at the *Chicago Tribune*, at the *Chicago Sun-Times* James Strong and Trina Cieply, and to Joslyn DiPasalegne at the *Chicago Defender*. Thanks, too, to the Hearst newspapers, the Associated Press, United Press International, and Reuters, all of whom have given their permission for the use of material.

Every effort has been made to secure permission to reproduce copyrighted material. If there has been any omission, it is unintentional and will be corrected in subsequent editions of this book.

Chicago Christmas

INTRODUCTION

Once upon a Christmastime, in 1979 to be exact, I found myself working the editor's desk at Chicago's WBBM Newsradio. This is not unexpected, nor is it unusual. Reporters, writers, and editors in all daily media often must take their holidays whenever they can.

Working on Christmas Day, however, often proves to be an unusually difficult task. Most people, after all, are home with their families enjoying the holiday. The courts are closed, so are most businesses, and aside from the rare breaking or continuing story, there usually isn't much news.

With this in mind, I approached WBBM's then news director, John Hultman, with a proposal: why not let me put together a series of Christmas specials, summing up not only the news, but holiday stories and trends of past Christmas seasons.

John agreed, and radio's *Christmas Past* was born. The research involved hours of staring at microfilms of old newspapers. Instead of being a tedious and laborious job, this activity became an enjoyable hobby, even a kind of treasure hunt. Many were the moving stories of Christmastime that I found in those pages; many were the now forgotten details of "history in the making," or some unusual or enticing nugget of trivia. Much of the writing was wonderful, but some of it was strange to the eye and ear of the late twentieth century. These are the Christmas memories not of any single person, but of the people who have lived in the Chicago area over the past hundred years or so. Much of it was the kind of stuff you'd want to share with your friends. My colleagues at WBBM have long urged me to do just that, to adapt my *Christmas Past* radio shows into book form.

This is not a scholarly endeavor to explain why certain things happened at certain times, or what effect, if any, world events have had on Christmas celebrations in Chicago—or vice versa. But rather, this is a sort of scrapbook of Christmases long ago, an evocation of Christmas memories not unlike those described by Charles Dickens in "A Christmas Chapter" in *The Pickwick Papers:*

> Numerous indeed are the hearts to which Christmas brings a brief season of happiness and enjoyment. How many families, whose members have been dispersed and scattered far and wide, in the restless struggles of life, are then reunited, and meet once again in that

happy state of companionship and mutual good-will, which is a source of such pure and unalloyed delight, and one so incompatible with the cares and sorrows of the world, that the religious belief of the most civilized nations, and the rude traditions of the roughest savages, alike number it among the first joys of a future condition of existence, provided for the blest and happy! How many old recollections, and how many dormant sympathies, does Christmas time awaken!

We write these words now, many miles distant from the spot at which, year after year, we met on that day, a merry and joyous circle. Many of the hearts that throbbed so gaily then, have ceased to beat; many of the looks that shone so brightly then, have ceased to glow; the hands we grasped, have grown cold; the eyes we sought, have hid their luster in the grave; and yet the old house, the room, the merry voices and smiling faces, the jest, the laugh, the most minute and trivial circumstances connected with those happy meetings, crowd upon our mind at each recurrence of the season, as if the last assemblage had been but yesterday! Happy, happy Christmas, that can win us back to the delusions of our childish days; that can recall to the old man the pleasures of his youth; that can transport the sailor and the traveller, thousands of miles away, back to his own fire-side and his quiet home!

The book is organized along chronological lines—but only partly so. To examine each and every Christmas season of the past century would result in a tome much thicker than the one you now hold in your hands. So, some of the book is organized topically, to compress the wide sweep of certain traditions or consecutive years that go together well.

This is not a book meant to be read at one sitting. It is one, I hope, you will find a place for next to that favorite anthology of Christmas stories, one that you can go to from time to time or year to year to find something interesting and old (but new to you), or something nostalgic. You might even want to jot down some of your own Christmas memories in the blank pages at the end.

And may they all be merry Christmas memories!

1900-1909

1900: Turn of the Century

Just exactly when does one century turn into another? At what point does a new millennium begin? Does it begin with the turn of a year ending in "99" or "00"? To those of a mathematical or scientific mind, it is clear that the counting system begins with one. To most of us all those zeroes at the end of the new year are reason to celebrate.

In December 1999, however, there was an awful lot of planning and celebrating of the new millennium with the arrival of January 1, 2000 despite the protests of those who argued that the new millennium really wouldn't arrive for another 365 days..

This question was not an issue to the editors of the *Chicago Tribune,* who reckoned that December 25, 1900, was the last Christmas of the nineteenth century. In many ways, that day was like any Christmas Day. In many ways it was also different.

Here is how the *Tribune* reported that day, complete with the multiple headlines that were the journalistic fashion back then:

LAST CHRISTMAS IN THE CENTURY
Chicago Will Celebrate the Day in Elaborate Manner Fitting the Occasion

---

FEAST FOR EVERY PERSON
All Routine Business Throughout the City Suspended,
but Santa Claus Works Overtime

Under the Tree 1900

Many toys at the turn of the century are familiar to us today, others are not.

The Frank Brothers' store at 138-44 State St. advertised all iron velocipedes (known today as tricycles) for 98¢ apiece. Children's sleighs were 15¢. Dolls cost 19¢, or 25¢ if they had movable joints, or 35¢ if their eyes closed.

The Fair Store advertised mechanical toy train sets that ranged in price from 45¢ cents to $15.00. There were footballs (65¢ to $4.00), bicycles ($10.00 to $25.00), and toy tool chests (25¢ to $15.00). The Fair boasted a wide selection of jointed dolls in fancy gowns. They cost anywhere from 25¢ to $10.00. Tea sets could be had for as little as a dime, or as much as $6.00. Sleighs ranged from 18¢ to $5.00.

Hillman's Store was selling costumes: soldier, policeman, or fireman suits from 12¢ to 89¢ apiece.

For mom and dad, Carson Pirie Scott & Co. reduced $25.00 jackets and cloaks to $14.75. Marshall Field's advertised marble statuary and Christmas slippers and Lyon & Healy was selling gramophones for $5.00.

GAYETY IN EVERY HOUSE

County Institutions, Hospitals, Orphan Asylums, and Prisons All Will Furnish Special Programs

MUSIC IN THE CHURCHES

Good Christmas weather will prevail on Tuesday (today). There will be some sunshine and some cloudiness, with probably a few snow flurries. It will continue cold, the temperature ranging from 18 to 20 degrees above zero, with fresh westerly Winds. (Henry J. Cox, Professor of Meteorology, United States Weather Bureau.)

Thousands of Chicagoans will hallow Christmas by brightening with charitable effort the lives of their less fortunate fellows. I suggest that they go personally and carry their gifts to the families and individuals with whose worthiness they are satisfied. The giving of food or money to beggars at the door is inadvisable in the vast majority of cases. On Christmas day so many public dinners are served by charitable institutions that no worthy person need go hungry. (Ernest P. Bicknell, General Superintendent Chicago Bureau of Charities.)

I hope all persons who ask for food on Christmas day will be sent to Tatternall's, where the Salvation Army is prepared to feed, free of charge, 10,000 persons. No one will be turned away hungry. Only in case a person cannot reach any of the free dinners in the city would I advise the feeding of beggars at the door. (George French, Colonel of Salvation Army.)

Christmas—old-fashioned and up-to-date, lavish and modest will be celebrated in Chicago today for the last time in the nineteenth century. The good cheer will be abroad in the city, in every nook and cranny, from the cribs in the lake to the prairies of Cicero, in the mansions, the tenements, the prisons, the hospitals, and among the homeless of the streets. No worthy person will be forgotten in the feasting and dispensation of the gifts of the day.

Not enough snow has fallen to furnish the Christmas upon which the old settlers are fond of dwelling, and Chicagoans will have to content

Salvation Army Christmas Dinner

themselves with a happy mean of crisp breezes and plenty of skating. The temperature will give ample reason for gathering close about the hearth fires within doors.

PROGRAM FOR THE DAY

The day will be spent in the exchange of gifts and greetings of good will, in religious worship, in feasting, and in recreations of limitless variety. The Puritans and the Cavaliers will be in evidence just as surely as in the days of broad brimmed hats, plumes and slashed doublets. For the former there will be as many church services as can be crowded into the holiday, while the latter will find opportunity for more than the usual amount of levity. The average citizen will attend church in the morning, dine in family reunion in the early afternoon, and devote the remainder of the day to social visits, the theater, and other entertainment. Friendships will be renewed, and about the homecoming of other thousands of absent ones a special gayety will reign.

ROUTINE ACTIVITY SUSPENDED

All routine activity has been suspended and in the hush which will prevail this morning in the city preparations will be underway for the sacrifice of many hecatombs* of turkeys and other various fowl. . . ." It is estimated that 350,000 turkeys will be consumed by the Americans. . . . South Water street looked like the track of a storm last night after the heads of families had made their inroads there and carried home the Christmas feast.

Christmas really began yesterday afternoon between 3 and 4 o'clock, when a great clatter of closing desk lids was heard through the city and the exodus from the big office buildings commenced. By 6 o'clock the workingmen were pouring into the streets and the holiday was fairly inaugurated. State street was a place of wild excitement.

SANTA CLAUS WORKS OVERTIME

Santa Claus arrived in town shortly after supper and worked slavishly all night in the distribution of his freight. He was found early this morning, and though worn out, consented to be interviewed.

"I have visited over 500,000 families in Chicago,"

said he, "and have a few visits to make yet today before I leave. I don't know when I have been so overworked. The chimneys are extremely smoky and sooty here." (Copyright *Chicago Tribune.* Used by permission.)

In other news at Christmastime 1900, John D. Rockefeller had just presented the University of Chicago with a gift of $1.5 million. The Chicago school system, on the other hand, was having financial difficulties. Teachers were not being paid on time because of a dispute between the city comptroller and Mayor Carter Harrison II. At the same time, a report to the British government by Britain's vice-consul in Chicago concluded: "The system of education in the U.S., especially in the city of Chicago, can be stated to be the most practical in the world for fitting the youth of the country for the battle of life."

The city council had just passed a bill banning prize fighting except in clubs that didn't charge admission. Friends of saloon and bowling alley owner Frederick Jaeger were passing around a petition, hoping to convince Mayor Harrison to restore Jaeger's liquor license. The mayor had just lifted it, following complaints from parishioners at the nearby Saint Vincent's Church at Webster and Sheffield. It was the culmination of a dispute going back six years. Father F. J. Walsh of Saint Vincent's voiced the parishioners' complaint: "The place has a tendency to attract young men, who go to bowl there, and while there, learn to drink. It also attracts a class of idlers, and as the saloon is the greatest enemy of the Irish Americans, we are naturally opposed to it. The bowling, especially on

---

*From *Webster's New World Dictionary:* 1. In ancient Greece, the slaughter of 100 cattle at one time as an offering to the gods; hence, 2. any large-scale slaughter of turkeys and various other fowl.

summer nights, disturbs the neighborhood. The noise can be heard in the church when the services are held."

Fourteen-year-old Wilfred Johnson of Evanston was arrested Christmas Eve for stealing a pocketbook and two bottles of perfume from William S. Lord's department store. At the police station, the boy began crying and said he wanted to give his mother and sister Christmas presents because they had always been good to him. The boy's father was out of work, and so he had no money. Evanston police sent the boy home after he promised to tell his father what had happened; Wilfred was afraid he'd get a whipping.

Just before Christmas there was an unusual sight on Michigan Avenue: Barney the elephant ambled down the avenue from Lincoln Park, and then up four flights of stairs at the Chicago Athletic Club to perform in the club's circus. In 1900 telephones were all the rage in gift giving. There was the newspaper ad that read:

> The New Year is ever the time for new and better resolves. Resolve to start the New Year right by installing a telephone in home or office. The cost is 16 cents per day and up. Ask about measured service. The Chicago Telephone Company.

Predictions For Christmas 2000

On Sunday, December 23rd, 1900 the *Chicago Tribune* carried an editorial which might possibly resonate with today's readers. The editorial decried the cynicism surrounding Christmas. It pointed out that gift giving had become a matter of calculation and vulgar display. The happy occasion had left people with empty pocketbooks, blasted expectations, and the pains associated with overeating and indigestion.

In its feature section, the *Tribune* gazed into its crystal ball and decided that by the year 2000 very few people would be celebrating Christmas at all. The *Tribune* writer believed Santa Claus would be passé, his reindeer extinct, and Christmas trees environmentally unsound because of depletion of the northern forests.

The writer believed the tradition of gift giving would be frowned upon as vulgar, and that all church creeds would be "as dead as was Santa Claus," replaced by the preaching of the fellowship of man. He foresaw

On Stage 1900

The grand opera season opened on Christmas Eve with Aida *sung by the Metropolitan English Grand Opera company at the Auditorium Theater.* Martha *was the opera matinee on Christmas Day, followed by* Bohemian Girl *in the evening.* Quo Vadis *was on the bill at the McVicker's. The Klaw & Erlanger Comedy Company was presenting the* Rogers Brothers in Central Park *at the Illinois. At the Studebaker Theater* Rob Roy *was performed by the Castle Square Opera Company.*

The vaudeville card at the Olympic included Prelle's talking dogs, the dancing Collinis, and Professor Hillman. Seats were 10¢, 20¢, or 30¢ apiece.

Top Songs 1900

The most popular songs of the day were "When You Were Sweet Sixteen," "Because," and "Ma Blushin' Rosie."

On the Table 1900

The Christmas turkey of 1900 cost 10¢ a pound at The Fair Store. The store also offered a Christmas dinner basket, including a nine-pound turkey, celery, sage, plum pudding, canned corn, raisins, a pound of mixed nuts, a quart of cranberries, minced meat, sweet potatoes, and olives, all for only $1.95.

Under the Tree 1902

Teddy bears, named in honor of President Theodore Roosevelt, made their first appearance on toy store shelves shortly after Mr. Roosevelt refused to shoot a bear cub during a hunting trip in Mississippi in the fall of 1902. A newspaper artist drew a cartoon of the incident, and it was widely circulated. Several stuffed animal makers claimed to have produced the first teddy bear, but only one, Morris Michtom of Brooklyn, wrote Mr. Roosevelt and received permission to use his name on the bears he was producing.

The clerks at The Fair Store at State and Adams sold men's fur-lined gloves for $3.75 to $5.25 in 1902; women's silk shawls cost $2.50 to $5.00; Irish linen table-cloths could be had for as little as $1.00. For little girls, the most expensive doll carriage, made of willow and rattan, cost $3.95; for little boys there were tool chests and tools made of wood that cost 20¢ to $2.25.

Browning, King & Co., Wabash and Madison, was selling knit gloves, silk handkerchiefs, and flannel nightshirts for $1.00 and $1.50. Ties, kid gloves, silk suspenders, and umbrellas could be purchased for 50¢.

The Hub Store had overcoats and suits on sale for $20.00. Men's and women's shoes were $2.25 a pair.

Chicago as being a metropolis of four million people and a seaport to the world. He predicted that noiseless, dustless electric transit at eighty miles-an-hour would extend the city's suburbs to a radius of fifty-five miles. He wrote of cars running on compressed air and rolling on quiet, rubber-rimmed wheels. Adequate light, power, and heat would be distributed to all homes from a centralized location. Social problems would have been solved, and money will have "ceased to be the end toward which all people moved, and with the opportunity gone for the hasty piling up of millions society was looking to economy."

No doubt the writer would be horrified if he could see what society is like today, one hundred years in the future.

1901: *Fires at Christmastime*

It happened a few days before the intensely cold Christmas of 1901. The kindergarten class waited, their rosy-cheeked faces aglow for the arrival of Santa Claus at the Perkins Bass Elementary School on West Sixty-seventh Street.

When the appointed moment arrived, the classroom was all ready: the decorations were in place, including the Christmas tree, complete with candles alight with flame. With a jolly "Ho! Ho! Ho!" in walked Santa Claus with a bag of gifts slung over his shoulder for the forty children.

The revelry went on for a time—and then it happened. With an unfortunate twist of the head, Santa Claus's beard became entangled in the Christmas tree. The flame from one of the candles leaped onto the beard, and it caught fire!

Santa shrieked and began tugging at his beard as the little children looked on in horror. The smell of burning hair filled the room. Finally, Santa was able to remove his beard, and the children were aghast. There, in Santa's fur coat, face blackened and eyebrows singed, was the children's teacher, Anna Nichols.

Although the tragedy of a school fire had been avoided, there was a tragedy of the soul at the Perkins Bass School that day. The *Chicago Inter Ocean* reported that the forty children were "disillusionized" and had to be once again persuaded that there really was a Santa Claus.

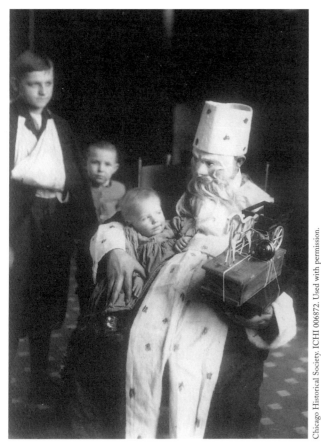

Christmas at County Hospital

The worst fire in Chicago's history, in terms of loss of life, was a holiday fire that occurred in 1903. In November of that year, the Iroquois Theater opened its doors, claiming to be "absolutely fireproof." A few days after Christmas, on December 30, with a standing-room-only holiday matinee crowd that included many parents and their children, a lamp somehow ignited a piece of drapery about fifteen feet above and to the rear of the stage. The asbestos curtain jammed while coming down. Despite the heroic efforts of comedian Eddie Foy to calm the crowd, there was a panic. Fire exits were poorly marked, locked, or frozen shut. Six hundred two people were killed, many of them trampled to death.

If there is any Christmas in Chicago's history that might have been utterly lacking in the joy of the season, it would have been the Christmas of 1871, which followed the Great Fire where as many as three hundred people died (some bodies were never found), 17,500 buildings destroyed, and one hundred thousand people were left homeless. That Yule fell on a Monday after a miserable weekend that brought cold and snow, and then rain, thunder, lightning, wind, and mud.

Yet, amid the aftermath of the calamity there was a great ray of hope, and the certainty that one did not need material wealth to share the joy of the season.

The main cause of household fires at Christmastime long ago was the practice of using real burning candles to decorate the tree. Chicago's fire chief urged aldermen to pass an ordinance requiring people who decorated trees with burning candles to purchase wire globes to protect the candles. The chief reported that nineteen fires had been started in Chicago in 1902 by candles burning on Christmas trees.

Chicago passed the most memorable Christmas in her history—not to be particularly memorable on account of any act of her own, but made so by the force of circumstance. To many persons it was inexpressibly sad, by the force of old associations. To all it had its somber side, in spite of all efforts to throw off the incubus and to forget the great calamity

Chicago Historical Society. ICHI 006872. Used with permission.

through which we have so lately passed. . . . There were the usual family gatherings except in occasional instances where families had been scattered and it was impossible to get domestic fragments together. The little ones were remembered, but not quite with the lavish generosity of former days. Friends remembered friends until the bottom of the purse was reached, and with many that happened very soon—much sooner than in former prosperous times. Where no gifts were exchanged, love and friendship were not less—perhaps for this reason they were stronger.

The Churches accustomed to such observances had their usual services, and the Sunday Schools even those in the burnt district had, or are to have, their festivals.

The day was characterized out-of-doors by subdued hilarity and quiet inebriation, and the harvest gathered in at night "by ye gentle policeman" was rather less than in former years. As a whole, the day was a success, and had less than ordinary drawbacks to happiness. A little more sunshine and happiness was shed into all lives, and a little more strength and courage gathered for a renewal of the battle with fate. (Copyright *Chicago Tribune*. Used by permission.)

A few days before Christmas, the Relief and Aid Society of Chicago issued a report saying that nearly $2.5 million had been sent to Chicago from all of the states and from abroad. The Society claimed to have helped eighteen thousand families so far, and aid continued to pour in daily: $1,000 from Dublin, Ireland; $1,472 from Bethlehem, Pennsylvania; more from the New York Chamber of Commerce, which reported that its Chicago relief fund had surpassed $996,000.

Chicago was rising from the ashes. Already, by Christmastime, the dining room at Anderson's European Hotel at 157 Dearborn Street had reopened, and an ad proclaimed it ready to feed the hungry multitude. Meals of roast beef, mutton, veal, or pork cost 15¢; roast chicken was 35¢ cents; roast turkey 40¢. Pure mocha coffee was 10¢.

1902: *Getting the Day Off*

In 1902 retail clerks in Chicago were fighting simply to get Christmas Day off. Even Scrooge begrudingly gave Bob Cratchit the day off. The *Chicago Tribune's* Christmas Day edition reported the hard fought victory:

HOLIDAY WON BY CLERKS

Retail clerks employed in the clothing stores of Chicago will enjoy a complete Christmas holiday for the first time. Reports received at the headquarters of their organization last evening showed that every merchant, with one exception, had yielded to the petitions of their men and would not open for business today.

Grocers and market men have agreed to close their stores before noon, and the majority of them will cease to do business by 10 o'clock. The smaller department stores in the outlying districts also will close.

Union clerks are jubilant over the victory secured by their organization, and they say it has strengthened their cause materially. While the employees have in some cases taken a day off on Christmas in former years it is said they lost a day's pay for their holiday. This year they will be allowed full wages for the day.

ONE FIRM BREAKS UNANIMITY

H. J. Conway, leader of the clerks union, said that

Stern Bros., Larrabee street and North avenue, was the only firm that had refused the request of the men, although competing stores in the neighborhood had agreed not to open their doors. Plans were discussed for picketing this store. There is a police station directly across the street, and the men were warned to be careful not to do anything that would cause them to end their holiday in a cell.

"This Christmas closing is the best thing we have gained since the retail clerks formed a union," said Mr. Conway. "When we first started out to get the stores to close we were met with much opposition. A number of merchants insisted they would do business the same as usual, and we thought we would have to spend the day appealing to their customers to stay away. Every merchant except Stern Bros. finally has agreed to close, and many of the employers went out and helped us."

TWO HOLIDAYS WITH FULL PAY

A notice was posted yesterday in the shops of the Morgan & Gardner Electric company, Shields avenue and Twenty-seventh street, that full holidays would be granted the employees on Christmas and New Year's, with full pay. The holiday has been granted in the past at the expense of the men. (Copyright *Chicago Tribune*. Used by permission.)

By all accounts 1902 was a banner Christmas for Chicago's merchants, closed or not on Christmas Day. Leon Mandel of Mandel Brothers estimated for the *Tribune* that Chicagoans had spent $14 million on their Christmas presents. Charles A. Stevens said, "Two million people shopped this year where 500,000 people formerly found themselves crowded. That accounts for the crush of holiday shopping. The season which ends with Christmas has been the most successful generally of any in the history of Chicago." It's no wonder the store owners felt magnanimity toward their employees.

1905: An American Always

The big news in Chicago's newspapers at Christmastime 1905 was the revolution then under way in Russia. "RUSSIA REEKS IN BLOOD; REBELLION FILLS EMPIRE" screamed the front-page headline of the *Chicago Inter Ocean* on Friday morning, December 22.

Under the Tree 1904

The Boston Store was selling rocking horses for 35¢ or 65¢. Double-runner skates were 38¢. The Fair Store offered a Ferris wheel with string clockwork for 39¢ and a printing press with type, cards, and ink for 59¢.

Marshall Field's had men's walking sticks for $1.50, $2.50, or $3.75 and women's silk petticoats for $5.00. A one hundred piece set of white and stippled gold patterned china sold for $37.75.

Under the Tree 1905, 1906

For $17.00 you could get you a Victor talking machine, which Lyon & Healy was advertising as "the most unselfish gift" of the season.

In 1906, little girls might have found a My Playmate doll with movable joints and closing eyes. They cost $1.25 at Siegel & Cooper. Little boys might have found a thirty-seven-inch iron toy train including locomotive, tender, and two coaches. They were 98¢ at the Boston Store.

Marshall Field's was advertising a wide variety of clocks: alarm clocks, 55¢ to $3.00; imported desk clocks, $5.00 to $45.00; automobile clocks, $4.00 to $35.00. Fields was also selling fur-lined coats for men and women for $50.00. French handmade night dresses cost $7.75.

Burning Palaces Light Shores of Baltic Sea for Forty Miles and Owners Slain and Thrown to Vultures

---

900 MUTINEERS BURNED IN PRISON
French Revolution Outdone in Livonia, Where Armed Bands Loot Estates and Hold Orgies in Historic Halls—General Strike Again Grips Country.

Special Cable Dispatch to the *Inter Ocean*

St. Petersburg, Dec. 21, Via Warsaw—The gloom which has settled over Russia tonight is the deepest this country has ever known, and the outlook the most desperate.

The palaces of the nobility are blazing from St. Petersburg to Odessa, and the mutilated bodies of the partisans of the Emperor fill the ditches of country roads and the gutters of the streets of the rebellious cities.

Nobles who have been able to escape the vengeance of the peasants in the country and the proletariat to the town are fleeing to the frontiers, leaving manorial halls and wide estates as lost for the now fully aroused people.

The memory of centuries of oppression seems to stir the masses to massacres of the most revolting cruelty. Believing that each blow struck the nobility reaches the desperate government, the peasants are striking deep and sure.

On all the snowy reaches around Riga nobles have been slain by scores, their bodies thrown to the vultures, and their ancient estates made scenes of orgies of drunken peasants.

The lands of the richest estates are divided among the men who drive away or kill the former owner, the rich tapestry, furniture, pictures and carpets go to the peasants' huts, and the castles are destroyed.

Sailors on the Baltic sea declare that the coast of Livonia for forty miles north of Riga is lit with the flames of burning estates. In Riga hotels down to the meanest lodging-houses are crowded with persons who bear the highest names in Russia, who have been glad to escape from the infuriated mobs with their lives, leaving all their property in the hands of the revolutionists.

From all other portions of the unhappy empire come reports as awful.

Two days later the *Chicago Tribune* reported, "It would seem that the vast empire has now commenced her last agony." Not quite. By year's end, the tide turned as elite troops, most loyal to Czar Nicholas II, bloodily repressed the revolution.

Matters of war and peace were on President Theodore Roosevelt's mind. As the fighting raged in Russia, he was preparing to appoint a delegation to an international peace conference at The Hague. A few days before Christmas, the president met with a delegation of Shakers, telling them that the disarming of nations was impractical, and that war was just and entirely proper when a nation's honor suffered a great and unprovoked wrong.

One Chicagoan who was professing not to be alarmed by the reports coming out of Russia was Mrs. Potter Palmer, leader of Chicago's high society. Her niece was the Russian Princess Cantacusene, formerly Miss Julia Grant. The princess and her husband were expected in Chicago later in the winter season. Their two children, Prince Michael and Princess Bertha, were expected to arrive the day after Christmas. According to the *Chicago Daily Journal*, one corner of "the big castle on Lake Shore Drive" was filled with Christmas gifts for them.

In an interview with the *Journal*, Mrs. Palmer strongly denied reports that she was planning on moving to London. "When you are an American once you are an American always," she said, and, "I'm American, a Chicagoan too, forever." The *Journal* described Mrs. Palmer as a recognized leader of American society abroad, a friend of King Edward's in England, and just as at home in Paris as she is on Lake Shore Drive.

As in so many years in Chicago's history, there was a building boom in 1905, and some developers wanted to tear down the old Chicago water tower at Chicago Avenue and Lake Shore Drive. The developers argued that the water tower had outlived its usefulness. The *Inter Ocean* tells that a similar suggestion was fought back just two years earlier:

There was a suggestion that it might be well to remove the tower and convert its site into a little park, or transform it into a broad turning point for carriages coming out of Lake Shore drive.

There were some who even ventured the suggestion that its architecture, of a pronounced German type, did not conform with the surroundings. When this project became known there was a storm of protest. Business men of the North Side lake front, who as boys had clambered to the top of the dusty, winding stairway, were opposed to any such action. Thirty years ago the tower was one of the "sights" of the city. Passengers on lake boats saw it as one of the things to be remembered about Chicago. Sight-seers who came by rail considered their visit incomplete until they had seen the tower which had endured against the great conflagration when surrounding structures, even a portion of the near by engine rooms, were swept away.

The Chicago Water Tower remains a prominent landmark to this day.

Christmas sales continued to grow, and there was something new to attract shoppers to stores: escalators. In 1905 the Boston Store prominently displayed the words "MOVING STAIRWAYS" in bold print in its ads. The *Chicago Inter Ocean* wrote up a short feature:

Moving Stairs Facilitate Shopping in a Big Department Store in Chicago

The delights of the escalators which have been installed in the Boston store have captured the thousands of people who have taken advantage of them to do their Christmas shopping. More than 200,000

Sports 1905, 1906

In 1905 Mayor Dunne led a crusade against ticket scalping at Christmastime. Incensed by the fact that he had to pay a scalper $11 for admission to a Thanksgiving football game, the mayor called for a meeting with all theatrical managers in Chicago. He wanted to ban the sale of theater and concert tickets from department stores and from the streets.

Tickets to baseball games in Chicago would prove to be a hot item in 1906. Cubs' president Charles Murphy was just back from the baseball meetings in New York, and he was ecstatic with his trading successes. He had acquired outfielder Jimmy Scheckard and catcher Pat Moran. He fully expected the Cubs to win the National League pennant in that year. Which they did with a record-setting 116 victories.

It was in 1906 that the Cubs and the White Sox met in the World Series. The Sox won the series and at Christmastime were making big plans for spring training. The Sox picked Mexico City for their camp, the farthest afield of any of the sixteen big league teams. The Cubs failed to get accommodations in San Antonio, Texas, and were looking at Waco as their spring base.

persons have taken advantage of them instead of using the elevators and they have worked to the satisfaction of all. The smiles of satisfaction on the faces of the shoppers when they were deposited safely on a floor without the crowding and shoving incidental to the old method of transit were extremely noticeable.

Both boys and girls regarded the innovation with pleasure while they proved an inestimable boon to tired mothers with children.

"Elevators have always frightened me," said an aged woman laden with packages, "but now I feel I can go from floor to floor with perfect safety. The features that appeal to me especially are that one is able to have a space for herself free from crowding, and the gentleness of movement with which the invention raises or lowers one to her destination."

The new mechanism has robbed Christmas shopping of most of its terrors, and there is no waiting, no crowding, and no jostling. The shoppers are kept in a good humor and leave the store in a happy frame of mind.

1906: An Automobile Romance

The *Chicago Inter Ocean* described the Christmas weather of 1906 as being "Spring-like." Perhaps that was a bit of an exaggeration. Temperatures ranged from the mid-twenties to the mid-thirties. About the holiday itself, the newspaper was equally exuberant:

Merry Christmas!—When Father Time raced under the midnight wire last night the old, time honored phrase was echoed and re-echoed in a thousand Chicago homes, on a thousand Chicago streets, in gayly bedecked restaurants, halls, churches, and in all the places where people congregate for cheer and jollity. The factory sirens yodeled it and the merry chimes of many belfries rang it up in all its changes. Chicago has never seen such a Christmas bedlam nor such a bumper Christmas. A jungle of trees bore $20,000,000 worth of variegated fruit. Tons of turkeys quietly folded their drumsticks in readiness for the turkey cemetery. The big stores, gutted of gifts, closed their doors on wreck strewn interiors. State street was a holiday riot. From Mayor Dunne, with eleven stockings to stuff, to the lowliest home in the city, to which the Salvation Army, the Volunteers, or some other charity ministered, the watchword last night was joy and cheer.

In 1906 a six-cylinder Franklin touring car sold for $4,000, and a four-cylinder light touring Franklin for $1,850. The Matheson Company of New York advertised its thirty-five horsepower runabouts for $4,000. A car salesman was happy to bring a vehicle to a prospective customer's home for a test drive in 1906. It was just such a demonstration that led to something much more, according to an article in the *Chicago Tribune* of Sunday, December 16:

CUPID DRIVES MOTOR CAR
Chauffeur Demonstrates and Wins Bride.

GEORGE B. BROWN, EXPERT ON "CHUG" MACHINES, GOES TO SELL ONE TO MISS JENNIE JOHNSON—

SALE ENDS IN ROMANTIC MARRIAGE OF COUPLE—

EMPLOYER OF SALESMAN FINDS OUT TOO LATE—

WHY

TRANSACTION REQUIRED SUCH A LONG TIME.

An "automobile romance," in which figured a northwest side young woman, an automobile demonstrator, and a $4,000 automobile, came to a climax last evening in the wedding of the young woman to the expert chauffeur. The young woman was Miss Jennie Johnson, 23 years old, daughter of the late A. J. Johnson, a pioneer west side furniture manufacturer, and the groom is George B. Brown, head salesman and demonstrator for C. A. Coey & Co., automobile dealers. The wedding ceremony took place at the home of the bride's mother, 196 Evergreen avenue, the Rev. H. A. Hanson, pastor of Trinity Norwegian Lutheran church, reading the service. When the bridal couple left the house in the automobile which was "the cause of it all" their friends showered them with rice and a collection of old shoes.

ROMANCE STARTED OCT. 1
The romance had its inception on Oct. 1.

C. A. Coey, head of the automobile firm, one bright, sunny day received a telephone call for a sample car and a demonstrator. The voice was a feminine one and it spoke in sweet tones from 196 Evergreen avenue.

On Stage 1905

More than 557,000 people went through the turnstiles of the International Amphitheater during the week before Christmas. That made the 1905 Live Stock Exposition and Horse Fair the most successful in the city's history.

On stage, on Christmas Day, Maxine Elliott opened in the comedy *Her Great Match* at Powers' Theater. It is the story of an American girl abroad who meets and falls in love with the heir apparent of a European principality. The musical *Fritz* in Tammany Hall premiered on Christmas Eve at the Illinois Theater. *The Wizard of Oz* was back for its annual Yuletide run at the Grand Theater. A notice in the Journal said: "The songs are all new this season, and include a new football satire. All the familiar features of the play have been retained."

The "Audubonesque" musical frolic *Woodland* was opening at the Studebaker Theater with Harry Bulger again in the role of the "bibulous 'King Blue Jay.'"

Transportation 1905

In 1905 $2,250 would buy a four-cylinder model S Olds. A Reo was $1,000 cheaper.

Under the Tree 1908

The Fair Store advertised a fourteen-inch, growling "teddy" for $1.45. The Fair's selection of Christmas toys included a painted wooden Noah's Ark, complete with animals. It cost 39¢. Twenty-five cents fetched a musical spinning top. Eighty-nine cents could purchase a magic lantern made of sheet tin with a dozen assorted slides.

THE "REO" $1250 CAR

Is crossing the country twice. It won the six-day 700-mile economy contest in New York. It is giving every day satisfaction It is kept in repair free of cost to you, both labor and material, "that's the guarantee." The Runabout costs $600. The Coupe Limousine is $1,800.

ALL MODELS OF "REO" ON HAND.

 **311 Michigan Ave.**

In a few minutes the car was selected and Brown was on his way to the residence of the young woman. The sale of the automobile was made on the first day of Brown's visit, after a lengthy demonstration in Evergreen avenue and other streets in the vicinity of Wicker park.

Meanwhile, Mr. Coey sat in his office awaiting the result of his employee's work, but he waited in vain on the first day, for the good and sufficient reason that Brown received an invitation to dinner from his fair customer and spent the evening with the young woman and her mother.

MORE DEMONSTRATIONS FOLLOW

Then followed daily visits to the Johnson home and daily demonstrations with Miss Johnson's newly acquired automobile. Mr. Coey noticed that Brown prolonged his visits more and more every day, but it had been a good sale and he said nothing about it at first.

Finally affairs came to such a pass, Brown was taking such an unreasonable amount of time for this one demonstration, that Mr. Coey decided it was time to call a halt.

So one day last week he called Brown into his office and asked him why it was necessary to spend so much time with Miss Johnson.

"Well, I'll tell you, Mr. Coey," said Brown. "I not only sold an automobile but I have won a bride."

"You don't say so," gasped the astonished automobile dealer, who is a bachelor himself. "The next time I get a telephone call like that I'll not send one of my employees, I'll promise you that."

The bridal couple will leave this morning on a honeymoon trip. (Copyright *Chicago Tribune.* Used by permission.)

Waterless Swimming

In 1906 Upton Sinclair published *The Jungle,* detailing the filth and inhuman conditions in Chicago's stockyards. The book helped bring about the nation's first pure food and drug laws. At Christmastime, Health Commissioner Charles Whalen delivered a lecture in the public library and displayed all manner of foodstuffs that had been seized in raids, including smoked fish that had been steeped in coal tar to give them a smoky smell, catsup made of apple and squash pulp and colored with poisonous aniline dye, dried and rotten eggs used by some of the city's bakeries, and olive oil contaminated with cottonseed oil.

At the Chicago Architectural Club's Christmas banquet the message was that good morals went hand-in-hand with beautiful building. Among the speakers was famed architect Daniel Burnham, who said, "Keep the beauty of the lakefront intact, improve its condition, and the health of Chicago will be improved."

Morals were also on the minds of Chicago's school officials. They were planning to introduce hugless dancing and waterless swimming to the 270,000 children in the city's public schools. The footwork would be called "fancy steps," and it was hoped that the practitioner would learn the mazurka, the waltz, two-step, and polka without even knowing it.

As for the waterless swimming, the plan was to teach children the various strokes while they were standing up, and then suspend them from hanging rings and a leather belt, so they could enjoy the sensations of swimming without fear of cramps.

Also in that same year, a battle was raging over the city's lax, even nonexistent, enforcement of the state law requiring taverns to be closed on Sunday. On one side were the clergymen, members of the Sunday Closing League. They had gone to court demanding an order requiring Mayor Dunne to shut down Alderman Michael Kenna's two Clark Street saloons.

Among those on the other side were members of the Bohemian Societies of Pilsen. At a mass meeting on the Saturday before Christmas, organizer Victor Sarner championed the principle of personal liberty: "If these blue laws were enforced Chicago would be as dead as the inside of a morgue. If we wish to drink beer in an orderly manner and the ministers wish to drink water, let each do as he wishes. There is plenty of water in the lake."

1907: The Tree at Marshall Field's

Every year, thousands of Christmas shoppers marvel at the big, beautiful Christmas tree in the Marshall

Field and Company State Street store. The tradition goes back to 1907, according to the Field's in-house publication, *The Field Glass:*

> The practice of having a large Christmas tree in the Walnut Room dates back as far as 1907 when the present Main Store was finally extended to include the whole block. It was not the Walnut Room back then, but it was a tearoom and it boasted a handsome tree—the envy of all other stores in Chicago.
>
> According to Mrs. Clara P. Wilson, who joined our Display Department back in 1916, the Christmas tree was begun "with bus boys in the tearooms decorating it." The tearoom furnished the lads with conventional ornaments, gilt balls and artificial icicles. I was the first official 'designer' of the tree's decorations," Mrs. Wilson recalled to a newspaper writer. "Before 1916, the bus boys merely threw ornaments on the tree. When I came to the store, Mr. Bunker (Charles C. Bunker, then store superin-tendent) asked me to plan the tree. So I made the drawings, assembled the decorations in the tearoom—and stood under the ladders and yelled at the bus boys up on the scaffolds. I also had to do a great deal of climbing around myself—but it was real fun. Finally, after several years, I convinced the store it should employ Christmas tree specialists for the job—I was getting worn out yelling at my young part-time decorators!"

Today, Marshall Field's big Christmas tree is artificial. In years past, however, the revolving doors at State and Randolph were removed to allow workmen to bring huge natural trees into the store. They were hoisted seven floors through the light well and erected with block and tackle. Whether natural or artificial, more than fifteen hundred ornaments adorn the Marshall Field's tree which towers at least fifty feet over the floor of the Walnut Room.

1910 - 1919

1910: The Stockyard Fire

At 4 a.m. on Thursday, December 22, 1910, a fire broke out at the Morris & Company plant in the stockyards. It was a huge brick six-story building, covering almost an entire block. Twenty minutes after a watchman gave the alarm, Fire Chief James Horan and several companies of firefighters were on the scene.
According to the *Chicago Inter Ocean*:

Along the east wall of this gigantic structure there was a platform used for loading and unloading freight. This was covered with a wooden loading shed twenty-five feet wide.

Chief Horan and about thirty of his men were on this platform waging their uneven battle against the seething furnace of flames in the building.

Suddenly a great roar came from the volcanic depths of the burning warehouse and the tall brick walls tottered and swayed threateningly.

"Run for your lives, men!" shouted Chief Horan. Assistant Chief Seyferlich, who, a second before, had been talking with his superior officer, leaped away to safety, but before Horan and the other men could rush from the platform the great wall of brick and burning timbers with a roar that could be heard for blocks away, crashed down upon them.

Instantly great forks of flames leaped up from this awful pile of debris so that many of the victims were literally roasted to death.

On Stage 1912

Variety estimated that George M. Cohan made $1.5 million a year with his productions. His musical farce Exceeding the Speed Limit *was playing at Chicago's Grand Theater at Christmastime 1913.*

Eddie Morton, one of the biggest stars of vaudeville, sang the popular "Oceana Roll."

On Christmas Eve, famed prima donna Mary Garden was making her first appearance of the season at the Auditorium Theater, appearing in the Jongleur de Notre Dame. *The opera star had shed twenty pounds since her last Chicago appearance, and she told a reporter for the* Inter Ocean: *"I love my beer, but I love my figure better; mineral water for me in the future."*

She also told a reporter for the Tribune: *"I just love Chicago and the Chicago people. Back east they laugh at me when I tell them that, but it is true, and I declare it wherever I go. It was here I received my first recognition, and then came Boston, and finally New York."*

Another opera prima donna, Madame Schumann-Heink, spent Christmas Eve in her sixth-floor room of the Auditorium Hotel, breaking all precedents and hotel rules. She stuffed a Christmas goose and prepared all the dishes needed for a German-style Christmas feast that she would cook for her children. "It is a mother's duty to be with her children. I am very proud of my cooking," said Schumann-Heink.

Hours after the wall had fallen piteous groans were heard coming from the ruins and it is believed that the mercy of an instant death was denied many of those who perished.

When the wall fell the other firemen and the hundreds of horror-stricken spectators rushed to the ruins in a frantic effort to drag out the bodies of the men pinned under the burning debris.

Men clawed desperately with bare hands among the crackling flames and bricks, which were as hot as live coals, in a wild effort to rescue the firemen lying crushed and baking under the smoking ruins.

But the heat was intense, rescue was impossible and the crowd was compelled to fall back and helplessly watch the flames like demons of death sweep over the scene.

Chief Horan, twenty-one of his men, and three civilians were killed by the explosion, caused by a buildup of gases, heat, and smoke inside the building. The cause of the fire was an electrical malfunction. Within two days, a drive to raise money for the victims' families had received a quarter of a million dollars in donations and pledges.

1912: Blue Christmas

In 1912, blue laws continued to make tempers in the pulpits of the city run red. The city had just announced a decision to allow saloons to stay open until 3 A.M. on New Year's Day, and clergymen were in a state of near revolt. "In the face of the stampede of crime it is amazing that the chief of police should see fit to set aside the law regulating the sale of liquor and substituting his own orders therefor," thundered the Reverend John Balcom Shaw in his sermon at the Second Presbyterian Church on Sunday morning, December 22: "It is this kind of civic course which encourages criminals to disregard laws and dare bolder crimes. Such action, on the part of the officials, should receive the censure of all law-abiding citizens."

The next day, under the headline "Clergy to March Upon the Mayor in War on Orgy" the *Chicago Inter Ocean* newspaper (whose slogan was "All the News That Is Clean") reported on plans for a march on city hall on December 30. Among those who would be speaking was Arthur

Burrage Farwell of the Chicago Law and Order League, who expressed his outrage:

> The city is overrun with criminals. Citizens are being murdered and the murderers are escaping. Vice and crime are being winked at by public officials.
>
> Every evidence shows that these New Year's Eve revelries are criminal in their excesses and start more young men and women on the road to ruin than a thousand ordinary saloons on ordinary nights.

While area ministers vehemently voiced their opinions on alcohol, it seems they were silent on defending civil rights. Discrimination against African Americans was casual and matter-of-fact, even if the victim was a wealthy boxing champion. The *Inter Ocean* carried a story illustrative of the times on December 22:

JACK JOHNSON BUYS LAKE GENEVA HOME

Purchases Property for $32,500 from J. E. Sherman, and Exclusive Chicago Society is Shocked

Jack Johnson, negro pugilist, has purchased a home at Lake Geneva, the exclusive summer resort of Chicago society. H. J. Evans, a director of the National Biscuit company, will be his neighbor on one side, and Charles W. Leland, of the Leland Derby Real Estate company, on the other.

The property, which was bought yesterday at the cost of $32,500 from Judson E. Sherman, a grain dealer, is a Christmas present for Mrs. Lucile Cameron Johnson, white wife of the fighter. It has a frontage of 125 feet on the lake, and lies near the homes of many of Chicago's wealthiest society people.

Julian Rumsey's home is two doors from the bungalow bought by Johnson, while J. J. Mitchell, president of the Illinois Trust and Savings bank; Samuel Allerton, S. B. Chapin, J. H. Moore, Edward Bosley and others are in close proximity.

Since it became known that the property had been sold to Johnson a strong sentiment has been aroused by both the citizens of the village and Chicagoans owning summer homes in that vicinity. Declarations that the pugilist has undertaken a more difficult task than he had planned were made freely.

On the Table 1912

The Christmas goose of 1912 cost 18¢ a pound at Rothschild & Company. Turkeys were 23 1/2¢ a pound. Libby's plum pudding was 23¢ for a one-pound can.

Transportation 1912

A brand new Abbott-Detroit motorcar sold for $3,050 in 1912. Overlands were selling for $1,100, Packards with enclosed carriages were $4,500 to $5,000. Chicagoans were so enthusiastic about all cars that the Chicago Motor Club was arranging for a special train to take enthusiasts to the big New York auto show in January.

Steps into and onto Society

"He seems to crave good society, and it looks very much as if he has stepped right into the center of it," said J. J. Mitchell last night. "The Sherman residence is a very comfortable and nicely located place, but I do not believe that Johnson will enjoy great solace if he attempts to occupy it. I would not be surprised if it had been purchased with the idea that residents will pay a large sum to buy the property from him."

"I absolutely cannot believe that it is true and until I am convinced I shall not talk about it," said Charles Leland, one of Johnson's next-door neighbors. "It certainly can be nothing but a wild rumor—I have never heard of such a thing."

"Johnson will not find Lake Geneva receiving him in open arms, nor will he find it pleasant," said J. J. Evans, the neighbor on the other side.

"I can hardly believe it possible. For years every one has guarded all the property with great care, so that none of it would be sold to anyone undesirable," declared Mrs. E. F. Bosley.

"It is a beautiful little place. Just what I have wanted for a long time," said Johnson. "I have had my eye on it for some time, and have purchased it at last. It is one of the best locations along the lake, has simply grand oak shade trees and a large lawn."

Johnson never did buy the house. In fact, there's some evidence that the whole thing was a scheme to drive up the price of the property by scaring a white buyer into paying more for it at auction.

1913: Chicago's Famous Christmas Trees

Imagine this: a cold, foggy, and rainy Christmas Eve afternoon, and Michigan Avenue, between Monroe and Washington, is a sea of humanity. The crowd spills out into Grant Park. The mood is festive and expectant.

It happened in 1913, when Chicago erected its first municipal Christmas tree. It stood thirty-five feet high and was festooned in a myriad of electric lights that, according to the *Chicago Tribune*, "the newsboy, the bootblack, the poor of the city can gaze upon and claim it as their own."

The program started with the Chicago Band performing for more than an hour and a half. The music began with "Onward, Christian Soldiers" and included selections from Rossini's "Stabat Mater" and the "Hallelujah Chorus" from Handel's *Messiah*.

Near the Art Institute a huge screen had been erected, and at five o'clock a series of safety-first films were shown. At just before six o'clock, Mayor Carter Harrison II mounted the platform that stood before the great tree. He was accompanied by trumpeters from the First Illinois Cavalry and by mounted police.

The *Tribune* says one small boy was disappointed:

"Papa," he said. "I thought Santa Claus was a great big fat man." "That isn't Santa Claus, sonny," responded the father. "That is Mayor Harrison." "But why isn't he fat?" queried the unsatisfied one. (Copyright *Chicago Tribune*. Used by permission.)

The mayor gave a short address and concluded by saying, "Let us hope the lights on this tree will so shine out as to be an inspiration to Christian charity and to inject new courage and new hope into the hearts of those not so fortunate as we are." Then he pushed a button.

Hundreds of multicolored lights went on. So did a Star of Bethlehem at the top of the tree. The lights reflected and played off clouds of steam from half a dozen idling Illinois Central locomotives specially stationed behind the tree, creating a kaleidoscopic effect.

The crowd cheered. The band struck up a "Salute to the Nations" and a medley of national anthems that concluded with "America." Then, from the third-story balcony of the Chicago Athletic Association, came a fanfare of trumpets from members of the Chicago Grand Opera Company, who were dressed in costumes from the period when Christ was born. An improvised sounding board was in place above the balcony, and Henri Scott broke into a solo of "Gypsy John." He was soon interrupted when one of the locomotives let off steam with a loud bang. "It's Chicago, after all," sighed one young woman.

The chorus of the Grand Opera Company from their perch on the north portico of the Art Institute followed with another song. Then there was more fanfare of trumpets, more solo performances, and it all wrapped up around seven o'clock when the crowd joined the band and the ensemble in singing "The Star Spangled Banner."

Selling Christmas trees near South Water Street

Under the Tree 1914

In 1914, The Fair advertised a mechanical train "outfit," consisting of a locomotive, tender, coach, station, and nine pieces of track. It was a $2.95 value, on sale for $1.98. For 25¢, a mechanical airplane could be bought that had a unique ability: "attach with a string to ceiling and when wound flies in circle," said the ad.

Since Theodore Roosevelt was no longer in the White House in 1914, teddy bears that year were reduced to $1.29. Papier-mâché dolls with bisque heads and moving eyes cost 98¢. A varnished child's kindergarten blackboard could be had for $1.67.

One official noted the huge size of the dissipating crowd and remarked, "There must have been over 100,000. This leads us to believe that we ought to continue the affair."

The huge tree was a gift to the city from Milwaukee Avenue tree dealer F. J. Jordan. He was a former partner of schooner captain Herman Scheunemann, who, with his brother August, in 1887 began making yearly voyages from Manistee, Michigan, bringing a shipload of Christmas trees to Chicago. When their ship arrived, Chicagoans knew that the Christmas season had really begun. It became a tradition for countless families to purchase their trees from the Scheunemanns, taking the evergreen right off the ship docked near a bridge at Clark Street.

August Scheunemann and his ship, the *S. Thal*, were lost in a Lake Michigan storm while bringing trees to town in 1898. Brother Herman met a similar fate with his schooner, the *Rouse Simmons*, in 1912, one year before Jordan decided to commemorate the brothers with his gift. The brothers were also memorialized by Charles Vickery who created a series of paintings of the "Christmas Tree Schooner." There also is a folk song and a musical about the ships and their cargo.

A latter day attempt at reviving the Victorian practice of fresh cut Christmas trees at the docks has taken place at Navy Pier. Nowadays the trees come to Chicago from North Carolina by train and truck, and then are loaded onto the ship parked at the pier and sold.

1914: Joe Tinker's Christmas

Sometimes in the hustle and bustle of shopping, decorating, cooking, and entertaining we may forget the essential meaning of Christmas. On the day after Christmas 1914, the *Chicago Daily News* told about the holiday celebrated in the true spirit by a man who is immortalized as part of the Tinkers-to-Evers-to-Chance Cubs' doubleplay combination.

JOE TINKER PLAYS SANTA
TO THE POOR
Carries Christmas Cheer to Fatherless
Family on the North Side

———————————

Loots His Own Pantry
Tonneau Full of Food and Toys Brings Happiness to Youngsters and Joe
by John O. Seys

Santa Claus had just finished decorating a tree in the home of Joe Tinker, manager of the Chifeds [Chicago's Federal League baseball team, the Whales]. It was near the midnight hour. All around the cozy flat there were signs of prosperity, good cheer and happiness. Joe and Roland, the two sons of the ball player, were tucked away in their warm beds dreaming of toys, candies and things of the morrow. Bundles were being piled up at the foot of the dazzling pine tree. Dr. Jay Pitts and wife and several friends had been called in to visit out the Christmas eve. Outside the wind was rattling the doors with the wireless message telling of the bitter cold.

"We're all feeling in good spirits tonight, but the poor are suffering, I'll wager," said Joe as he handed his wife a diamond dinner ring and in turn received a pair of red topped slippers, a reading lamp and other things. "That wind makes me shiver when I think of those who are half dressed, half fed and half clothed."

"We ought to go out and find such a family and give them something," said Mrs. Pitts.

"Well, my car is down in front and if the radiator is not frozen, we might go," said the ball player.

One of the guests was sent to the telephone and tried to find a needy family through the charity organization. It did not take long to find one. "There is a woman out on Sedgwick street with five children who needs assistance," said the agent on the other end of the line.

Start Out in Tinker's Car

"Come on, we'll all go," said Joe. Heavy wraps were thrown on and at 11:30 they started for the Sedgwick street number, determined to find out what was needed and get just what the poor mother was unable to provide for her flock, to make the Christmas eve a pleasant one.

On the second floor in the rear of a building one block south of Division street there was a faint light burning to show the way to the Christmas party. Down through a long hall the visitors, headed by Tinker, wound their way.

"Who's there?" came a feeble voice from within, in answer to the knock.

"Santa Claus," said Joe. He might have said Joe Tinker, but he feared possibly the person within might not know whether Joe Tinker was Santa Claus or a burglar.

The door opened and a thin but pleasant faced woman greeted the visitors.

Unlike most women who received help this one did not cry. When told the object of the midnight call she smiled as best she could with her pinched cheeks.

Scrubs for a Living

Out of another room came a little girl of about 11, while from another room there came the prattle of a child and the rattling of tin.

"This is my oldest girl, Clara," said the mother by way of introduction. "The baby, 3 years old, has a train of cars some one left him to-night and he just won't go to sleep. It's the first real toy he's had since he was born." In another minute the child appeared at the door. He was shivering in the chill of the cold flat, but he had a tin railway car in each hand. His little body was sticking out through the gaps in his pajamas, and he trembled as he tried to hook the engine on to the train at the time saying "Toot! toot!"

"He is a twin, but his little brother died," said the mother. "They were born six months after my husband died. I was married fifteen years ago and I have had eight children, but buried three of them. Yes, it's hard work sometimes to keep these little ones fed and clothed, especially in the winter. I scrubbed a big store today and it took me all day. That's why I'm all in to-night. Clara, there, is the little mother while I'm away working. She got down on her knees to-day and scrubbed the floors while I was working. She said Santa Claus might come to-night and she wanted to have the house clean."

YOUNGSTERS SAVE CARFARE

Just then the outside door burst open and in came two more girls, 8 and 10 years old. Over her shoulder the larger carried a basket.

"There, mom, is the dime you gave us for car fare," said the little one. "We walked down and back and saved the money."

The mother then explained the girls had attended a Christmas tree entertainment in a hall at North Clark street and West Washington street. They had been given a basket containing a chicken and other necessaries of life. The girls had walked home from that point to Sedgwick and West Division street in order to save the paltry 10 cents.

That big raw boned athlete, who had been in baseball for years, who could tell an umpire things not in the book, and fight at the drop of his hat, just brushed away a tear as he looked on and thought of his own happy home with the two Tinker kids tucked away in their warm bunk, a big turkey in the ice box, and toys by the dozens hanging on the Christmas tree.

"Come and see our tree," said one of the little girls. In one of the three rooms occupied by the family was a good sized tree trimmed with tassels and a few little ornaments.

MOTHER SECURES THE TREE

"I carried that tree all the way home from South Water street," said the mother. "It was given to me. I knew I could not get on the street car with it so I lugged it home. It was a task after a hard day's work scrubbing, but it made the babies happy."

"Would you permit any one to adopt that baby boy," asked Dr. Pitts, who had been watching the little chap playing with his train.

"No, I'm afraid I couldn't do that," said the mother. "I find it difficult at times to feed and clothe them but I couldn't part with one of them. I've had some rough obstacles in my way but always climbed over them. My children are all good ones. They go to school and Sunday school. The county gives me some coal, oat meal and flour and, with my work, I manage to keep the little family together. They may grow big enough some day to take care of me when I break down under the hard work."

CHILD PLEASED WITH RIBBON

"Oh, Mom, see the pretty hair ribbon I got on the tree," said one of the little girls as she waved a big red bow before her mother. Then she turned to her sister, the little mother, who had remained at home, and said twittingly, "Now don't you wish you had gone?"

"Yes, but I had to take care of the baby," said little Clara.

The woman slipped the "little mother" a coin and told her to buy herself a ribbon. Tinker slipped a roll of bills in the mother's hands. The visitors found out what was needed and yesterday Joe Tinker's automobile drew up in front of that home loaded with potatoes, coffee, flour, bread, sugar, clothes, toys, fruit, canned goods, jelly and lots of good things.

"They just cleaned out my pantry," said Joe, "and I'm glad of it. This is the best Christmas I've ever had and I guess it's this little bit of charity that makes it so." (Reprinted with special permission from the *Chicago Sun Times*.)

Ironically, it was about a week earlier that ballplayer-turned-evangelist Billy Sunday scorched the ears of a crowd at the YMCA, telling them that "Chicago doesn't believe in God anymore," and "If the devil was looking for a new headquarters to install his furnaces, his imps and his minions, he wouldn't look any further than Chicago."

Not Joe Tinker's Chicago.

A popular toy for children four to eight years old was the 1914 version of those plastic foot-powered cars we have today. It was a buggy, called "The Horsemobile":

A handsome turnout. Horse is flexible so that head turns with the guiding rein. Unbreakable (laminated) horse in cart, enameled in dapple gray, glass eyes, best hair mane and tail, leather ears. HARNESS, strong webbing and leatherette, ornamented in brass. CART has fine shaped body, bent thills, steel dash and whip socket, seat padded with corduroy. GEAR especially made for this vehicle, enameled black. WHEELS, best 1/2-inch rubber tired, tandem spokes, 6 inches and 16 inches high [the smaller wheel was under the horse]. Entire height, 25 inches; length, 48 inches. Painted bright red or deep blue. A whip furnished free with this outfit. Actual value, $8, special for this sale: $4.89.

1916: Toy Story

The name of Milton H. Samson should go down in the laurels of Chicago's history as a real children's hero of Christmas.

Once upon a time, Mr. Samson was the proprietor of a toy store that stood near Lake and Dearborn Streets. He made it his business over a series of years to give away his stock at Christmastime to each and every poor child he could find—or rather, who could find him.

On Saturday, December 23, 1916, the *Chicago Daily News* reported that when Mr. Samson entered his shop by a back entrance that morning, he found about five hundred eager faces already pressed against the front window. He had announced his plans a few days earlier in the *News:*

An hour and a half after the doors were opened 1,500 tots of 10 years or under had scampered away, each with an arm tightly wrapped about a precious package. Mr. Samson's stock was half gone. Mrs. Samson paused in handing out boxes of miniature battle ships to catch her breath. Mrs. Samuel Kuit, assisting with the doll houses leaned against the depleted shelf. Policeman W. P. Creagh, who with broad grin and assumed gruffness, had been keeping the line of youngsters in order, mopped his brow. So did Mr. Samson.

"Great!" gasped Mr. Samson.

"Oh, such excitement!" gasped Mrs. Samson.

"I never had such a good time," said Mrs. Kuit.

"Lord bless 'em, they look happy," said Officer Creagh. "Here, ye young spalpeen, get back in line."

"If I only had twice the stock," Mr. Samson regretted. "We'll be cleaned out by the middle of the

afternoon. I'll have to call off the plans I had for distributing tomorrow. We won't have a toy left by tonight."

Over 150 letters from people too far removed and too poor to pay carfare were received within a day or two after the announcement in The Daily News. To take care of these pleas Mr. Samson sent out 300 or more toys.

The crowd today came from all parts of the city. Many walked downtown.

"I didn't mind walkin'," said Emily, aged 6. "Look at my dolly house."

"I wish I had more toys," lamented Mr. Samson. (Reprinted with special permission from the *Chicago Sun Times*.)

Now there was a *real* Santa Claus.

One might argue that it was easy to be generous in 1916. Prosperity was riding high in the United States, much of it from the sale of goods and materials to the belligerents fighting in Europe. There were jobs aplenty, profits too, and the idea of a Christmas bonus was sweeping across the nation. That 5.75 million salaried workers and wage earners were getting bonuses was front-page news.

In Chicago, the employers—and their gifts—were noted in the newspaper columns. The Fitzsimmons Steel and Iron Company was giving $25, $50, and $100 in gold to employees who had served a year or more. The Corn Exchange National Bank was giving gifts of 10 percent of its employees' annual salaries. American Express was pledging to give an amount equal to one month's salary to employees who were making $2,000 or less and who had been on the payroll for the entire year. The Spitfire Battery Company announced a 10 percent increase for all of its employees. The Herman H. Hettler Lumber Company gave every employee a $10 gold piece. The Gulbransen-Dickinson Company, in addition to distributing an $8,000 bonus among its employees, announced plans to install a profit-sharing system.

The *Daily News* predicted that Chicago was at the brink of its biggest Christmas ever, a $100,000,000 spending spree that had "Chicagoans fairly atingle with the Yuletide spirit."

In the now long-ago days before the ascendancy of suburban shopping malls, *the* place for doing one's Christmas shopping was the Loop. The names Marshall Field's, Carson Pirie Scott & Company, the Fair Store, Wieboldt's, Goldblatt's, and the Boston Store, among others, resound through the history of Chicago merchandising. Tracts have been written about the development of the modern department store, of the effort to make it cozy and comfortable, laid out like a small city unto itself. Shopping was transformed from a necessary chore into a joy, and much more so at Christmastime.

1918: The Plight of the Alabama

As Chicagoans awoke on Tuesday, Christmas Eve, 1918, one look out of the window would have convinced most of them that the prudent course of action would be to turn over and go back to sleep.

Outside their homes a blizzard was raging. Heavy snow was coming down, being driven by forty-eight mile an hour winds. By noontime, five inches had accumulated.

The storm brought transportation to a crawl. Thousands of Chicagoans abandoned the streetcar lines, which were hardly moving, for the elevated trains, which were slow. Suburban trains were running up to thirty-five minutes late.

On the southwest side, a Santa Fe passenger train, groping its way through the blizzard, collided with a line of stalled freight cars, catching

Under the Tree 1918

Christmas presents of 1918 may have included auto robes; they were selling for $3.48 to $6.98 at The Fair Store. Ansco cameras cost from $17.00 to $21.00.

Marshall Field's advertised boys' knitted caps for 40¢ apiece. Winter overcoats cost $21.00 to $24.00. Wool serge dresses were $16.75. Field's general manager David Yates declared the 1918 Christmas shopping season "the largest trade in history."

On the Table 1918

The Christmas turkey of 1918 cost 42¢ a pound at Wieboldt's. Coffee was 27¢ a pound.

them on fire. Passengers on the train panicked, but the only injury recorded was to a railroad switchman.

While this was occurring on land, a drama was being played out on the waters of Lake Michigan. The *Daily News* reported that the steamship *Alabama*, with two hundred people aboard, was caught in a tossing world of gray and green waves and wind-driven snow. At 7 A.M. Christmas Eve, the ship was only half an hour out of Chicago, but at that point, the captain decided the best course of action was to turn back and head for safety on the Michigan shore. All through the day, the passengers suffered from the cold, the tossing, and the worry that their lives would be lost in a wintry maelstrom.

Then the ship's engines stopped. Motion grew perceptively less. There was a noise, a scraping sound along the ship's hull. The *Daily News* reporter, Ruth Russell, wrote some thought it was a lifeboat being lowered. It was, in fact, a gangway. The *Alabama* had made it to safety in Grand Haven. It was midnight Christmas Eve.

Many of the passengers would take the train to Chicago. Most trains bound for the city were packed in the days leading up to Christmas. America's servicemen were coming home from World War I and Chicago was in a mood to welcome them.

On Christmas Eve the *Daily News* reported that any soldier or sailor who spent a lonely Christmas Day would do so only because thousands of ready friends were unable to get in touch with him:

Preparations for the entertainment of soldiers and sailors have been made on a huge scale, both by organizations formed for that purpose, by clubs and societies and by private families, whose tables will be resplendent and dehooverized.* There will be "blowouts" for the boys to-night and every day until New Year's.

Another story in the *Daily News* noted that the Hotel Men's Association of Chicago had decided that eight- and ten-course meals in hotel restaurants were to be curtailed to comply with a request from Mr. Hoover.

*A reference to the end of restrictions imposed by domestic food and European relief administrator Herbert Hoover.

Among the organizations hosting dining and dancing for servicemen were the Khaki and Blue Club, the Red Cross, the Garfield Girls Navy Recreation Club, the Soldiers and Sailors club, and—note the segregated military—"the new War Camp Community Service Soldiers and Sailors club, at 3033 South Wabash Avenue, which caters especially to colored men in uniform."

Not every returning serviceman would find the city so accommodating, however. Among this set was Pvt. Bert Gunderson of Ontonagon, Michigan. The *Daily News* found him propped against his rucksack at Union Station on the Saturday before Christmas. Although his overseas cap was tilted at a rakish angle, Private Gunderson was not very happy.

He had a nine and a half hour layover in Chicago, and to his dismay he discovered that Chicago had forgotten about the men who had served in the war.

"It's the overcharging that makes me angry," he said. "My overseas uniform seems to be the signal to soak me for everything I buy."

The end of the war meant the introduction of certain technologies into civilian life. Illustrative of this is an interesting ad, run by the Underwood Typewriter Company at Monroe and Wabash:

> War demanded of the Underwood factory—the largest in the world—over 100,000 typewriters for the use of the United States and its allies. That we were able to supply this demand is a bright page in our history of success. Peace now recalls us to the needs of the public to which we owe our thanks, not only for its continued endorsement of our product, but for the patriotic patience it has shown during the period when all Underwoods were devoted to the necessities of war.

Another example of postwar technology was the start-up of airmail service. A plane piloted by Leon D. Smith, formerly of the U.S. Army Air Service, left Elizabeth, New Jersey, at 7:20 A.M. on December 18, bound for Chicago, with an expected arrival time of about 5 P.M. Also the *Daily News* printed a photo of the "world's largest seaplane." Built for the U. S. Navy, it could carry fifty people.

A couple of days before Christmas, city health authorities shut down the Woodlawn Theater on East Sixty-third Street. A health department worker had been in the crowd on the Saturday before the holiday, and he

Sports 1918

In 1918 America's celebrity athletes, particularly baseball players, cut short their 1917 season because of the war. John McGraw, manager of the New York Giants, told the Daily News *he feared that even the great stars, like the Cubs' Grover Cleveland Alexander, had ruined their careers:*

"I am afraid that Alex and the other boys who have seen active service on the battle field will find it impossible to play the old game as they did before they went through that experience," said the Giant leader. "The life which they have led for the last few months has been sterner than anything they ever knew before, and while they have gained the glory which is the due of all of our fighting men they have lost something, I believe, which they can never get back. That which they have lost is the physical condition and the mental poise so necessary to the major league ball player."

Although McGraw may have been right about some ballplayers, he was wrong about Alexander. "Alex" would pitch for eleven more seasons, including a 1920 season in which he would win twenty-seven games and post a 1.91 earned run average. Not only did Alexander maintain his mental poise while in the service, he was scouting talent for the Cubs' management, recommending spring tryouts for players he had met while "over there."

On Stage 1918

The Ziegfeld Follies of 1918 opened at the Colonial Theater three days before Christmas. Daily News *critic Amy Leslie was enthusiastic: "The splendor of it all, the delightful modernity of the wit, the prettiness of melody and superb beauty of the women have never been surpassed anywhere at any time."*

Opening Christmas night at Cohan's Grand was the George M. Cohan musical farce Going Up. *Lionel Barrymore was on stage at the Studebaker Theater in* The Copperhead. *A Christmas Tree Festival and Animal Circus was at the Chicago Coliseum.*

Best-Sellers 1918

At McClurg's bookstore in 1918, the popular new fiction of the day included The Cross of Fire *by Robert Gordon Anderson,* The American Family *by Henry Kitchell Webster,* The Magnificent Ambersons *by Booth Tarkington, and* The Treasure Trail *by Marah Ellis Ryan.*

Top Songs 1918

In 1918 the most popular music of the day included "I'm Always Chasing Rainbows," "Oh, How I Hate to Get Up in the Morning," and the "Tiger Rag."

had noticed a large number of people coughing, with no attempt by theater management to ask the coughers to leave. This occurred one month after the end of what's generally considered to be Chicago's worst flu epidemic. In the fall of 1918, more than 8,500 people died from influenza and pneumonia.

1920 - 1929

1920: Prohibition Christmas

The Roaring Twenties in Chicago were filled with cops-and-robbers stories, tales of Prohibition peccadilloes, celebrity adulation, and reaction and overreaction to the technological advances of the day.

On Christmas Eve, 1920, Chicago police rounded up 150 suspected criminals and just threw them in jail. No worries here about civil rights—it was a campaign to clear Chicago of crooks by Christmas. Among those arrested was a West Side doctor accused of running a million-dollar booze ring.

The cops weren't busy only chasing robbers. On Christmas Eve, 1920, there was a story in the *Chicago Tribune* about a tailor, a traffic cop, and spurned love. It began this way: "Mrs. Gertrude Rosner told the world yesterday at Madison and Wells Streets that she positively would not be a bird in a gilded cage for Samuel Markin."

The audience for her soliloquy was one traffic cop, William R. Murphy, the aforementioned Markin, and Samuel Shatz, the owner of the tailor shop at which both Rosner and Markin worked. Markin had been pressing his courtship by giving Gertrude a wristwatch and planning to buy her a diamond ring. But Gertrude would have none of it.

Markin sought to express his love by kneeling before her right there on the street. But his foot slipped on the icy pavement, pushing open a manhole into which he promptly fell, feet first. As Officer Murphy pulled him out, Gertrude told the officer to "run the shrimp in and keep him in the hoosegow."

To make matters worse for poor Markin, his boss, Sam Shatz, fired him. "Why should I keep a man who is so lovesick," asked Shatz, "that when he should be cutting out trouser seats, he cuts out hearts instead?"

What's so remarkable about this story is that when it was retold as part of WBBM Newsradio's *Christmas Past* series, it prompted a phone call from a relative of one of the principal figures who actually remembered the story—sixty years later!

In an interview with the *Chicago Tribune* at Christmastime 1920, the president of U.S. Steel, Elbert H. Gary, said the steel industry would like to adopt an eight-hour workday for its employees instead of the current twelve hours. But then, he said, the industry would have to pay workers almost as much for less work, and that, he said, would force the price of steel up. Gary also worried that a shortage of labor would mean an insufficient work force if the eight-hour day were to become the standard.

1923 & 1924: Bootlegging

By 1921 Chicago's courts were clogged with suspects arrested in Prohibition raids. So many raids were being carried out that the city's chief chemist, Frederick Toomey, complained that he didn't have enough help to test all the evidence that was pouring into his lab: everything from "white mule" to the very best Scotches and ryes.

In Washington in 1922, the chairman of the U.S. Senate Rules Committee urged a crackdown on those who were soft on Prohibition. The chairman, Senator Curtis of Kansas, was ordering the sergeant at arms to arrest anybody who solicited orders for liquor in the Senate wing of the Capitol or the Senate Office Building. Senator Curtis deplored reports of some senators illegally acquiring alcohol, while others appealed for more money to enforce Prohibition.

About a week before Christmas, 1923, the *Chicago Tribune*'s Arthur Evans wrote from New York that smugglers had redoubled their efforts to bring liquor across the Canadian border. Evans quoted a prominent New Yorker as saying, "When I go to Montreal, I tuck a couple of bottles in my pockets and bring

them home. I'm scared of the stuff sold here. Before prohibition we rarely had liquor in the house. I don't know what the exact psychology is, but many resent what they deem an infringement upon personal rights guaranteed by the constitution."

An article published in 1924 illustrates this phenomenon.

DRINKING ISN'T AN ADVENTURE IN CHICAGO NOW BOOTLEGGING GROWS HONEST IF NOT HONORABLE
by Arthur Evans

Purveying of the real stuff in hard likker among the de luxe trade which can pay the price seems now to have settled down to a matter of fact basis. Much of the fussing and ceremonial and door locking over the pouring of a libation in the busy marts of trade seems to have vanished the last twelve months.

The parade of Sandy MacDonald and Old Squire and the Hon. John Walker has become a commonplace. The novelty has worn off. Gone too is the bloom from the secret joy or satisfaction many were wont to display over the hoisting of forbidden drinks just to show it could be done.

THREE OUTSTANDING FACTS

Nowadays nobody seems to take the trouble to feel naughty over it. This has been a marked psychic development in this year of grace 1924, fifth year of the Sahara epoch.

Demand for the high priced real stuff is less than a year ago. Less is being bootlegged to the gilt-edged trade, but what there is of it is of better quality.

Demand has decreased, but authenticity has increased.

Implement dealers declare there are more fruit

presses in Cook county than washing machines. Concomitants of this phenomenon are a 45 per cent increase in the amount of grapes sold this year, and a probable volume of 15,000,000 gallons of wine made in the Chicago area.

More moonshine is being consumed than a year ago. The closing of the saloons and the drive against beer has increased the consumption of distilled stuff, fearsome stuff. (Copyright *Chicago Tribune*. Used by permission.)

The main opposition to drinking came from the church. At Christmastime, 1923, in Joliet, the Reverend Henry Rompel, pastor of the First Methodist Church, organized twenty prohibition agents for ten raids on the Saturday night before Christmas. Among those arrested at a saloon was a Will County supervisor and the brother-in-law of Joliet's captain of police.

The church also opposed a new dance sweeping the nation. At Christmastime 1923, Americans were dancing the Charleston. A preacher in Elkhart, Indiana, denounced the evils he perceived in the dance. According to the *Chicago Tribune*, the Reverend W.W. Denham told a crowd at the First Christian Church: "We do not say that every person or even a majority of those who dance are vicious or degraded, but that the ballroom is inimical to the highest attainment intellectually, morally, and spiritually, 28,000 young women who were ground up in the vice mills of Indiana last year declare. Every Christian minister in this city knows it, feels it, and believes it, yet some try to ignore it."

Santa Claus called on Mayor William Dever of Chicago in 1923. Santa Claus came in the guise of city department heads. They brought the newly elected mayor mahogany office furniture, a desk, a table, eight straight chairs, and an armchair. They also brought a bouquet of roses for Mrs. Dever. Such gifts from underlings would certainly raise eyebrows and questions today, but in 1923 Dever was known as the reform mayor, an honest man who won his election between the terms of Big Bill Thompson, who is considered one of Chicago's most corrupt mayors.

In 1923, Lyon & Healy was calling on consumers to "Make This a Radio Christmas!" Sets cost $25 and up. The Fair Store advertised a four-tube set for $98.50.

Under the Tree 1922

Walgreen's had cast iron Ford model cars for 49¢ and yellow cabs for twice that. For $1.98, the family could provide daughter with a Puss-in-Boots doll that meowed like a cat, a Ma-Ma talking doll cost $1.00 more. For Mom, Mandel Brothers were selling women's slippers with fur-trimmed tops for $2.50, and H. M. Paradise at 17 North State had a women's coat sale for $75.00 to $115.00. Dad might be interested in those Stetson hats for $12.00 on sale at Maurice L. Rothschild's, or those Hart Schaffner & Marx silk-lined two-trouser suits for $50.00.

Transportation 1922

If the family had time and money enough, then a six-month round-the-world trip on the SS Empress of France might be the ticket. Clark's Cruises advertised tours starting at $1,800.00.

On the Table 1922

Christmas dinner roast turkey, goose, or duck with all the trimmings cost $1.50 at the Blackhawk Restaurant on Wabash Avenue. The Blackhawk was calling itself "Chicago's Greatest Restaurant."

At the Movies 1922

At the movies, Mary Pickford starred in Tess of the Storm Country, *opening Christmas Day at the Roosevelt Theater. At the McVickers, the movie was* Making a Man *starring Jack Holt. But the McVickers also had a symphony orchestra on hand to present a Christmas spectacle called* Snow Flakes *and Paul Whiteman and his band to perform* The Romance of the Rhythm Orchestra.

On the Table 1925

The Christmas turkey of 1925 cost 37¢ a pound at the General Market House. Geese were 25¢ a pound.

A full Christmas dinner at the Hotel LaSalle cost $2.00 per person.

Radio was booming in the early 1920s. It was a new force, uniting the nation. Most Americans still lived on farms, and radio proved to be a useful tool for farmers, giving them the most up-to-date market prices.

City-dwellers also enjoyed this new form of entertainment; they could hear music being played by live musicians without having to leave the comfort of their homes. Just the idea of turning on this little box and hearing sounds coming through the air, or ether as was the common term, was extremely exciting and ever so modern. In 1922 alone, more than five hundred new stations went on the air.

In the industry itself, there was chaos. There was no regulation of station power or frequency, and frequently stations interfered with each other. Secretary of Commerce Herbert Hoover arranged a series of national radio conferences in the early 1920s, at which executives discussed ways to pay for their programming (Secretary Hoover was among a large group of Americans who were horrified at the thought of advertising on the radio) and how to deliver programs to a national audience.

The *Tribune*'s Robert M. Lee looked into his crystal ball and wrote:

The Future of Radio—a Forecast:

1. Fifty powerful broadcasting stations controlled as a unit will stretch from coast to coast, giving simultaneous service. The present 550 or more stations, which fill the air with a wild medley of sounds and cost a king's ransom every year, will be eliminated.

2. Control of light rays may make possible the transmission of pictures, even to views of actual happenings in progress. And two persons may carry on a direct conversation by wireless over great distances.

3. Centralization will be so perfect that the common desk telephone in the home will be a combination of telephone and radio receiving set, and a receiving set may be carried with no more inconvenience than a wrist watch. (Copyright *Chicago Tribune*. Used by permission.)

One year later, by Christmastime 1924, government concerns about program content were front-page news in the *Tribune*. Commerce Secretary Hoover told the newspaper in an interview that "the radio industry can't live on an endless diet of jazz." He said radio was becoming more important in the life of the country each day. As for paying for programming, he said, "This country would never stand for licensing or taxing radio listeners," which was the system then being set up in Great Britain.

Jazz, of course, wasn't the only music on the air. The very next day, December 23, the *Tribune* carried a story that described a different content. Headlined "Ether Throbs with Music of Christmas," the story told listeners how they could tune in stations from various distant cities, like St. Louis, Pittsburgh, and New York, and hear soloists, choruses, and orchestras all performing music of the season.

In other news of the day, many Chicagoans were being warned not to use candles on trees at all. Chicago's Fire Commissioner, Joseph Connery, appealed for the use of electric tree lights rather than candles.

The Commonwealth Edison Company was more than happy to oblige. The utility had a number of appliance stores scattered about the city, and its newspaper ads touted the electrical wonders of the day: Christmas lights for the tree, eight to the string, were selling for $2.45.

1925: The Volstead Act

In 1925, a Christmastime debate was raging in Congress over how the Volstead Act was being used to enforce Prohibition. One of those leading the charge against it was Sen. William Bruce (D-Maryland). He thundered, "There is more moral degradation in a spoonful of illicit liquor than in a whole barrel of licensed liquor." A colleague argued that while there had been a huge increase in the number of arrests for drunkenness since the start of Prohibition, still the amount of liquor consumed in this country was far below what it had been in pre-Volstead times. Bruce replied: "Has it come to this? What desperate straits

are they driven to when they say the volume of drink is not so much as before prohibition. A veritable army of spies and snoopers spent more than $42 million last year in a vain attempt to enforce this law and yet that is the most advanced ground they can take."

Indeed, during a House Appropriations Committee hearing, a record of which was made public a few days later, Assistant Treasury Secretary Lincoln Andrews admitted that twenty-five citizens had been shot and killed by federal Prohibition agents during the previous fiscal year, and that federal courts had issued writs of habeas corpus to save them from local murder charges. A total of 122 federal agents had been arrested, indicted, or discharged from the service for various criminal acts.

There was also congressional outrage over the admission by one agent that he had spent more than one thousand dollars on a lavish party at the Mayflower Hotel in Washington in an attempt to trap a hotel waiter as a bootlegger.

Congressman James Gallivan (D-Massachusetts) noted that, "The taxpayers' money [was being] used to buy Prohibition agents 'Supreme of Cantaloupe Au Porte' and Corona cigars at seventy cents apiece. On this expense account I see he had thirteen guests and that for the thirteen he had to have invitation cards that cost $10.11. Then they had several quarts of 'Old Smuggler,' two rounds of cocktails and cordials, but later they bought a quart of whisky for $10 as evidence. Oh, they had evidence all right, and it was safely ensconced with them. It would have taken a stomach pump to produce it in court."

The outrage on the Hill led to the quiet admission in Chicago that plans were being redrawn for

Prohibition enforcement on New Year's Eve. The city's fifty-two regular agents and twelve undercover men were no longer expected to make reservations for themselves and women companions at a Chicago cabaret. The move would save Uncle Sam at least $7,600.

At the same time the *Tribune* noted that "there still is enough good liquor in town to form the bases of many happy mixed drinks—those charming concoctions that almost had been forgotten during the swigging period when bourbon, Scotch, and moon were plentiful." Then, after dutifully noting that to manufacture, barter, sell, or give away intoxicating liquors was illegal, the *Trib* went on: "Judging from extensive preparations revealed by a survey, many individuals seem hazy on the scope of the Volstead Act." The newspaper went on to name the bourbons, Scotches, and champagnes that were available, such as "Cedar Brook—Most of this is guaranteed instantly to kill pyorrhea germs, but care should be taken that it does not dissolve the teeth."

It was also lethal stuff. Every year there would be reports of fatal alcohol poisoning in the news. In 1926, thirty-seven deaths were counted in four cities. Seven of those deaths were in Chicago, and they led to the resignation of Cook County Sheriff Peter Hoffman. He considered it impossible to enforce the Volstead Act because so many people did not support it.

On the Sunday before Christmas in 1925, evangelist Billy Sunday expressed his view, telling three packed houses at Moody Memorial Church that "Demon Rum has been knocked out; he's whipped. Prohibition is here to stay." He said, "It's as permanent as the forty-eight stars and the thirteen stripes of our flag." Sunday also thumped modernists and science, saying the two could never be reconciled with old-time religion. But he did give his approval to bobbed hair and lipstick.

Also in the news shortly before Christmas, 1925, the Illinois Supreme Court ruled that women did not have the right to serve on juries in Illinois. The court agreed with attorney Alfred Austrian, who represented the election commissioners of Chicago. He argued that when the state legislature used the word "electors" in granting women's suffrage, it did not contemplate them as being qualified to serve as jurors. Mrs. Hannah Fyfe of Oak Park had brought the suit. Her reaction was that "Illinois remains old-fashioned and unaware of the trend of the times."

A popular trend of the past was coming-out parties planned for the daughters of the rich and famous. One such Chicago family were the Glessners of 1800 Prairie Avenue. At Christmastime 1925, the house was bedecked with flowers for the coming-out party of Miss Martha Lee, the granddaughter of the Glessners. Miss Lee was from Littleton, New Hampshire.

She was dressed in silver lace for the occasion, and carried a bouquet of orchids and roses. Among those who were represented at the tea in her honor were members of the faculty of the University of Chicago, many people associated with the Chicago Symphony Orchestra, and many other prominent Chicagoans. Today the Glessner House is open for tours, thanks to the the Chicago Architectural Society.

Also around Christmastime in 1925 the *Tribune* and the *Chicago Herald and Examiner* were reporting on plans for Chicago's greatest building project. It was to be called the American Agricultural Mart, and it would be the largest commercial structure in the world, measuring fifty-nine million cubic feet in volume, with three million square feet in retail space. The building was to be erected on the site of an old Chicago & Northwestern railroad terminal at Kinzie and Wells. It would be eighteen stories tall with a tower rising to thirty-four stories. In the tower would be a super radio station, broadcasting agricultural reports to the nation. The tower and the radio station are not there, but today that structure is known, of course, as the Merchandise Mart.

Marshall Field's Ads

Starting in the 1920s, Christmas advertising became real works of art. On Christmas Eve, 1925, Marshall Field & Company, calling itself "The Store of the Christmas Spirit" ran a seven-column, page-length ad. Inside a border defined by the titles of Christmas carols and sketches appropriate to each there was a half-page oval showing three children singing in front of a full moon.

Below were the words:

SANTA WILL COME TONIGHT!

And little children all thrilled with thoughts of the presents, of stockings filled to the brim, of the sparkling tree will sing their carols lustily this evening. No one will be disappointed if we can help it, for every gift purchased here for a child or grown-up before six o'clock tonight will be delivered tonight. Great fleets of trucks are ready to carry their gay packages all over the city and its suburbs. If just one truck could cover every one of these distances and should travel straight ahead, it would go half way around the world.

Santa will deliver all gifts as early as possible, but you must forgive him if he has to ring your doorbell in the wee small hours.

On Christmas Day, 1925, Marshall Field's waxed poetic. A full-page ad showed the interior court of the State Street store, calling it "The Cathedral of All the Stores," and presented the reader with a poem written by Irvin Clay Lambert, who had been with Field's since 1892:

Untrammeled and fair like a thing of dreams,
Its granite walls uprise;
Four square to the world, symmetrical, true,
It tow'rs 'neath bending skies.
To the north and south, to the east and west,
Swing gates to wondrous floors
Builded for service, aye, proudly it stands,
Cathedral of all the stores.

Santa Will Come Tonight!

AND little children all thrilled with thoughts of the presents, of stockings filled to the brim, of the sparkling tree will sing their carols lustily this evening.

No one will be disappointed if we can help it, for every gift purchased here for child or grown-up before six o'clock tonight will be delivered tonight. Great fleets of trucks are ready to carry their gay packages all over the city and its suburbs. If just one truck could cover every one of these distances and should travel straight ahead, it would go half way around the world.

Under the Tree 1925

In 1925 a player piano went for $195.00 ($2.00 per week). You could buy a Chevrolet touring car for $525.00, a Hupmobile for $1,285.00, a Peerless sedan for $1,595.00, or an Auburn Straight Eight for $1,795.00.

Walgreen's was selling black-and-white walking and barking pull dog toys for 98¢ apiece. Felix the Cat dolls with revolving heads and movable joints were only 23¢. A steel toy piano said to be "strong as the Rock of Gibraltar" and able to play two full octaves cost $1.98.

American Flyer was advertising ungrammatically that its toy trains would make a boy say, "Gee! Dad, this is the swellest train in the world." Sets cost $5.75 and up.

John T. Shayne & Company, at Michigan and Randolph, was selling men's and women's raccoon coats for $295 apiece.

And radiant stretch the passes within.
Like fairied aisles they run
Mid postured columns, uplifted and white
As snood of cloistered nun.
Ever and ever press myriad feet,
Expectant thru the doors
Builded for scrvice, securely it stands,
Cathedral of all the stores.

And here ingathered from places anear,
And lands beyond the sea;
Are wonderful wares for uses of men,
Rare works in artistry.
And so shall it stand with fame unmatched
Here, or on distant shores.
Builded for service—the marvel of men
Cathedral of all the storcs.

Dem Bears

All through the day on Friday, Christmas Day, 1925, the mercury kept falling, and falling, and falling. Christmas, 1925, was extremely chilly. By 9 P.M. the mercury registered twenty-six degrees. Twenty-four hours later it was down to an official reading of six degrees, but many readings in the outlying areas were below zero.

The cold and a strong north wind contributed to a very busy day for Chicago firefighters. They handled 110 calls on Christmas Day According to the *Tribune:*

> The cold snap and Christmas celebrations, staged in the traditional white of Yuletide in Chicago, resulted in the overheating of many furnaces and the abnormal number of fire calls.
>
> All day long the youngsters, their attention attracted by the passing fire engines, deserted Christmas trees and laden stockings to rush to windows. All through the day firemen, rushing from spot to spot in the bitter wind, fought the blazes. Most of them were of the minor variety. (Copyright *Chicago Tribune.* Used by permission.)

Even though it was cold and windy, it was also a sunny Christmas Day. Thousands of people spent part of their holiday skating on the lakes, lagoons, and artificial rinks in the area. Park officials couldn't remember such a big turnout on a Christmas Day.

But it was in the seventies in the Miami area, where, on Christmas Day, the Chicago Bears and their newly acquired star running back, Red Grange, were on a barnstorming tour.

Grange scored a touchdown and the Bears beat a team of eastern collegians 7-0. The game was played in suburban Coral Gables, in a seventeen-thousand-seat stadium built in just ten days for the event, which was attended by notables wintering in Miami and the local high society. The game was the Bears' first on a month-long seventy-five-hundred mile tour through the South and West. Earlier in the month the Bears had gone east, where they had played eight games in twelve days.

Grange was the main attraction. His fame had come from his football exploits at the University of Illinois, and his name was as dominant in the sports pages in the mid-twenties as were those of Babe Ruth and Jack Dempsey. *Time* magazine called him an "eel-hipped runagade."

After the University of Illinois's last game, Grange signed with the Bears and made his pro debut on Thanksgiving Day. For many in America, this was a moral disaster. Professional football had a reputation of being dirty and profane. Grange's friends and many in the public had been advising him to go into acting or business. They were especially outraged because Grange went professional before graduating.

From the standpoint of the Bears, however, the addition of a true American sports hero could do nothing but help the pro game, and they wanted nothing more than to capitalize upon Grange.

Their tours did just that. The Bears with Grange drew thirty-five thousand fans in Philadelphia, then seventy-three thousand the very next day in New York City. The Bears won both games. By the time they got back to Chicago for a rematch against New York, the entire team was battered and bruised. Grange had a badly swollen arm and had to stay on the sidelines. After the Bears lost to the Giants 9-0, the *Tribune* editorialized that pro football was in danger of killing the goose that laid the golden egg.

Top Songs 1925

The top tunes of the day, and the artists who made them popular, included "Oh, How I Miss You Tonight" by Ben Selvin, by the Benson Orchestra of Chicago, by Lewis James, and by Irving Kaufman; "Manhattan" by Ben Selvin and by Paul Whiteman; "Remember" by Isham Jones and by Jean Goldkette; and "The Prisoner's Song" by Vernon Dalhart. The latter sold a million copies and was number one in the nation for twelve weeks during the year.

At the Movies 1925

Cecille B. DeMille's The Road to Yesterday *was playing at the Orpheum Theater at State and Monroe. Blanche Sweet, Holbrook Blinn, and Ben Lyon were starring in* The New Commandment *at the Chicago Theater. At the Roosevelt Lon Chaney and Mary Philbin were starring in* The Phantom of the Opera.

On Stage 1925

The Ziegfeld Follies with W. C. Fields was playing at the Illinois Theater. The Daughter of Rosie O'Grady *starring Pat Rooney and Marion Bent, was at the Garrick. Al Jolson, "the world's greatest entertainer," was opening Christmas night in* Big Boy *at the Apollo Theater. At the Woods, it was Eddie Cantor and Mary Eaton in* Kid Boots.

Best-Sellers 1925

Best-selling fiction books of the day included: Christopher Morley's Thunder on the Left, *Martha Ostenso's* Wild Geese, *and Frank Swinnerton's* The Elder Sister. *In nonfiction, the best-sellers included Viscount Grey's* Twenty-five Years, The Diaries of George Washington, *and* Aaron Burr *by Samuel Wandell and Meade Minnegerode.*

Scandal was also besmirching the game's reputation. In the week before Christmas justice came swiftly for four Englewood High School football stars who confessed to playing for the pro Milwaukee Badgers team on December 10, in their game against the Chicago Cardinals. They said they played because they had been led to believe that it was a practice contest and that they would learn some of the finer points of the game. They did not get paid for their services, but none of that held any sway with the board of control of public school athletics, which found them guilty of violating the rules of amateurism and barred them from future high school play. That ruling also cost the boys any hopes they might have had of playing football in college.

At the same time, the city of Chicago and the state of Illinois, through a committee of aldermen, park board members, and patriotic and civic groups, were trying to convince the army and naval military academies to hold their 1926 football game in Soldier Field.

One year later another scandal was front-page news at Christmastime. In 1926 two of baseball's biggest stars were defending their good names. Baseball commissioner Judge Kenesaw Mountain Landis was investigating allegations that Ty Cobb and Tris Speaker had fixed a game back in 1919, the same year as the Black Sox World Series scandal. In 1926 the stars were still active as players and as successful managers. Both men had just appeared before the judge, and both had offered their resignations, their "voluntary involuntary retirement" from baseball.

Cobb was vocal in objecting to the proceedings. The *Chicago Herald and Examiner* recorded his words:

> Is there a God? I am beginning to doubt it. I know there is no gratitude. Here I am after 22 years in hard, desperate and honest work, dismissed from baseball in disgrace without ever having a chance to face my accuser.
>
> It is enough to try one's faith. I am branded as a gambler on ball games in which my club took part. I have never in the 22 years I have been in baseball made a single bet on an American League game.

The day after Christmas, the public found out who their accuser was: Dutch Leonard, a former ball player who apparently was disgruntled because he had been released by both Cobb and Speaker, when each was his manager. When Leonard refused to leave California to testify, Landis cleared both men and reinstated them. Cobb and Speaker went on to play a couple more seasons.

1927: Capone Christmas

One of Chicago's most notorious figures, Al Capone, was often in the news. On the Friday before Christmas, 1927, Mr. Capone was in a courtroom in Joliet, paying a fine for himself and four of his lieutenants for carrying guns. All had been arrested when they got off a train from the West Coast.

The *Chicago Tribune* related the conversation in the courtroom:

"I hope," said Judge Adams, "that this will be a lesson to you not to carry deadly weapons." Capone grinned.

"Yes, judge," he replied, "it certainly will be a lesson to me not to carry weapons—in Joliet."

Capone then pulled out a roll of bills, peeled off one $1,000 bill and six $100 bills and tendered them to the county clerk, A. F. Delander, father of the 1927 "Miss America."

"The fines are $1,500 and the charges are $89.80," said the clerk. "Here's your change, $10.20."

"Please take that down to the Salvation Army

Al Capone in the courtroom

<small>Chicago Architectural Society. Used with permission.</small>

4-A
Merry Xmas and a Happy New Year
COME TO HARMON'S
DREAMLAND
BALL ROOM
VAN BUREN AND PAULINA STREETS

DANCING — Thursday, Friday, Saturday Sunday Afternoon and Evening

Learn the new songs-Between dances - "Melody Dan-Sing a Song Man"

ALL CHORUSES REPRINTED BY SPECIAL PERMISSION
All Dance Numbers Specially Arranged by "Dr. Cook" "The Man Who Knows Music"

1 A LITTLE MUSIC IN THE MOONLIGHT

A little music in the moonlight,
On a sleepy old lagoon,
There's a lot of magic in a June night,
When the ukuleles croon,
Give me a birch canoe, made for two, there
  with you,
While night birds softly coo, the world's in
  tune,
To float along while stars are gleaming,
On a night of joy and bliss,
A little song, a little dreaming,
A little love, a little kiss,
All that I ask is this, my whole life thru,
A little music in the moonlight, a June night
  and you.
Copyright 1926 by Milton Weil Music Co.

2 ALONG MIAMI SHORE

Down beside the summer sea
Along Miami shore,
Someone waits alone for me
Along Miami shore.
Paradise I'll find among the palms,
Paradise in someone's empty arms,
Then how happy we will be,
Along Miami shore.
Copyright Transferred 1926 to Forster Music
  Pub., Inc.

3 BLAME IT ON THE WALTZ

If you feel my arms caressing,
Blame it on the waltz;
If you hear my lips confessing,
Blame it on the waltz;
If my yearning eyes should haunt you
Tho' the dreamy music halts,
If forevermore I want you,
Blame it on the waltz.
Copyright 1926 by Jerome H. Remick & Co.

4 BREEZIN' ALONG WITH THE BREEZE

I'm just breezin' along with the breeze,
Trailin' the rails, roamin' the seas;
Like the birdies that sing in the trees,
Pleasin' to live, livin' to please;
The sky is the only roof I have over my head
And when I'm weary Mother Nature makes
  me a bed;
I'm just goin' along as I please,
Breezin' along with the breeze.
Copyright 1926 by Jerome H. Remick & Co.

FRIDAY IS CLASS NIGHT
Over 311 Instructors
Learn To Dance In One Evening

5 'DEED I DO

Do I want you, oh my, do I?
Honey, 'deed I do!
Do I need you? Oh my, do I,
Honey, 'deed I do!
I'm glad that I'm the one who found you,
That's why I'm always hangin' 'round you.
Do I love you? Oh my, do I?
Honey, 'deed I do.
Copyright 1926 by Ted Browne Music Co., Inc.

6 WHEN I FIRST MET MARY

Ev'ryone nice mp. brings back days of long
  ago,
When I first met Mary, my sweetheart Mary,
There's a farmer in the dell,
Games we played and loved so well,
When I first met Mary.
Belive me, eyes of blue, her heart was true,
The whole wide world knew,
Just like kids, the things we did were innocent
  too,
Now that we are old and gray,
I just live and bless the day,
When I first met Mary, my own.
Copyright 1926 by Milton Weil Music Co.

7 EVERYTHING'S PEACHES

Ev'rything's peaches for Peaches and me,
Oh, how she teaches, you ought to see;
Our little flat, the dog and the cat,
That's the whole family.
We're not much on wealth, but we've got our
  health,
Plenty of this and plenty of that,
We're just as happy as can be.
Gee, we're always smiling, we're never blue,
Bills keep on piling, that's nothing new;
We laugh it off when the comes due,
We're saving up for a farm, you never know,
We may want our own peaches to grow.
Ev'rything's peaches for my little Peaches and
  me.
Copyright 1926 by Lewis Music Publishing Co.

8 FOR MY SWEETHEART

Love made the birds that sing,
The flow'rs in spring and ev'rything for my
  sweetheart;
Love made the skies of blue,
The morning dew, the sunbeams too for my
  sweetheart.
Love built a bungalow where roses grow,
Where we will go and never part;
I know that I'm glad as can be,
Love picked a little boy like me for my sweet-
  heart.
Copyright 1926 by Jerome H. Remick & Co.

Santa Claus on the corner," said Capone. "Tell him it's a Christmas present from Al Capone." (Copyright *Chicago Tribune*. Used by permission.)

One year later, Capone wasn't even in Chicago for Christmas. The *Chicago Herald and Examiner* explained it this way:

Nice little politicians who used to believe in Santa Claus and call him "Al" are just about ready now to admit that if the prodigal old saint ever did exist it must have been at least two years ago.

The sad evidence which has brought them to this desperate conclusion is a brief dispatch that came from Miami.

"Al's here," it said, and went on to explain that Scarface Capone, alias St. Nick, alias Claus, who used to give away $100,000 along about this time of year in Chicago is down there at his winter home for a quiet—and inexpensive—Christmas.

Last year at this time, it will be remembered, Mr. Capone, bitterly complaining that his most favored customers had ungratefully called him "bootlegger" and other hard names, hurried away to Los Angeles, and afterward (at the suggestion of the Los Angeles police) to Florida.

And he cut out his whole Christmas gift list, so far as the Chicago names were concerned.

The disappointed ones, however, found consolation in the belief that this year would be different.

Just why he decided to absent himself again this year is a matter in which anybody is entitled to guess. (Reprinted with permission of the Hearst Corp.)

Within a couple of years, Capone would be spending Christmas behind bars after being convicted of income tax evasion.

1929: The Crash

At the beginning of the Roaring Twenties, the amount of money that Chicagoans spent on Christmas shopping had expanded fivefold. As department store cash registers rang with delight and throngs of last minute shoppers packed the Loop on December 23, 1922, the *Tribune* reported, "The surging masses reminded one of the pre-Prohibition New Year's eve crowds, though packages took the place of confetti." It was being estimated that Chicago shoppers were spending $70 million on their Christmas gifts, $20 million more than the year before. What were they buying? Player pianos, cast iron toys, and raccoon coats for $295.00 apiece.

The high times of the 1920s came crashing down with the stock market in October of 1929. By Christmastime 1930, unemployment was soaring and prices were dropping. Food was down 10 percent. Hillman's was selling turkeys for 39¢ a pound, four pounds of coffee for 79¢, butter for 31¢ a pound, and apples were 29¢ for four pounds. It was not unusual to see people selling apples on street corners.

Even the price of Prohibition beer fell. Reports in both the *Tribune* and the *Chicago Times* said mobsters had cut the price of a stein of beer from 25¢ to 15¢. The papers credited northwest side wholesaler William "Klondike" O'Donnell with the idea for the price cut. It was designed to regain customers who weren't drinking as much because they couldn't afford to.

1930 - 1939

1930: Depression Christmas

The 1930 census made Chicago the fourth largest city in the world, with a population of 3,376,438. Only New York, Berlin, and London were larger.

Snow fell several days leading up to the holiday, but mild temperatures and clear roads were the rule for Christmas Eve and Christmas Day. The forecast hinted at the possibility for more snow or rain on Christmas night.

For many Americans, the Christmas of 1930 was cautiously lean. The full effect of the stock market crash of 1929 had not yet settled in, but all around there were signs: more than twenty-six thousand business failures, more than thirteen hundred bank failures.

Unemployment was going up. The Labor Department estimated that between 2 and 3 million American workers were out of jobs by the end of the year. The American Federation of Labor put it at 5.3 million. By Christmastime 1932, 15 million people were out of work. These figures made for an unemployment rate between 6 and 11 percent. Rising unemployment was on President Herbert Hoover's mind at Christmastime. He spent part of his holiday working out the details of a $116 million emergency construction plan, just approved by Congress to relieve unemployment.

Economic worries were on the minds of Christmas shoppers and were reflected in the kinds of articles chosen for Christmas gifts. According to a report out of Washington in the *San Francisco Chronicle*, shoppers were buying more carefully and choosing practical gifts, not gifts that would wind up in the attic or the dust bin. One particular item that was in demand was rubber footwear.

On the Table 1930

The Chicago Tribune *reported a 10 percent decline in food prices over the past year. The Christmas turkey of 1930 cost 39¢ a pound at Hillman's. Coffee was four pounds for 79¢, butter 31¢ a pound, apples four pounds for 29¢.*

Under the Tree 1930

In Chicago, Commonwealth Edison's electric shops were advertising electric refrigerators at Christmastime, $10.00 down and total prices ranging from $140.00 to $310.00. Commonwealth Edison was also boasting the "largest electric toy department in Chicago—every toy in motion." Complete Lionel or American Flyer train sets could be had for $7.00. Single cars could be purchased for 75¢ and up.

As the Christmas of 1932 approached, Assistant U.S. Commerce Secretary Julius Klein reported a $170 million toy trade in the United States. Ninety percent of the toys were made in Chicago. Klein said: "Little girls of 1932 are demanding home-making gadgets the demand for such merchandise as toy vacuum cleaners, electric irons and electric stoves has more than doubled in the past two years."

Walgreens advertised American Flyer mechanical train sets for $1.19. Sears offered men's shirts for $1.29, suede leather jackets for $6.79, and flannel robes for $3.45.

A Christmas Reunion

On Christmas Eve, 1930, the *Chicago Tribune* told the story of Orris Wattles, who had left his parents' home in downstate Clay City ten years earlier at age nineteen and hadn't been heard from since.

On the Sunday before Christmas, a man was killed by a train in Naperville. The body lay unidentified for forty-eight hours until the proprietor of a Naperville hotel identified the body as that of Wattles, a bricklayer. The authorities notified Wattles's parents, who were "too old" to make the trip, so other family members came north to claim the body.

A sister, a brother, and two brothers-in-law confirmed that the body was indeed that of Wattles. In the meantime, the authorities had determined that Wattles lived at an address on the Chicago's West Side. Family members telephoned to that residence.

"Yes," said the voice on the other end of the line. "This is where Orris Wattles lives. This is Orris Wattles talking."

After Wattles drove out to Naperville to confirm his existence to his unbelieving relatives, plans were made for a big Christmas celebration and reunion down in Clay City, Illinois, his hometown. The body in Naperville remained unidentified.

1933: New Beginnings

From the vantage point of Monday, Christmas Day, 1933, a look back at the year just ending revealed a multiplicity of momentous changes. Some were good, others decidedly not, and the judgment about others still depends on one's point of view.

Even the weather at Christmastime 1933 was a change. It was Chicago's first white Christmas in four years. Snow fell the afternoon of Christmas Day, following a morning cold snap that plunged the mercury to seven degrees.

The Christmas of 1933 was Franklin Roosevelt's first in the White House. In the nearly ten months since he gave his famous "The only thing we have to fear is fear itself" inauguration speech, President Roosevelt had been busily at work, battling the depression with bank

holidays, big public works spending, the National Recovery Administration, and a new relief program to help the needy. The *Chicago Tribune* described Christmas at the White House:

> Washington, D. C. Dec. 25—[Special.]— President and Mrs. Roosevelt celebrated today their "happiest Christmas" surrounded by a family house party representing four generations and including also an uncle and several nephews as well as sisters and cousins and aunts.

Accompanied by Mrs. James Roosevelt, the President's mother, and their children, Mrs. Curtis B. Dall, Franklin Jr., and John, the President and Mrs. Roosevelt attended the morning service at St Thomas' Episcopal church, where Mrs. Roosevelt went at midnight last night to the Christmas eve service.

CHILDREN TAKE THE LEAD

But long before they left the White House the Christmas festivities were at their height. "Sistie" and "Buzzie" Dall, the two grandchildren who helped to "make Christmas" at the White House this year, were up shortly after daylight, and the rest of the household, wakening one by one as the joyous cries of the children rang through the house, hastened to join in the fun.

Meeting in the President's bedroom, the stockings, including those of the President, hung in a row over the fireplace, where they were emptied with celerity, the children bringing them to the bed to be assisted in the opening of packages and to watch "grandfather" open the gift packages Santa had left in his stockings.

GIFTS FROM AFAR

There were other gifts also for the President and Mrs. Roosevelt, by which they were deeply touched. From far and near, and from people in all ranks of life, came presents, inexpensive, many hand made, but each accompanied by good wishes, and in many instances, by grateful thanks. (Copyright *Chicago Tribune.* Used by permission.)

There's no doubt that some of those thanks came from Chicagoans, who, like the rest of the nation, were struggling through a depression-era Christmas. Yet, in keeping with the significance of the holiday, there was hope. The Christmas of 1933 was being described as the happiest since 1929. Thousands of unemployed workers and their families received Christmas baskets and dinners throughout the city. The railroads reported passenger traffic up 40 to 60 percent higher than the year previous. The *Tribune* said the busy train stations were reminiscent of 1928 or 1929, when entire families journeyed back to their hometown to celebrate Christmas with the old folks.

Rise of Nazi Germany

The Christmas of 1933 was also the first for the new dictator of Germany, Adolf Hitler. The *Tribune* reported:

NAZIISM RIVALS CHRISTIANITY IN GERMAN HOLIDAY
Hitler Given Place with Santa Claus.
By Sigrid Schultz.

BERLIN, Dec. 24.— "Our leader has given us a new and united Germany," is the chant of the Nazis, echoed by the bulk of the German people, in praise and gratitude to Chancellor Adolf Hitler this Christmas. But pleas to put uppermost the thought of Jesus Christ and the spirit of clemency even over events of the day, were voiced today in many churches of Germany, which were more crowded than they have been for years.

Tremendous party and state machinery was set in motion to collect gifts for the poor. Santa Claus, private and official, was given greater publicity than ever before in German history and always pains were taken to include Naziism with Santa Claus.

"No Germans Hungry" Is Slogan

"No German is to be cold or hungry this Christmas," was the slogan of the government and government officials feel they have accomplished their aim. Their newspapers this Christmas eve are full of a story of how Hitler himself when driving along the roads of south Germany, was accosted for a ride by two volunteers in a labor camp, and how he not only gave them a ride but his famous mustard-colored trench coat and $2 each. The Polish minister, fired by the spirit of sacrifice, offered presents made in Poland for the winter relief.

The release of prisoners from concentration camps went on for days before Christmas and was given much publicity. In the course of the releases camps were mentioned whose existence was not known before. Yet when one tries to get close to those released from a prison camp, one realizes that the presence of a foreigner is not desired. Many of those held on suspicion for months are without jobs now, and their families are still in the throes of worry and apprehension.

Church Still Divided

While the Nazi press was celebrating the new German unity, Christmas eve found the Protestant church more divided than ever. This correspondent listened to services in the parish where the Rev. Walter von Rabernau openly spoke of the new dangers threatening Protestants this Christmas day.

"Great changes took place this year," he said. "The danger of godlessness coming from Moscow is eliminated, but there is a strong movement of those who do not want Christ or the Bible."

Von Rabernau warned that these people "want a human Christ, one who can be inserted into their political system."

"We firm believers in the gospel insist that Christ should be brought close to school children, that he should rank above any humans," he continued. "Only the thought of Christ can give persons the sense of the all supreme duty they need."

WILL STRUGGLE ON

Von Rabernau left no doubt in the minds of his listeners that Protestants are "determined to struggle on to reestablish the supremacy of Christ and eliminate a mental attitude similar to the one which reigned in Germany before Christendom reached this country." (Copyright *Chicago Tribune*. Used by permission.)

Pope Pius XI was critical of a recently announced German program to sterilize 400,000 people whom the German government deemed unfit because of hereditary defects or incurable diseases. Meanwhile in Italy, Benito Mussolini was trying to boost the birthrate by honoring mothers, specifically ninety-two women who had brought 1,288 children into the world. The most prolific was a Naples woman who had mothered twenty children.

In Moscow, the All-Union Godless Society was campaigning to convince 100 percent of the labor force to work on Christmas Day.

End to Prohibition

The Christmas of 1933 was the nation's first legally wet Christmas since 1919. Prohibition had come to an end on the afternoon of December 5, when Utah became the last of thirty-six states to ratify the Twenty-first Amendment to the Constitution, repealing the Eighteenth. President Franklin D. Roosevelt called on the nation to practice moderation in order to prevent the "repugnant conditions" that had brought about Prohibition in 1920.

The Chicago City Council was hard at work on that matter. The city was wrestling with legislation covering taverns and retail liquor outlets. The council passed, and Mayor Ed Kelly signed, a bill forcing such establishments to close their doors at 1 A.M. or 2 A.M. on Sundays. Meanwhile, ads for liquor were once again appearing in the newspapers. Walgreens, for example, was selling nine-year-old wine for 98¢ a bottle.

Cook County State's Attorney Thomas Courtney declared Chicago's judiciary "rotten" with political domination. He asserted that crime

Transportation 1930

The fare on Chicago Rapid Transit trains in 1936 was 10¢. It was 7¢ on Chicago Surface Line streetcars. The Chicago City Council was also making building plans, voting forty to one to construct a subway line under State Street.

On the Table 1933

A seven-course Christmas dinner at the Stevens Hotel (now the Conrad Hilton and Towers) in 1933 cost $1.25.

Kroger had butter for 19¢ a pound, ham for 13 1/2¢ a pound, and a one-pound loaf of white bread for 5¢. Stop and Shop advertised turkey for 29¢ a pound, and three-and-a-half ounce cans of caviar for $1.00.

Top Songs 1933

The most popular music of 1933 included "Who's Afraid of the Big Bad Wolf" by Don Bestor and Victor Young and Ben Bernie, "Did You Ever See a Dream Walking?" by Eddie Duchin, "The Last Round-Up" by Guy Lombardo and by George Olsen, and "Love Is the Sweetest Thing" by Ray Noble.

Transportation 1933

You could fly to Philadelphia from Chicago on United Airlines planes for $41.95 one-way. The trip took five hours.

At the Movies 1933

At Christmastime, the Marx Brothers were playing in Duck Soup *at the Chicago Theater,* Katherine Hepburn *was starring in* Little Women *at the Roosevelt, at the McVickers it was* Alice in Wonderland *starring Charlotte Henry, Gary Cooper, Cary Grant, and W. C. Fields, and at the Oriental it was* Design for Living *with Frederic March, Gary Cooper, and Miriam Hopkins.*

Transportation 1935

In 1935 riders on the Burlington train to San Francisco or Los Angeles paid $86.00 for a Pullman or $61.75 for coach. A one-way ticket to New York on American Airlines cost $47.95. The trip took four hours and twenty minutes.

On December 21, 1935, the Douglas DC-3 made its first flight. The plane was capable of carrying twenty-one passengers at a speed of nearly 160 m.p.h. The original version of the plane was supposed to have fourteen beds instead of twenty-one seats. American Airlines had ordered the planes so that they could compete with Pullman rail service.

would never be routed until judges were appointed to their posts because of their merit, rather than because of some politician's favor.

The alderman perhaps best known for his crack that "Chicago ain't ready for reform," Ald. Paddy Bauler of the Forty-third Ward, was in trouble with the law. A few days before Christmas Bauler was arraigned in court on a charge of assault with intent to murder a police officer. The officer in question was wounded in a gun battle outside Bauler's tavern on North Avenue in the early morning hours of December 19. Bauler claimed self-defense in the shooting, which erupted after the officer tried to enter his tavern at 4 A.M.

Meanwhile Mayor Kelly publicly extolled Chicago's police force. This boost of confidence came after a raid on an apartment in Rogers Park, which police believed to be a hideout for the notorious archcriminal John Dillinger. Dillinger wasn't in the flat, but three other gunmen were. Two of them were jail escapees and bank robbers, the third an ex-convict. When the shooting stopped, three gunmen were dead. None of the officers involved suffered a scratch. Said Kelly of his police: if we just let them alone, they would make the city too hot for the type of criminals who were killed.

The city fathers of Berwyn celebrated the arrival of a new police patrol wagon, but the event turned into an embarrassment. The first passengers in the wagon for a ride from city hall to the police station were the police chief, an alderman, the president of the Berwyn Taxpayers Association, and a representative of the company which sold the vehicle. Officer Tony Weber was behind the wheel, and when he pulled up to the police station, lo and behold, he couldn't find the key to the locked rear door. From within, the police chief assigned the entire detective force to search for the key. It took them forty-five minutes to find it at curbside; it had slipped through a hole in Weber's pocket.

1935: State Street Parade

Chicago's Christmas of 1935 was a cold one. The mercury plunged to minus two degrees on that Wednesday Christmas Day, making it the coldest day so far that season.

A few nights before Christmas sixteen thousand people jammed the Chicago Stadium to hear the stars of stage, movies, and radio perform on Mayor Ed Kelly's second annual *Night of Stars*. It was a benefit performance to raise money for the mayor's fund for the needy. Among the thirty-five acts that performed were Herbie Kay and his orchestra, George Olsen with Ethel Shutta and the College Inn Orchestra, Earl Hines and his orchestra, Amos and Andy and the WLS "Barn Dance," the male chorus of the Cook County Council of the American Legion, and various stars of the Cubs, the White Sox, and the Bears. The show started at 8:45 P.M. and didn't wrap up until well past midnight. It raised more than one hundred thousand dollars for the needy children of the city.

On Christmas Eve there was a Santa Claus parade down State Street. Escorted by mounted Chicago police, the jolly old elf drove a wagon pulled by six horses, and in the wagon was Senn High School's a cappella choir. The parade was sponsored by State Street's merchants, who were celebrating what they called the return of good times, namely the biggest shopping boom since the crash of 1929.

The Christmas of 1935 was not a merry Christmas for American aviation hero Col. Charles Lindbergh. He, his wife, and their three-year-old son Jon spent the holiday on a ship in the Atlantic, bound for a new home in Europe. The Lindberghs were worried about threats they had received against the life of their son. They were worried that accomplices of Bruno Richard Hauptmann might try to do the boy harm. Hauptmann had been convicted of the 1932 kidnapping and murder of the Lindbergh's first baby, Charles Jr. Hauptmann was scheduled to be executed in New

Jersey in January, but in the month before the execution, the governor of that state, Harold Hoffman, was still expressing doubt that the case had been solved to his complete satisfaction.

The Europe to which the Lindberghs were escaping was itself a pretty scary place. Italy was at war with Ethiopia, and Benito Mussolini had ordered women to sacrifice their jewelry and gold wedding rings to the cause of Fascism. In Germany, four days before Christmas, Hitler ordered all Jewish doctors to give up their practices at private hospitals.

Chicago Historical Society. ICHI 24311. Used with permission.

Christmas decorations on State Street, 1936

The Christmas turkey of 1935 cost 33¢ a pound at The Fair Store. Coffee was 25¢ a pound at Jewel. Bread was 9¢ a loaf at the A&P.

At the Movies 1935

The Littlest Rebel *starring Shirley Temple was having its world premiere at the Chicago Theater. Just finishing up at the United Artists was* Mutiny on the Bounty *starring Clark Gable and Charles Laughton. At the Palace Theatre the movie was* Sylvia Scarlett *with Katherine Hepburn and Cary Grant. The Palace also featured a stage show entitled* Round the Town *with the WBBM Air Theatre and Dell Coon and his orchestra.*

Top Songs 1935

On the Saturday before Christmas, the songs featured on Your Hit Parade *included "Pennies from Heaven," "In the Chapel in the Moonlight," "I'll Sing You a Thousand Love Songs," "I've Got You Under My Skin," "It's De-Lovely," "The Way You Look Tonight," and the "Organ Grinder's Swing."*

The state of the world was such that a lot of people wanted to get away from it all—if only for an hour or so—through the movies. *The Littlest Rebel* starring Shirley Temple was having its world premiere at the Chicago Theater.

1936: Black Cloud of War

Chicago's Christmas of 1936 was the warmest in forty-one years. The mercury hit the mid-fifties both Christmas Eve and Christmas Day.

The year 1936 was filled with important news events. Hitler sent his Nazi troops to reoccupy the Rhineland; Italian forces conquered Ethiopia; Spain exploded in civil war; and Japan joined Germany and Italy in forming the Axis bloc.

In August of that year, black American track stars, most notably Jesse Owens, made a shambles of Hitler's racial theories. Owens won three gold medals individually and was part of the United States' winning 400-meter relay team. He was a favorite of the crowd, who chanted his name whenever he came onto the field.

On opening day, Hitler personally congratulated two German gold medalists and a Finnish winner. Later, with darkness falling and rain threatening, all the German high jumpers were eliminated from the competition. Hitler left his box to avoid congratulating the two black Americans, Cornelius Johnson and David Albritton, who had finished one and two in the competition. Count Baillet-Latour, the president of the International Olympic Committee, sent word to Hitler that he must either congratulate all winners or none. Hitler chose the latter alternative.

In this country, the presidential campaign was dramatic and filled with high emotion. There were many predictions that Gov. Alf Landon of Kansas would beat incumbent President Roosevelt. Landon's sunflower campaign buttons seemed to be popping up everywhere. A record number of Americans cast ballots in the election, resulting in a landslide for Roosevelt and his New Deal.

As December rolled around, all of the events of the year were being pushed off the front-page by a royal drama being played out in England. On December 11, King Edward VIII announced his decision to abdicate the throne and marry an American divorcée, Mrs. Wallis Warfield Simpson.

The *Chicago Tribune* and the *Chicago Daily News* were calling her "Wally" in headlines, as in "CHURCH ATTACK ON FORMER KING VEERS TO WALLY; Empire Never Would Have Stood Her, Bishop Avers," and "EXILED EDWARD AND WALLY LAY WEDDING PLANS; Long Distance Courtship Carried On by Courier."

Indeed, at Christmastime 1936, the former king was staying at the castle of Baron Eugene Rothschild in Enzesfeld, Austria. Mrs. Simpson was in Cannes, France. News coverage of the two, and of the controversy left behind in England, was akin to today's blanket coverage of some news events.

The ex-king was getting thirty-five pounds of gifts and fan mail a day. Mrs. Simpson needed special police protection just to go shopping for stockings and gloves. There were "inside" stories telling of Edward's homesickness for England, and of the "real story" of this great love affair.

In England, leaders of the Anglican church were in a dither, according to the *Tribune*.

The archbishop of Canterbury followed up Edward's abdication of Dec. 11 with a severe denunciation over the radio of Edward's "fast international set" and lack of "Christian principles of marriage." The archbishop repeated his attack in the house of lords on Monday, deploring the "painful past," expressing "immense satisfaction" in the rise of the duke of York to the throne as George VI, and praising his attachment to the church of England. The archbishop's flaying of Edward brought quick resentment among commoners and a part of the press. On Thursday before the commons Independent Laborite Jack McGovern shouted a retort to the archbishop, Prime Minister Stanley Baldwin, and all church leaders and cabinet ministers who opposed King Edward's marriage to Mrs. Wallis Simpson. McGovern called the ministers "a lot of huffy old women" and said, "Let the bishop get out and deal with unemployment . . . instead of kicking a man when he's down." (Copyright *Chicago Tribune*. Used by permission.)

Chicago and the rest of the world heard the voice of an ailing Pope Pius XI on the radio on Christmas Eve. The pontiff spoke from his bed, with his doctor nearby. He was suffering from uremia and the partial paralysis of his legs. The *Chicago Herald and Examiner* described his broadcast this way:

Twice during his dramatic speech the Pope's voice broke into low sobs that were heard in the hovels and mansions of London and New York, the dwellings and gathering places of the high and the humble, wherever men live. . . .

His Holiness, after pausing to drink a glass of water, fairly shouted into the microphone as he warned of the dangers recumbent in the civil war in Spain. . . .

The Pope's voice throbbed with emotion as he alluded to the events in Spain as a "new menace, more threatening than ever, for the whole world, and principally for Europe and its Christian civilization."

He revealed his grave concern over the war clouds darkening the horizon with the words: "Here are signs and portents of terrifying reality of what is being prepared for Europe and the whole world, if they do not hasten to adopt the necessary remedies of defense." (Reprinted with permission of the Hearst Corp.)

On the Radio 1936

The Daily News's *"Pick of the Air" listings for Christmas Eve 1936 included The Royal Gelatin program on WMAQ-NBC—Rudy Vallee and his Connecticut Yankees, guest artists included Edgar Bergen, ventriloquist, and Len Hammond, newsreel cameraman;* Band Wagon *on WBBM-CBS, featuring Kate Smith and the Paulist Choristers; Tchaikovsky's* Nutcracker Suite *on WLS-NBC;* Major Bowes' Amateur Hour *on WBBM-CBS;* Amos 'n' Andy *on WMAQ-NBC; and* Jamboree *on WENR-NBC with Don McNeill, master of ceremonies, plus an interview with Mary Christmas, and Christmas carols sung by students from the International House of the University of Chicago.*

Transportation 1936

The Chicago Park Commission had just won its battle with the Chicago Surface Lines. The Illinois Commerce Commission ordered the trolley company to tear out its tracks along Lake Shore Drive between Chicago and Grand Avenues.

In his Christmas Eve message to the nation at the lighting of Washington's community Christmas tree, President Roosevelt noted that he had just been engaged in his usual custom of reading Charles Dickens's *A Christmas Carol* to his family. Mr. Roosevelt called on the American people to observe the lesson of that great story, and he quoted Scrooge's Christmas pledge: "I will honor Christmas in my heart and try to keep it all the year. I will live in the past, in the present and the future. The spirit of all three shall strive within me. I will not shut out the lessons that they teach."

In what was becoming an annual tradition, "A Christmas Carol" starring Lionel Barrymore as Scrooge was broadcast over WBBM and the Columbia network on Christmas night. In the radio column of the *Chicago Daily News* on Christmas Eve, Barrymore explained:

> One of the reasons why I enjoy playing the role of Scrooge . . . is the fact that I believe in ghosts.
>
> Although Scrooge was confronted with three ghosts; namely, the ghost of Christmas Past—his memory, the ghost of Christmas Present—his intuition, and the ghost of Christmas Future—his imagination, people today may have as many as seven or eight ghosts haunting them. It all depends upon their experiences, for in the innermost recesses of every human mind there are the memories of the past, the intuitions of the present and the imagination of the future.
>
> It is foolish to harbor awesome thoughts about ghosts, for they are in reality man's conscience and therefore his best friend. If man refuses to accept them as such, they will force themselves upon him anyway as they did upon Scrooge when he closed his eyes and heart to the spirit of Christmas season and the joy of living. (Reprinted with special permission from the *Chicago Sun-Times,* Inc. © 1999)

Many people wanted to escape the news of foreign conflict and the drudgery of the depression by listening to such popular radio shows as *Buck Rogers of the 25th Century, Kate Smith's Coffee Time, The Camel Caravan,* and *The March of Time.* On Christmas Day 1935, WBBM carried the international broadcast of Christmas greetings from Britain's King George, a performance of Handel's *Messiah* from Cleveland, and the *Burns & Allen* program including Gracie Allen's Christmas drama, entitled "Scram Scrooge."

Nevertheless, certain sinister "foreign agents" were the villains in many a movie and radio program. Escape from Nazi Germany was even a theme in novels such as Phyllis Bottome's *The Mortal Storm*, published in 1937.

PHILCO

$174⁹⁵

Philco combination radio and cocktail bar

On the Table 1936

Hillman's was selling turkeys for 23¢ a pound and fruitcake for 35¢ a pound. Hills Brothers coffee was 26¢ for a one-pound can at the A&P. Butter was 35¢ a pound.

At the Movies 1936

Gold Diggers of 1937 starring Dick Powell and Joan Blondell was playing at the Roosevelt Theater. Shirley Temple in Stowaway was at the Apollo. Jack Benny, George Burns, Gracie Allen, and Martha Raye were starring in College Holiday at the Chicago Theater. And Clark Gable and Joan Crawford were featured in Love on the Run at the United Artists Theater.

Swing music was the beat of the land. In 1936 dance instructors had met in New York City to decide exactly what swing was. Their conclusions were that it was done in 4/4 time with the drums accented instead of syncopated. The most popular swing bands were those of Duke Ellington, Count Basie, and Benny Goodman.

The recording of music was becoming a bone of labor contention. It was just before Christmas that the Chicago Federation of Musicians announced that as of February 1, 1937, no union member would be permitted to make any kind of recording. Union president James Petrillo

On the Table 1939

The A&P was selling the traditional Christmas turkey for 24¢ a pound. Eggs were 37¢ for two dozen. A three-pound bag of coffee cost 39¢.

expressed concern that "canned" music was seriously affecting the employment of live musicians.

A radio under the Christmas tree in 1935 cost $19.95 at Sears for a six-tube model or $49.95 for an eight-tube version. If one had the money to be extravagant, Lyon & Healy was advertising Philco's combination radio and cocktail bar for between $99.50 and $347.50.

Teacher Declares There Is No Santa Claus

In 1936 school officials in Michigan City, Indiana, were publicly apologizing for the actions of a grade school teacher who had told her pupils there was no Santa Claus. Chicago school officials assured parents that teachers in the system would encourage children to believe in the Christmas spirit for as long as they could.

Trains, Planes, and the Story of Curly Top

In 1936, to fly meant risking danger and adventure. The Hindenburg disaster was still five months in the future, so dirigible travel was not yet out

Used with permission of Marshall Field's.

Toy center is open

of the question. Commercial airlines were in their infancy. At Christmastime, an Eastern Airlines plane got lost in a rain-and-snow storm and crash-landed on a mountainside in New York state. None of the eleven people aboard was injured. A report from San Francisco noted that passengers aboard Pan-American's Philippine Clipper celebrated Christmas twice: once at the Pan American Airways Inn at Wake Island, then the next day after crossing the international date line, at their stop at Midway Island.

In 1936 most travellers, however, were still riding the railroads. The Burlington Railroad's Denver Zephyr set a world long distance speed record, going from Chicago to Denver in twelve hours, twelve minutes. That was an average speed of more than eighty-three miles per hour. The Burlington was advertising its new Twin Zephyr service between Chicago and Minneapolis-St. Paul:

> They're here! Burlington's two new wonder trains, the 7-Car Twin Zephyrs. Diesel-powered and built of the strongest of all modern alloys—stainless steel, these latest Silver Streaks afford *three times the passengers capacity* of the original Twins they replace! Twice daily, the new Zephyrs streak between Chicago and the Twin Cities, following one of the country's most scenic routes—three hundred miles along the historic Mississippi river.

Twin Zephyr service would be short-lived. Because the trains were articulated, their lengths could not be varied. Hence, they were inefficient. Today at the Museum of Science & Industry in Chicago and at the Illinois Railway Museum in Union, Illinois, two of these silver beauties are on display.

The crew and some of the passengers on the Twentieth Century Limited made the Christmas of 1936 very special for a little girl in Elkhart, Indiana. The *Chicago Herald and Examiner* carried the story:

TRAINMEN BRING CHRISTMAS TO LITTLE GIRL NEAR TRACKS

TWENTIETH CENTURY STOPS WITH GIFT OF TOYS AND DOLL

ELKHART, Ind., Dec. 23—Pretty little 8-year-old Violet Schmidt, "Sweetheart of the Twentieth Century," who waves to the crew of that crack train as it passes through here every morning at 7 o'clock, is having the best Christmas she has ever had. The train crew of the "Century," who nicknamed Violet "Curly Top" because of her beautiful curly hair, played Santa Claus to the little girl today—a bit prematurely, to be sure, but then it has been getting cold in Elkhart, and the crew decided the sooner the better.

For the last three years "Curly Top," who lives with her parents in a small and humble cottage alongside the railroad tracks, has never failed to get up in time every morning to wave merrily to the crew of the "Century" as it roars through Elkhart.

It has gotten to be a daily ritual with the crew to look for "Curly Top" as the train passes through Elkhart and wave a cheery greeting back to the little girl. Even some of the passengers on the "Century" who rise early enough join in the ceremony.

A Happy Cinderella

In the last few days "Curly Top" shivered a bit with the cold—and the trainmen noticed it. But today as the flier roared through Elkhart "Curly Top" was a happy, warm Cinderella. Bundled snugly in Santa Claus' presents—a new coat, hat and a red, sweater-scarf-and-mitten set—she hugged a brand new doll in one arm and waved more gleefully than ever before with the other. Twenty-three passengers, including some celebrities got up to see her wave. This is the gayest Yuletide season "Curly Top" can remember. Her parents, Mr. and Mrs. George Schmidt, are in poor circumstances. Mr. Schmidt, a chef by trade, has not had a regular job since the depression caught him in its clutches five years ago. For the last three years he has been on relief as a first aid man on a Works Progress Administration project.

Take Up Collection

As the Century raced past "Curly Top's" home last week, Brakeman E. B. Gulmyer and Stewart Labbe noticed that the little girl shivered as a freezing gust of wind cut through her shabby coat. They took up a collection from seventeen trainmen, and two passengers insisted on joining in so Santa Claus could remember "Curly Top" handsomely this year and erase the memory of other years when Saint Nick ran out of good things before her home was reached.

Brakeman Gulmyer appeared at the door of the Schmidt home in person and made his first speaking acquaintance with the "Sweetheart of the Twentieth Century," as he presented her gifts. "Curly Top" danced with joy. Her brown eyes sparkled with gratitude.

Weep For Joy

Her mother and father both wept with appreciation of the unexpected kindness. Visited by a reporter tonight like a real celebrity, "Curly Top" declared the greatest ambition of her life is to ride on the train with her "friends." She said: "I have never ridden on a train. Santa has been wonderful to me! Some day I hope he will give me a ride on a train." The child, whose fame has reached a hundred grimy roundhouses spread over 10,000 miles of railroad track, is an alert, almost sophisticated youngster. She is in the fourth grade at the St. Vincent's Catholic School in Elkhart and she proudly displayed her last report record. It bore five grades, each of them 100. (Reprinted with permission of the Hearst Corp.)

1940 - 1949

This generation of Americans has a rendezvous with destiny. —Franklin D. Roosevelt

1940: A Tale of Two Cities

Worry had its place at Americans' Christmas tables in the late 1930s and 1940. How could it not? Wars had been or were being fought in Spain, China, and Ethiopia. Hitler and Mussolini were on the rise in Europe. German armed forces were once again in the Rhineland, Austria had been "anschlussed," and Czechoslovakia dismembered.

When war broke out in Europe on September 1, 1939, it was hardly a surprise. On the first Christmas of the war, with America on the sidelines, the front-page news was about the naval battle off Montevideo and the scuttling of the German pocket battleship, *Admiral Graf Spee;* it was also about the scuttling of the German liner *Columbus,* 420 miles east of the coast of Delaware, and the rescue of 578 passengers and crew members by the U.S. cruiser *Tuscaloosa.* The passengers were to be held temporarily at Ellis Island.

Front-page news was also about the cold fighting high above the Arctic Circle, where Soviet armed forces were being battered by the Finns. In temperatures of minus twenty-two degrees, there were no wounded in this battle, according to the *Chicago Tribune*'s Donald Day: "The men became frozen into rigid icy figures quickly after they were shot down. Many lie locked in an embrace, with expressions of hate and death frozen on their unshaven faces." Day estimated more than two thousand Soviets dead, and two hundred to three hundred Finns killed in the battle near Kuolajarvi, Finland.

From Berlin, the *Tribune*'s Sigrid Schultz reported that the war was having a negative effect on traditional German Christmas celebrations. There was a shortage of geese, the traditional centerpiece of German Christmas feasts, and of Christmas trees, which had been snapped up by Nazi welfare groups and other government organizations.

Top Songs 1940

Lyon & Healy advertised records for 35¢ apiece. Titles included "Beat Me Daddy, Eight to a Bar" by Woody Herman and his orchestra, "Hit the Road" by the Andrews Sisters, "Only Forever" by Bing Crosby, and "Maybe" by the Ink Spots.

On the Radio 1941

On the radio Christmas Eve, you could have heard Quiz Kids *on WLS at 7 P.M., or at the same time* Big Town *with Edward G. Robinson and Ona Munson in* Dear Santa Claus *on WBBM. On WMAQ at the same time it was* Adventures of the Thin Man *with Claudia Morgan, and Les Damon in* Santa Comes Across. The Lone Ranger *was on WGN at 7:30.*

WMAQ broadcasted a Red Cross variety program at 8 P.M. featuring Eddie Cantor as emcee, with Deanna Durbin, Fiorella La Guardia, Dinah Shore, Loretta Young, and Fibber McGee and Molly. At the same time on WBBM it was the Star Theater *with Fred Allen, Portland Hoffa, Kenny Baker, and Al Goodman's music.*

Mayor Ed Kelly asked everyone in Chicago to keep all the lights on in their homes from dusk until midnight on Christmas Eve. The mayor said it would be a contrast between America's freedom and the darkness enshrouding Europe's cities and democratic institutions.

Although one report in December 1940 said Santa Claus had adopted blitzkrieg tactics (he was planning to parachute from an airplane into a crowd of twenty-two hundred children celebrating in Elmwood Park), the mood of the season was somewhat subdued.

On Christmas Day, the *Chicago Tribune* contrasted conditions in Chicago and London, calling it a "Tale of Two Cities": "Chicago carolers sang last night. Toddlers hung their stockings beside glowing hearths. Neighbors visited each other, bearing gifts, exchanging greetings, sipping Christmas cheer."

The Loop had been jammed with shoppers on Christmas Eve, and it was being estimated that more merchandise had been sold during the 1940 holiday season than during any other dating back to 1929.

London, on the other hand, was without church bells for the first Christmas in a thousand years. The British capital was under a blackout order, but on Christmas Day, at least, death did not rain from the skies. Hitler had told a newspaper correspondent, "We do not fly at Christmas if the British do not fly."

On Christmas Eve, a cartoon on the editorial page labeled "The World's Most Unpopular Man" depicted Hitler sitting next to Scrooge, who was saying, "I can't compete with you so I might as well go out and make somebody happy."

Christmas Day, 1940, marked the seventy-fifth anniversary of the opening of the Union Stockyards. During those years, 896 million animals—cattle, sheep, hogs, and horses—had been sold in its confines for $21.5 billion, or about 1 million animals and $24 million in sales each month.

1941: Pearl Harbor

Just about every American who was alive at the time remembers what he or she was doing on December 7, 1941, when news came that the Japanese had bombed Pearl Harbor. Eighteen days later, the news wasn't

Christmas shoppers on State Street, 1940

much better. The big bold headline across the top of the *Chicago Tribune* on Christmas morning read: "U.S. MAY QUIT MANILA." With Japanese forces pouring onto the shores of Luzon, the U.S. considered removing the island's government and all military forces from Manila, declaring it an open city and thus saving its residents from bombardment.

Off the U.S. West Coast, Japanese submarines were punishing American shipping. Two days before Christmas two American tankers were shelled and torpedoed within sight of the coast. That made half a dozen attacks since December 11. On Christmas Day, a newspaper report told of thirty gaunt and exhausted seamen who finally reached shore, nine and a half days after their freighter had been sunk.

One of those who was fortunate enough to have made it to the U.S. mainland safely was UCLA football star Jackie Robinson, the man who six years in the

At the Movies 1941

The usual pasttimes entertained Chicagoans that first Christmas after Pearl Harbor. Walt Disney's Dumbo *opened at the Palace Theater. Other movies playing in town included* Sergeant York, Honky Tonk, The Little Foxes, Scarface, *and* I Wake up Screaming *with Betty Grable and Carole Landis was new at the* Chicago.

Da Bears 1941

On the Sunday before Christmas, December 21, the Bears beat the New York Giants 37-9 to win the NFL title. Arthur Daley was effusive in his praise in the New York Times, *calling the Bears "that greatest of football teams."*

The crowd which saw the game was one of the smallest for a post-season game ever—only 13,341. Daley attributed the small turnout not to the war, but to the fact that "potential spectators had read so much about the mayhem that the Bears were to inflict on the Giants that the soft-hearted customers stayed away in droves."

future would break baseball's color line. Robinson arrived in Los Angeles aboard the *Lurline,* telling reporters that while in Honolulu he had booked two passages home, one on December 6 and one on January 2. Homesickness caused him to take the earlier passage, and thus miss the Japanese attack by one day.

"The California coast is in a panic. They are expecting air raids hourly," gushed actress Lillian Gish to a *Tribune* reporter on December 22, as she stepped off the Santa Fe Chief in Chicago to change trains for a Christmas visit to her mother in New York. She said so many people wanted to flee inland that it was difficult getting reservations on eastbound trains. All windows on the coast were blacked out with paint, and nobody wanted to venture out after 6 P.M.

British aviation editor William Courtenay was visiting Chicago at Christmastime. In an address to the University Club, he gave the assurance that Chicago was unusually safe from enemy air raids because of its midwestern location. He did warn, however, that Chicago's defense plants could be the targets for saboteurs.

At the same time, the president of the International Chiefs of Police, Capt. Don Leonard, told 150 state highway officials from across the nation that it was a bad idea to turn off traffic signals during blackouts. Leonard recommended putting caps over the signals to make them invisible from above.

Chicago mayor Edward Kelly declared that Chicago had already won one important battle: "Emotion has given place to action. Facts are what we want now. We have no time for idle rumor. We have a job to do and we will let nothing distract us from it. Because Chicago has accepted the challenge calmly and with resolve, our worst enemy—hysteria—is already licked," he said in a broadcast over several local stations.

The mayor urged citizens not to be "frightened by talk of that bogeyman called blackouts." He said it was even possible that Chicago would not be called upon in the near future to impose a blackout. He promised a quick installation of a complete air raid signal system, and he noted that he was ordering the police and fire departments to replace the sirens on their vehicles with gongs, so they wouldn't be confused with an air raid siren.

Chicagoans were ready to fight, and the *Tribune* used the latest enlistment statistics to strike a blow in the city's rivalry with New York City. The *Trib* noted that, based on enlistment tables and in relation to their respective populations, Chicago was contributing nearly three men to the armed services for every two New Yorkers who signed up.

Cook County officials reported that filings for divorce were down sharply since the start of the war. For the first time in years, Christmas midnight masses were once again being celebrated in the archdiocese's Catholic churches.

1942: Ration Cards

The Christmas of 1942 might best be summed up by a cartoon that appeared in the *Chicago Daily News*. The caption was "Under the Mistletoe, 1942." The drawing showed a masked riveter hard at work. In the background one workman says to another, "Now's your chance, Joe. The prettiest girl in the plant."

America was fully at war, and most people were doing their part, either on the battlefronts or on the war production home front. Col. Paul Armstrong, the state's selective service director, complained that men aged fifty or older had been failing to answer occupational questionnaires they had been sent. He said many had the mistaken belief that their age would preclude them from participation in war activities.

The Chicago City Council ordered the immediate restoration of service on four of seven bus lines that had been eliminated earlier in December by a federal order seeking to save tires. The council's special traction attorney would take the matter up with the Illinois Commerce Commission, which handled appeals to the Office of Defense Transportation. To compensate and to save the requisite amount of rubber, the council ordered a 15 percent reduction in service on all city bus lines.

The Office of Civilian Defense for Metropolitan Chicago okayed outdoor Christmas light displays, though they were subject to emergency blackout orders. The War Production Board asked that such lighting be eliminated entirely.

Top Songs 1942

The number one song on Your Hit Parade *in 1942 was "White Christmas," just recorded that year by Bing Crosby. Other tunes on the* Hit Parade *and the artists who made them popular were: "Mr. Five by Five" by Freddie Slack, the Andrews Sisters and Harry James, "Praise the Lord and Pass the Ammunition" by the Merry Macs and Kay Kyser, "There Are Such Things" by Tommy Dorsey, "When the Lights Go On Again" by Vaughn Monroe, "Dearly Beloved" by Dinah Shore, "Why Don't You Fall in Love with Me" by Connee Boswell and Dinah Shore, "I Had the Craziest Dream" by Harry James, "Manhattan Serenade" by Harry James and Jimmy Dorsey, and "There's a Star-Spangled Banner Waving Somewhere" by Elton Britt.*

The weather that December was unseasonably cold, in fact the coldest on record according to the U.S. Weather Bureau. Heating oil was being rationed, and people were afraid that they would run out. Just before Christmas, federal price administrator Leon Henderson acted to ease their fears by increasing the fuel oil allotment for Illinois and twelve other midwestern states, and by moving up the start of the next rationing period by two weeks, to December 23.

The newspapers were filled with the names of Illinois's sons winning promotions in battle or becoming victims of the conflict. Heavy fighting was raging in Russia, where the German army was retreating in hasty defeat, the battle of Stalingrad lost, the eastern front in shambles. A *Daily News* cartoon showed a Volga boatman crossing the River Styx, his barge piled high with German corpses. The Belgian news agency reported that two wings of the prison in Brussels were filled with German troops who were refusing to accept transfer to the east.

U.S. and R.A.F. bombers pounded Nazi positions on the continent. American fliers were expressing amazement at the amount of punishment their sturdy B-17s could take and keep flying. American bombers were also hitting Japanese installations on Kiska in the Aleutian Islands chain.

Lt. Col. Eddie Rickenbacker, just rescued from a twenty-one day ordeal adrift in the Pacific Ocean, was quoted in the *Chicago Tribune* about his mission to the southwest Pacific:

> I found a real hellhole of mud and corruption at Guadalcanal. If only the people back home could know what those boys are doing for us and putting up with, I think they would take this war more seriously.

Thirty-five thousand servicemen were stationed in the Chicago area at Christmastime 1942, and Chicagoans were doing their part to make them feel at home. There were three servicemen's centers in the city, decorated appropriately and providing special dances, dinners, gift exchanges, and Christmas caroling for servicemen. The Civic Opera House was selling tickets for a big benefit performance. Irving Berlin's *This Is the Army* was to open on January 4, and opening night tickets for the first twenty-two rows were priced high at twenty-two dollars apiece.

Most midwestern trains were reporting standing room only as servicemen and their families hoped for one last holiday together. Forty restaurants took out a newspaper ad suggesting that families dine out with their serviceman. The ad pointed out that most of the restaurants were close to public transportation, which was important in those fuel-rationed times.

In Blue Island, the Kiwanis Club had decided to play Santa Claus for eight children whose mother was in the hospital. The woman was in such dire straits that she had told the kids that Santa had been killed in the war. The Kiwanis Club members went all out to change that message.

1943:

Nazis Can't Kill Santa!

Chicago's temperature reached forty-six degrees on the Christmas Saturday of 1943. It was a dry day, and it also was a holiday for most of the thousands of war plant workers in the Chicago area. Those plants included the Buick plant in Melrose Park, where engines were being built for *Liberator* bombers, the Douglas Aircraft corporation plant near Park Ridge, which was assembling C54 cargo planes, and the Dodge plant in Chicago, which was making aircraft engines, just to name a few. Although Christmas was to be a holiday at most factories, New Year's Day, 1944, would be just another regular working day.

American fighting forces were advancing in New Britain in the South Pacific and up the Italian boot toward Rome. American bombers pounded German targets, and in December 1943, CBS News correspondent Edward R. Murrow went along on one mission. His report is a classic:

> Boz called his direction: "Five Left, Five Left.". . . And then, there was a gentle, confident, upward thrust under my feet and Boz said, "Cookie gone.". . . A few seconds later the incendiaries went. And D-Dog seemed lighter and easier to handle. I began to breathe, and to reflect again. . . that all men would be brave if only they could leave their stomachs at home. . . I looked on the port beam at the target area. There was a red, sullen, obscene glare. The fires seemed to have found each other. And we were heading home. Berlin was a kind of orchestrated hell, a terrible symphony of light and flame.

Murrow returned to an England where American soldiers were busy making Christmas merry for Britain's younger victims of Nazi bombing raids. The *Chicago Tribune* carried this report.

NAZIS CAN'T KILL SANTA!
YANKS IN BRITAIN PROVE IT
Plan Yule Parties for Child Raid Victims

LONDON, Dec. 18 (AP).—A bigger and better American army in Britain began a bigger and better round of Christmas parties today—with the accent on old fashioned frolics, which may produce an occasional stomachache but won't have a hangover in a thousand.

Soldiers of an American supply depot began the celebrations in London's bomb-ridden east end. Their guests were 100 Cockney children and many of their dock yard working parents. At least 15,000 other children will go to Yank parties or the parties will be taken to them.

For this second American army Christmas in Britain, about 50 Red

On the Table 1943

Turkeys were 50¢ a pound at Stop & Shop.

At the Movies 1943

Movies of the season included Sahara, *starring Humphrey Bogart, at the Roosevelt Theater;* Northern Pursuit, *starring Errol Flynn, at the Apollo; Dorothy Lamour got top billing in* Riding High *at the Chicago Theater; Alan Ladd was starring in* Gangs Inc. *at the Woods.*

Top Songs 1944

The top song on Your Hit Parade *two nights before Christmas was Bing Crosby's and the Andrews Sisters' "Don't Fence Me In." W. W. Kimball was selling the most popular records of the day for 53¢ apiece.*

On the Table 1944

Turkey was 49¢ a pound at the A&P, although supplies were limited. Eggs were 49¢ a dozen. Cranberry sauce was 20¢ for a sixteen-ounce can plus forty blue ration points.

Under the Tree 1944

Under the Christmas tree, little boys might have found metal trucks. Mandel Brothers was selling them for 59¢. Electric football or baseball games were $1.39. For little girls, there were baby dolls with their own suitcases, bottles, and changes of clothes. The dolls drank and wet, and cost $1.98.

Da Bears 1944

The War Department announced that films of Chicago Bears' games would become a part of the movie GI Weekly, *for troops at home and overseas.*

Cross clubs thruout the island are sponsoring children's parties for about 2,500 youngsters. As many more pairs of young eyes will pop at gay doings arranged by army units or small Red Cross field clubs. It is estimated that a single infantry division will have 9,500 young guests at 40 parties.

PARTIES AT HOSPITALS

Because bombs have left so many children unable to go to parties, the parties will go to them. At Exeter soldiers will move Santa Claus and company into the Princess Elizabeth orthopedic hospital and in Leicester the GIs will make the rounds to children's hospitals to deliver gifts and candy.

No one knows how much candy has been saved from none too ample rations or how many thousands of toys have been made, bought or received.

"Uncle Sam" is providing a well proportioned fir tree, 6 to 8 feet in height, for every 250 soldiers in the European theater. In this land where shiny ornaments long ago vanished from stores, bright bits of ribbon, stars cut from ration cans, odd bits of colored paper and cotton have been pressed into service for tree decorations.

WACS "ADOPT" LOST FLYER'S GIRL

Amid all this festivity more lasting help to unfortunates also has been provided. One WAC unit in London is "adopting" a 7 year old daughter of a missing R. A. F. flyer with a fund of $400. (Copyright *Chicago Tribune.* Used by permission.)

A week before Christmas the Selective Service System announced that two million more men would be drafted by July 1944. Half of them would come from the less than five million draftable fathers still home with their families. The army's casualty report for that week listed 197 killed, 5 from Illinois, and 273 missing, 23 of those were from Illinois.

On Christmas Eve President Franklin D. Roosevelt announced to the nation that Gen. Dwight D. Eisenhower would be the commander of the planned Allied invasion of Europe.

It was a traditional Christmas dinner for the sixty-six thousand sailors and WAVES stationed at the Great Lakes Naval Training Center. The government had purchased 10,000 mince pies, 35,000 pounds of sweet potatoes, and 61,000 pounds of turkey for the feast. This meant a shortage of turkey on the civilian market.

1944: The Last Push

In Chicago, the Christmas of 1944 was cold and snowy. Temperatures hovered in the lower twenties during the day, then plunged to seven degrees by late Christmas night. The icy conditions meant slippery sidewalks. On the weekend before that Monday Christmas, more than two dozen people required hospital care for injuries suffered from falls. William McFetridge, the president of the Chicago Flat Janitors Union, told his ten thousand members to do more to make Chicago's sidewalks safe.

It was bitterly cold and snowy on the European front as well, where Allied and German forces were engaged in the Battle of the Bulge, Hitler's last-ditch offensive. On Christmas morning, the *Chicago Sun* trumpeted the good news. "YANKS STOP NAZIS; U.S. LAUNCHES GREAT DRIVE." A UPI report datelined Paris began, "American troops halted the German winter drive dead in its tracks and opened a mounting counter-offensive against the exposed Nazi flanks today." This Christmas Day of fire and ice, a number of reporters filed personal accounts of what they had seen. Perhaps the most moving appeared in the *Sun*:

BOMBS VIE WITH SINGER IN YULE RITES AT FRONT
By John B. McDermott
United Press Staff Correspondent

WITH U.S. FORCES ON THE WESTERN FRONT,

Dec. 25. "Silent night, holy night, all is calm. . ."

A bomb crashed down through the misty, moonlight darkness.

But the middle-aged baritone's voice didn't waver. He never lost a note. Not a single person in that little cathedral moved for the exit, although the drone of Jerry's planes were vying with the singer for attention.

It was midnight Mass at a Catholic cathedral in the battle zone—the first Christmas night time service in five years. The Germans hadn't permitted such when they were here.

A few G.I.'s nervously wiped sweat from their brows and two, I noticed, reached down and picked up their rifles off the floor. The church shook again as another Jerry bomb crashed a short distance away.

The priest mounted the pulpit to the sputtering roar of anti-aircraft guns. He spoke in heavily accented English, "Happiness and peace in this world is the biggest treasure you can find. We are trying for that now. Tonight is holy night—but not silent night."

Many of the GI's who were kneeling in the church I had seen a little earlier, crowded around a piano singing Christmas carols at the Red Cross club. Tears glistened in the eyes of many young, homesick boys at this night of nights. Others in the canteen tried to forget the roaring guns, exploding grenades and their mission of killing. (Copyright United Press International. Used by permission.)

At the Movies 1945

The movies of the 1945 Christmas season included The Stork Club, *starring Betty Hutton and opening Christmas Day at the Chicago Theater;* Weekend at the Waldorf *with Ginger Rogers, Walter Pidgeon, Lana Turner, and Van Johnson at the State-Lake;* Yolanda and the Thief *starring Fred Astaire, Lucille Bremer, and Frank Morgan at the United Artists;* Shirley Temple in Kiss and Tell *at the Roosevelt; and Bing Crosby and Ingrid Bergman in* Bells of St. Mary's *at the Woods Theater.*

There was also a brief notice from Paris in the Christmas Day papers. It said that dance orchestra leader Maj. Glenn Miller had been missing since December 15 when his plane disappeared while on a flight from England to Paris. Before entering the service in the fall of 1942, Miller had been the most popular dance band leader in America. His long list of number-one tunes includes "Wishing (Will Make It So)" (1939), "Stairway to the Stars" (1939), "In the Mood" (his signature theme, 1939), "Tuxedo Junction" (1940), "Imagination" (1940), "Song of the Volga Boatmen" (1941), "You and I" (1941), "Chattanooga Choo Choo" (1941), "Elmer's Tune" (1941), "Moonlight Cocktail" (1942), "Don't Sit Under the Apple Tree" (1942), and "I've Got a Gal in Kalamazoo" (1942).

At Christmastime 1944, five-time Chicago mayor Carter Harrison II announced plans to retire as collector of Internal Revenue, a post he had held since 1933; he was eighty-four years old.

In the midst of war came a heartwarming story of a man who found the true meaning of Christmas. His name was Franz Kurz and he worked as a boilerman in a war plant. He had never believed in Christmas, never had enough money to celebrate it. He had never believed that eating out was a good idea because his family would have had to starve the rest of the week to pay for it.

Two days before Christmas a hit-and-run driver ran Kurz down. He suffered a fractured skull and several broken ribs. From his bed in Cook County Hospital he told his wife, "Christmas is the bunk anyway."

But then several Chicago police officers learned of his plight, and they passed the hat around. They came up with seventy-five dollars, which was a lot of money in 1944. They gave it to Kurz so that he and his family of six could afford a Christmas turkey, new shoes, and more. Kurz changed his tune: "So there is a Santa Claus," he said. "Who would've believed he'd ever come to us?"

1945:

I'll Be Home for Christmas

" 'PEACE ON EARTH' TO MEAN MORE THIS CHRISTMAS" was a headline above a story about church services in the December 23, 1945, edition of the *Chicago Sun*. It spoke volumes about the tenor of the time. "This is the Christmas that a war-weary world has prayed for through long and awful years," declared President Harry Truman as he lit the national tree on Christmas Eve. "In love, which is the very essence of the message of the Prince of Peace, the world would find a solution for all its ills. I do not believe there is one problem in this country—in the world—today which could not be settled if approached through the teaching of the sermon on the mount," he told a nationwide radio audience.

Top Songs 1945

The songs on Your Hit Parade *on the Saturday before Christmas, and the artists who made them popular were "It Might As Well Be Spring" by Dick Haymes and Paul Weston, "I Can't Begin to Tell You" Bing Crosby with Carmen Cavallaro, "It's Been a Long, Long Time"—four recordings made the top ten that year: by Bing Crosby with Les Paul, Harry James, Charlie Spivak, and Stan Kenton— "Symphony" by Freddy Martin and Benny Goodman, "Chickery Chick" by Sammy Kaye and Gene Krupa, "That's for Me" by Jo Stafford and Dick Haymes, "White Christmas" by Bing Crosby, "Put That Ring on My Finger," and "Till the End of Time" by Perry Como, Les Brown, and Dick Haymes.*

On the Radio 1945

On the radio Christmas Eve, you might have heard The Lone Ranger *(WLS),* Melody Lane *(WBBM),* Skip Farrell, baritone *(WMAQ),* Easy Aces *(WGN),* Cavalcade of America *(WMAQ),* Lum and Abner *(WLS),* Bing Crosby Records, *(WCFL),* Hedda Hopper *(WLS),* Sherlock Holmes *(WGN),* Screen Guild Players *(WBBM), and* Bulldog Drummond *(WGN).*

On the Table 1945

Turkey was 42¢ a pound at Goldblatts. A one-pound jar of Hills Brothers coffee was 31¢. Eggs were 64¢ a dozen at A&P. The manager of the American Dairy Association was warning of a shortage of butter at Christmastime, because the price of the cream used to make it was too high compared to the government-controlled price of butter at the market.

Under the Tree 1945

The Fair Store advertised a Battleship Bombing Game, complete with a nineteen-and-a-half inch wood reproduction of a Japanese flat-top (aircraft carrier) that could be blown up. The game sold for $2.98.

Much of the news of that Christmas was about a world recovering from war: the Selective Service System was immediately discontinuing the drafting of fathers; the Price Administration was announcing the end, as of January 1, of the rationing of automobile tires; the Federal Housing Administration was out with a plan to provide four hundred thousand new homes for veterans; the Chicago chapter of the Red Cross was sending gifts to as many as thirty-five thousand veterans and their families in an attempt to help them forget, according to the *Chicago Tribune*, "the parched yuletide. . . spent on a hot Pacific island or that bitter Nativity in the Battle of the Bulge."

From Tokyo that Christmas week came word of the suicide by poison of former premier Prince Fumimaro Konoye, who chose to end his life rather than surrender and be tried as a possible war criminal. Gen. Douglas MacArthur, meanwhile, was ordering the end of Japanese state support for Shintoism, which his staff believed helped lead the Japanese into war. More a tradition dating back to ancient times than a religion with a code of morals, state-supported Shintoism was widely seen as a factor in the creation of the Japanese fighting machine, with its fanaticism, its contempt for all things foreign, and its demand of utter loyalty to the emperor.

In Nuremberg, American prosecutors wanted to convict six hundred thousand "little fuehrers" of war crimes for their membership in pro-Nazi organizations. That figure was being called conservative by American staff officers; they estimated that Nazi leadership down to the unit and block leader levels would number two million individuals. The exact figures eventually came out at the war crimes trial of the top twenty-one Nazi officials.

From Berlin, the *Tribune* reported on big-hearted GIs, embellishing the reputation of Americans:

YANKS RANSACK BAGS TO SPREAD CHEER IN BERLIN
by Henry Wales

BERLIN, Dec. 24—Nineteen thousand "angels in khaki battle dress" were spreading Christmas cheer thruout Berlin this evening as the

American army garrison celebrated its first yuletide after victory.

It seems as if every GI has adopted some German child or the youngsters of an entire family, and singly and in groups the soldiers were visiting in shattered buildings to distribute gifts and toast the holiday with schnapps and "prosits."

Pockets which a year ago were crammed with grenades and ammunition today bulged with candy bars, chocolates and loot picked up in the long campaign across France, Belgium, Holland and Germany.

HAUL OUT SOME TRINKETS

Today in a magnificent outburst of generosity, the Yanks ransacked foot lockers, duffle bags and hauled out all the trinkets, souvenirs and keepsakes—even presents from home—to gladden the hearts of a despairing, beaten people among whom they are quartered.

This evening Brig. Gen. Clay Stayer, Carlisle, Pa., Col. Frank Berry, former chief surgeon of the Roosevelt hospital, New York, and I visited a giant bunker on Frichte-Strasse where 3,000 German children evicted from the area that is now Poland, celebrated Weinachtsabend [Christmas Eve] with cardboard toys, sugar crackers and American chocolate.

CHILDREN SING CAROLS

Mrs. Elly Wedekind, in charge of the bomb proof [bomb shelter] led the children's shrill treble voices in carols.

Despite fatigue from days of trudging across country en route to their new homes, laden with knapsacks and bundles, the youngsters whooped with joy at wooden Mickey Mouses, Donald Ducks

and papier-mache wagons, tanks and self-propelled guns.

Newly arrived children who had been robbed of most of their clothing en route were outfitted warmly by peeling a layer of garments off luckier children and giving them extra articles.

SIMPLE, IMPROVISED GIFTS

Thruout the city tonight parents dwelling in damp underground air raid shelters or in shell shattered apartment houses celebrated the Nativity according to ancient Teuton tradition and with the simplest improvised gifts at their disposal. And youngsters, always appreciative if the gift giving is sufficiently dramatized, enjoyed their homemade presents just as much as expensive, fascinating objects of other years.

(Copyright *Chicago Tribune.* Used by permission.)

From Heidelberg came word of the death of an American war hero. Gen. George Patton died in his sleep on December 21, twelve days after breaking his neck when his car collided with a truck near Mannheim; he had been on his way to hunt pheasants.

"This is a hell of a way to die," Patton said as he was being put in an ambulance after the crash. Doctors said it was a blood clot in his lungs that turned gangrenous that caused Patton's death; he was sixty years old. His wife was at his side when he died. She decided that he would be buried somewhere along the route of his victorious Third Army.

Since the war was over, Mayor Edward Kelly was hoping that the air force would surrender its Douglas Air Field near Park Ridge, so that Chicago could turn it into a new, modern Chicago airport. Cook County officials, at the same time, were making plans to ask the Illinois Postwar Planning Commission for $320,000 to pay for engineering work on the proposed Northwest Superhighway that would link downtown Chicago with the airport—all of which is now O'Hare International and the Kennedy Expressway.

To the average GI, the end of the war and the approach of Christmas meant trying to get home in time to spend the holiday with family and loved ones. In the weeks leading up to Christmas, transports were docking every day at nine ports on the East and West coasts, discharging fifty thousand soldiers, sailors and airmen. They were filling up trains faster than the railroads could accommodate them.

On December 15, Maj. Gen. Homer Groninger, commander of the San Francisco port of embarkation, told reporters the four installations that were staging areas were filled, and it would be necessary to tie up troop ships at piers and leave the men aboard until the railroads could clear out those who had arrived earlier.

That was already the case in Los Angeles, where 1,900 soldiers were being held aboard the *Olmstead* because the staging camps were filled. To the north, Seattle, Tacoma, and Portland were awaiting the

Crowds jam Union Station

arrival of 75,000 soldiers. Three days later, the situation worsened. Forty-five thousand men were stacked up awaiting trains in San Francisco, 27,000 in Los Angeles, 17,000 in Seattle, and 4,500 in Portland. An additional 110,700 soldiers were expected to arrive on the West Coast within the following week. Every available coach was put into service on the seven train lines between Chicago and the West Coast. The Southern Pacific Railroad reported that 94 percent of its eastbound passengers were military personnel. To complicate matters, many trains were running late.

The transportation crunch came to a head on Saturday, December 22, in Chicago. Every one of the city's railroad stations was packed in what one veteran transportation official described to the *Tribune* as "far beyond even my worst nightmares."

Schedules went to the wind. Special trains were being made up as rolling stock became available. Fifteen thousand people were reported stranded at Union Station. A small scale riot broke out at the Dearborn Station when four hundred would-be travelers broke through gates to board a train even before it was stopped. Passengers stood shoulder-to-shoulder. The crowd was so closely packed at the LaSalle Street station that police were summoned to make a way through the crowd for a stranded train crew. A. R. Shaw, the trainmaster at the Illinois Central station, said he'd never seen such huge crowds in his twenty years of experience. A spokesman for the Western Association of Railroad Executives said the situation bordered on hysteria. "There is so little space that many civilians don't have a chance," he told the *Sun-Times.*

Finally, Gov. Dwight Green called up five hundred reservists and more than one hundred jeeps and trucks to help shuttle servicemen between terminals, or sometimes even to take them to their homes. That, plus the number of discouraged would-be holiday travelers who canceled their plans, finally ended the transportation siege.

Among the rail passengers who passed through Chicago in the days before Christmas was Col. Jimmy Stewart. He was on his way to Indiana, Pennsylvania, to spend the holiday with his mother. Stewart told reporters that after he received his air force discharge in February, he planned to start work on a new picture: *It's a Wonderful Life.*

1946 & 1947: The Postwar Boom

The lesson Chicago police officer Marshall Pidgeon learned as the Christmas of 1946 rolled around was that it was a good idea to tell your wife what you want for Christmas—even if you intended to buy it for yourself. Pidgeon had purchased a clock to install in his new car (clocks were not standard equipment in new cars in 1946). The clock was in a box wrapped in paper. The box was in the pocket of a coat Pidgeon had left draped over a chair in his home.

He had gone out again, wearing another coat. His wife, Agnes, had some friends over, and one of them heard a mysterious ticking. Mrs. Pidgeon traced it to the box in her husband's coat pocket.

Now, Marshall Pidgeon had a special rank in the Chicago Police Department: he was a detective in the bomb squad. The *Chicago Sun* reported that the notion came into Agnes Pidgeon's head that some fiend was trying to do away with her husband with an infernal machine. But she knew exactly what to do, and she wasn't afraid. She dumped the box into a tub of water. It was not a waterproof clock.

At Christmastime 1946, several stores were advertising the new Thor Automagic Washer:

It's the wonder washer of all times, streamlined, compact, occupied only a two-foot square of floor space in kitchen or laundry. The new Thor Automagic not only washes dirty clothes CLEAN— it provides two kinds of rinses—first agitated and then overflow—so the soap and soil are floated to the top and drained away. The Thor Automagic whirls clothes better than wringer dry. Then with a simple change of its TWO separate inner tubs (in 1 1/2 minutes!) it can be turned from a clothes washer into a dishwasher. Both operate at the flick of a dial . . . both have washing features never before possible.

The Thor Automagic Washer did not change the world, but one year later, an invention was unveiled that would do just that.

It was on December 23, 1947, that a team of Bell Telephone lab scientists announced the invention of the transistor. William Shockley, John Bardeen, and Walter Brattain would be awarded the Nobel Prize in physics for their work nine years later.

Another new idea catching the attention of motorists in southern California was self-service gas stations. Gas was a nickel a gallon cheaper at the self-service stations, and pretty girls in tight slacks on roller skates scooted around the stations, acting as cashiers.

Marshall Field's began marketing a new idea in 1947: something called an "improved model snow slider," basically a snow shovel on wheels, for $11.95. Other postwar prizes included a heavy, sheepskin-lined, leather B-3 flight jacket which cost $16.88 at the World War Surplus Store in South Halsted Street. Community Surplus Stores were selling children's gas masks for 49¢ each, saying they were "easily worth $3.95 as a toy value."

By 1947, Illinois was the third-ranking state in the nation in toy production, with an output that year worth a quarter of a million dollars. Radio Flyer wagons sold for $9.95, rider fire trucks for $5.98, Marx mechanical trains for $4.29, and miniature dolls for $2.98.

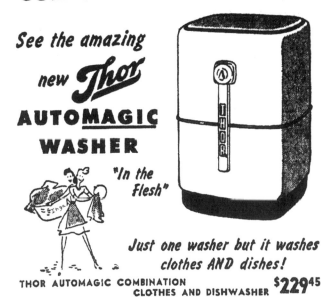

Come in! Come in!

See the amazing new *Thor* AUTOMAGIC WASHER

"In the Flesh"

Just one washer but it washes clothes AND dishes!

THOR AUTOMAGIC COMBINATION CLOTHES AND DISHWASHER $229⁴⁵

Many people could afford to be generous during the postwar boom. Every year, amid the stories about shopping and spending, there are stories in Chicago's newspapers like this one from the *Tribune* on December 24, 1947:

CHICAGO DONS RED SUIT AND PLAYS SANTA GIVES TO NEEDY AND CHILDREN

Chicago should wear a long, white beard and a red suit this week. With traditional good-heartedness, it is playing Santa Claus to those to whom Christmas belongs, to the poor and needy, and to children.

More than 5,000 Catholic Charities children will have a happy Christmas because of the generosity of many Chicagoans. Twenty Santa Clauses will visit 10 Catholic charities homes for children to delight 4,000 youngsters who have no homes of their own. Foster parents will make it a joyous occasion for 1,200 wards of the Catholic Home bureau living in private homes.

Gifts of toys, games and clothing will make it a happy Christmas at several other Catholic Charities agencies, including Angel Guardian Orphanage, St. Vincent's Infant Asylum, St. Joseph's Home for the Friendless, House of the Good Shepherd, St. Joseph's Bohemian Orphanage, Guardian Angel home, Ephpheta School for the Deaf, and Illinois Technical School for Colored Girls.

Funds contributed to the Volunteers of America's Santa helpers, were distributed yesterday to needy families in the form of Christmas dinner certificates. Hank Henry, comedian of "The Firefly," which opens at the Blackstone Theater Christmas night, was at the Volunteers headquarters, 1128 N. Dearborn St., to add cheer to the distribution.

Santa's rounds also included the Home for Destitute Crippled Children at the University of Chicago, 970 E. 59th St. He attended the annual Christmas party for the children and presented each one with a special gift.

The coeds of De Paul University became Santa's helpers and delivered 45 Christmas baskets to the poor. Mandel Brothers Post of the American Legion proved there was a Santa Claus too, when Siegfried Frank, child welfare officer of the post, began distribution of Christmas packages to 12 war widows and their children. (Copyright *Chicago Tribune*. Used by permission.)

Under the Tree 1948

Men's shirts were $7.95 at Baskin's. Lytton's had a "Shirt-a-Month" club for $3.65 to $4.50. Lionel train sets sold for $15.95 or eighteen-and-a-half inch pressed wood dolls for $3.50. The Fair Store was selling Royal portable typewriters for $79.50.

On the Table 1948

The Christmas turkey of 1948 cost 69¢ a pound at the A&P. Pepsi was 6¢ for a thirteen-ounce bottle, plus deposit. Stop 'N' Shop was advertising Cuban pineapples for 49¢ each.

Transportation 1948

Cunard Lines was offering an eleven-day holiday cruise to the West Indies for $335.

At the Movies 1948

Movies of the season included Cary Grant in Every Girl Should Be Married *at the RKO Palace, Olivia de Havilland in* Snakepit *at the Garrick, and Bob Hope and Jane Russell in* Paleface *at the Chicago Theater.*

Best-Sellers 1948

Postwar best-sellers included Frances Parkinson Keyes' Came a Cavalier, *Frank Yerby's* The Golden Hawk, *Norman Mailer's* The Naked and the Dead, *and Dale Carnegie's* How to Stop Worrying and Start Living.

Lithuanian Christmas dinner, breaking the wafer

1948: Postwar Strife

A moderate to heavy snowfall was predicted for Chicago on Christmas Eve, 1948, but it didn't happen. There already was up to six inches of snow on the ground. The Christmas of 1948 was one of those leaden gray winter days with temperatures hovering around twenty degrees.

There was considerably more drama to the weather in another part of the world. In southwestern Greenland, high atop a seventy-seven hundred-foot icecap, eleven U.S. Air Force fliers were struggling to survive, following the crash-landing of their C-47 airplane on December 9. The temperature was below freezing, and one-hundred-mile-an-hour winds were frustrating rescue attempts. On Christmas Day, two would-be rescuers landed their glider on the icecap, but found themselves joining the ranks of the stranded when their tow-rope broke. The U.S. Navy hurried the carrier *Saipan* toward the area, with a special complement of Marine Corps personnel and helicopters, but the air force made the rescue three days after Christmas with a C-47 specially equipped with skis and rocket boosters.

C-47s, or "Gooney Birds," also made news in another part of the world. The Soviet blockade of West Berlin and the Allied airlift to keep the city afloat was six months old, and the *Chicago Tribune* told its readers what Christmas was like in both sectors of the divided city:

SOVIETS CURB YULE CAROLS BY BERLINERS
By Larry Rue

BERLIN, Dec. 24— "Silent Night, Holy Night," was sung only behind closed doors in the eastern sector of Berlin and other parts of Russian occupied Germany this Christmas.

But in the western sector good will to men was lifted over the Russian blockade by British and American planes and the children of the "island of Berlin" got probably the best Christmas they have had since the war.

An order of the soviet military government forbade the singing of Christmas songs in schools or public places and ordered the substitution of Russian folk songs. Yet the Russians displayed some sign of Christmas spirit, altho this policy was not carried thruout the occupied zone. They issued additional rations of one pound of flour, a half pound of sugar, and another half pound of candy for children.

CHILDREN SHOW CONTRAST

"They are only doing this for us," a woman living in the Russian sector said, "because they want to make it appear that we are as well off as the Germans in the American sector."

She was shabbily dressed, her feet wrapped in burlap. She was watching a merry-go-round at the traditional Christmas market in the Lustgarten, near Unter den Linden, and remarked how even the children of the Russian zone, riding the merry-go-round, like their elders, hardly laughed or smiled. She added wistfully:

"I wonder how many eastern Berliners gladly would exchange their Christmas trees and extra rations for freedom if they only could."

The sight of German children shivering in the cold, their feet in stockings and homemade contraptions for shoes, present a grim contrast

Top Songs 1948

The line about "its two front teeth" was a reference to the Spike Jones tune "All I Want for Christmas Is My Two Front Teeth" which was just gaining in popularity. It would not be on Your Hit Parade *on Christmas night, but it would make the top ten one week later.*

Much of the postwar music reflected an upswing mood. The songs that made Your Hit Parade *on December 25, and the artists who made them popular were "Buttons and Bows" by Dinah Shore, "On a Slow Boat to China" by Kay Kyser, "My Darling, My Darling" by Doris Day & Buddy Clark, "A Little Bird Told Me" by Evelyn Knight, "Until" by Tommy Dorsey, "Lavender Blue" by Sammy Kaye, "You Were Only Fooling" by Blue Barron, "White Christmas" by Bing Crosby, "Cuanta La Gusta" by the Andrews Sisters & Carmen Miranda, and "Maybe You'll Be There" by Gordon Jenkins. Records cost 79¢ apiece.*

to those of the western sectors, warmly dressed, laughing and playing on the way to school or screaming with delight at the numerous Christmas parties given by American army units and civilians. (Copyright *Chicago Tribune.* Used by permission.)

In Japan, General MacArthur announced a Christmastime clemency for seventeen suspected war criminals. They were freed one day after Hideki Tojo and six other militarists had gone to the gallows.

In this country, the famous "Pumpkin Papers" case was breaking. Former State Department official Alger Hiss had just pleaded innocent to charges of lying about passing secret government papers to a Soviet courier. Another former State Department official, Laurence Duggan, had jumped to his death from a New York City skyscraper after his name came up at a hearing of the House Committee on Un-American activities.

In local news, the *Tribune* reported on a West Side bar where its dancers entertained in little more than their birthday suits. The next day Police Commissioner Prendergast expressed shock at the disclosure. Mayor Martin Kennelly was quoted as saying, "We don't want any girls around Chicago wearing nothing but smiles." But when in doubt order a study, and that's just what the police commissioner did. A team of willing specialists was assigned to conduct a survey of the West Side night spots.

At the same time Mayor Kennelly supported the decision of Commissioner Prendergast and the head of the police department's crime prevention division to ban Jean Paul Sartre's play *The Respectful Prostitute,* which was to have opened at the Studebaker Theater on December 27. The police censors said the play was immoral and presented the Negro race in an unfavorable light. The American Actors League said the decision made Chicago the laughingstock of the nation.

Provident Hospital was in financial trouble, just as it would again be some forty years later. A drive was just getting under way to raise $150,000 for the hospital.

Radio was still the nation's most popular medium for entertainment, but TV was causing a lot of soul-searching in the industry, as Larry Wolters reported in the *Trib* a few days before Christmas:

> If comedians keep on quitting at the current rate, radio won't even have its two front teeth by Christmas. Al Jolson, the mammy singer and funny man, announced that he is getting out of broadcasting at the end of this season. Fred Allen had previously disclosed that he is quitting at the end of the year to write a book, and Edgar Bergen says he will retire after December 26th to do some thinking about television and other things. (Copyright *Chicago Tribune.* Used by permission.)

As of yet, the medium hadn't become a household appliance.

Finally, 1948 was a tough year for Santa Claus. In Spokane, Washington, a three-year-old girl accused a department store Santa of being an "impothtor!" when he denied that he had a wife. In Newark, when Santa refused to write down a little boy's requests, the boy got back in line and screamed, "I told you you'd forget," when Santa didn't recognize him. In San Francisco, the question, "And what do you want, little boy?" drew the response, "I want to go to the bathroom."

1950-1959

1950: Christmas in Korea

The Christmas Monday of 1950 found the United States under a state of emergency. President Truman had declared it nine days earlier in an effort to accelerate military and industrial mobilization against the advance of Communist armies on the Korean peninsula. Christmas marked six months to the day that the North Koreans had invaded the South. Things were looking desperate.

In an "epic seaborne withdrawal," more than two hundred thousand hard-pressed American, Republic of Korea (ROK), and British troops as well as many Korean civilians were evacuated from the demolished port of Hungnam. All but the southern tip of the peninsula was in Communist hands. At the same time, the Chinese Communist army had driven to within twenty-eight miles of Seoul prompting an exodus from the South Korean capital.

A few days before Christmas, the *Chicago Daily News* carried the story of a young Chicago marine in Korea:

BELIEVES MOTHER'S PRAYERS SAVED LIFE IN KOREA HORROR
MARINE SURVIVES MASS ATTACKS,
TELLS OF 15-BELOW-ZERO COLD

A young Chicago marine wrote his mother that her prayers helped pull him through the horrors of "nightmare alley."

"The only reason I can give is the prayers you said for me," wrote Pfc. Frank M. Weir, 18, a 1st Marine Division tank driver, to his mother, Alice, 10235 St. Lawrence avenue.

"This is the worst beating the division has taken since Guadalcanal," he said.

Weir told of the retreat under fire from the Chongjin reservoir near the Manchurian border to the Hungnam beachhead.

He had been wounded at Seoul, hospitalized in Japan and returned to action just as the Chinese Reds attacked.

On the Radio 1950

One of the most popular programs on the radio in 1950 was Amos 'n' Andy. *In a classic broadcast on Christmas Eve, Amos explained the meaning of the Lord's Prayer to his little daughter, Arbadella.* Our Miss Brooks, Jack Benny, Charlie McCarthy, *and* Red Skelton *were also on the radio that Christmas Eve.*

Top Songs 1950

The number one song on Your Hit Parade *was "Rudolph the Red-Nosed Reindeer," which would become a million-seller for Gene Autry.*

The rest of the Hit Parade *lineup included: "A Bushel and a Peck," "Tennessee Waltz," "The Thing," "Harbor Lights," "Nevertheless," "A Marshmallow World," "Thinking of You," "Frosty the Snowman," and "All My Love."*

At the Movies 1950

Movies of the season included Harvey *starring Jimmy Stewart,* For Heaven's Sake *with Clifton Webb, Joan Bennett, and Robert Cummings;* Mr. Music *starring Bing Crosby, and* Let's Dance *with Fred Astaire and Betty Hutton.*

"We were hit hard by six divisions of Chinese Commies. They kept attacking, sniping. And then this cold weather.

"It went down to 15 below zero at night. During the day you got wet feet because the snow melts. Then it freezes and you freeze. Lots of guys froze to death.

"They try to give us a warm meal. You try to take the chill off your mess gear by putting it in boiling water. By the time you get through the chow line, your gear is frozen and your chow is cold.

"We have 10 tanks left out of 21 in this company. The company is just a memory. We've lost so many men.

"But it's only now that I know why I'm proud to be a marine. We have the finest fighting troops in the world, and I don't care what anybody says." (Reprinted with permission of the *Chicago Sun-Times.*)

At home the state of emergency meant a million more men were to be drafted into the armed services. It also meant tighter controls on wages and prices. The big automakers at first balked. General Motors (GM) even announced it would stop selling its 1951 model cars. But the protest fizzled after four days when GM, Ford, and Nash finally announced they would comply with the government order to roll back prices. Nonetheless, the Bureau of Labor Statistics released a new report saying the cost of living had never been higher.

A demand for higher wages led to a wildcat railroad strike in mid-December. It created a freight jam and forced the post office to place an embargo on mail. Trainmen started going back to their jobs the morning after President Harry Truman made a speech appealing to them, and contrasting their strike with the sacrifices being made in Korea. A federal judge had also threatened to hold the strikers in contempt, and there were rumors that a wage settlement was imminent. By Christmas trains were rolling once again.

In Chicago the head of the Chicago Teachers Federation, Frances Kenney, called on the board of education to give teachers a pay raise in 1951. She said it could be done without a tax increase if the board trimmed extra services. The highest paid elementary school teachers in Chicago made $4,300 in 1950. Top pay for high school teachers was $5,160.

A few days before Christmas, a congressional committee was in Chicago to hold hearings on organized crime. Bold headlines declared that the mob had made profits of $278,000 in Chicago in 1949 on policy wheel operations.

Mayor Martin Kennelly made the announcement that one and a half million copies of a pamphlet informing citizens of what to do in case of an atomic attack would be distributed in Chicago. Chicago's population at the mid-century mark was 3,620,962.

All over the world it was an uneasy Christmas, according to one respected wire service:

NOTE OF ANXIETY BROODS BENEATH CHRISTMAS JOY

ALL OVER THE WORLD THERE IS GREATER ABUNDANCE, YET FEARS OF WAR DISTURB GAIETY OF SEASON
By the Associated Press

Americans in the midst of plenty face Christmas seriously this year with their minds on fellow countrymen fighting in Korea's barren wastes.

Shops never were more abundant, Yule decorations never more lavish.

An outward air of Christmas cheer could not obscure ominous world events and thoughtfulness at what the future might hold.

War worries tempered the joyful anticipation in most European homes of the most prosperous Christmas in a decade.

While carolers sang of good will among men, many persons talked of Korea and the Kremlin, and how far you have to be from a falling atom bomb to survive.

POPE'S MESSAGE

Broadcasting from the Vatican, Pope Pius XII observed in his annual Christmas message that "the most urgent problem is that of the internal peace of each people."

In Europe, the extent to which the fear of war encroached on the Christmas spirit seemed marked in Czechoslovakia, West Germany, and the Netherlands. It lay below the surface in Britain, France and Italy.

The grim outlook placed added emphasis on home ties as Americans across the country gathered for Christmas reunions.

Under the Tree 1950

A new Buick two-door sedan sold for $1,964.00 in December 1950. A seventeen-inch Motorola TV cost $239.95. One year later the same model would sell for $199.95.

On the Table 1950

Jewel had Christmas turkeys from 45¢ to 65¢ a pound, Bluebrook coffee was 75¢ a pound, and a six-pack of six-ounce bottles of Coca-Cola cost 25¢ plus the deposit.

You could eat an eight-course Christmas turkey dinner at the Blackhawk Restaurant in the Loop for $3.00 (all you can eat), and you could ride the CTA to get there, paying just 15¢ on buses or streetcars, 17¢ on El trains.

President Truman flew from Washington to Independence, Mo., for a quiet Christmas observance in the family home with his wife and daughter, Margaret.

BETHLEHEM STAR

One of the impressive Christmas observances in the nation is at Bethlehem, Pa., where the original Star of Bethlehem scene is symbolized with a 90-foot lighted star on South Mountain, augmented by seven miles of Christmas lights. Bethlehem also planned its 194-year-old Christmas Eve candle light ceremony in the old Moravian Church.

Yet many were determined to be gay. Some reflected the attitude "Let tomorrow look after its own troubles." Holiday business boomed to new highs in most Western European countries, despite soaring prices. In West Germany, merchants said shoppers bought more because of a feeling that there is no use saving money with war so threatening.

The Christmas dinner turkey cost $1.05 a pound in England. Czechoslovak housewives paid almost $1.20 a pound for chicken and $2.50 a pound for pork.

FRENCH SPEND FREELY

There were no signs of austerity in Rome and Paris, even though prices were up. The French had their biggest Christmas spending spree since 1939 with all the food, drink, toys, and other goods they could afford.

A practical demonstration of good will toward men was under way tonight [Christmas Eve] in the Holy Land, where Arab Jordan and Israeli troops opened the historic Pilgrimage Road from Jerusalem to Bethlehem. More than 300 Christian clergy, nuns and diplomatic personnel were permitted over this route to attend midnight Mass in the Church of the Nativity. Many Christians in Israel also traveled to the little town of Nazareth, in the hills of Galilee, for midnight Mass in the basilica marking the place where Mary is said to have spoken to the Angel Gabriel.

Uncle Mistletoe

For millions of Chicagoans through the years, the idea of Christmas shopping was and still is synonymous with a visit to Marshall Field's State Street store. In the early 1950s, the store windows were the responsibility of Field's then display division chief, John Moss. He was also one of the creators of the Uncle Mistletoe character, which made its debut in Field's windows in 1948. Moss was the successor to Arthur Fraser, who initiated the idea of the grand department store window display at Field's in 1895.

In December 1952, as Field's was celebrating its 100th anniversary, its in-house magazine, *The Field Glass,* looked back over the store's many Christmases:

CHRISTMAS AT FIELD'S - WAY BACK WHEN

Getting ready for Christmas is nothing new at Marshall Field & Company. Ever since 1887 we have been busying ourselves with holly, tinsel and brilliant baubles for the magical season. When a man named Harry Selfridge became superintendent in '87, he immediately began plans for our first Christmas decorations.

That year, he merely put a few decorations around the rotunda at the Washington Street entrance. They were small and forlorn—compared with today's magnificent Main Aisle displays—but people all over Chicago crowded into the store and wondered at the beauty. Prior to those years, there were hardly any Christmas decorations to speak of in

Chicago stores. Christmas Fashions of the Hour [another Field's publication] for 1915 quoted a venerable matron of the city who recalled what Christmas was like way back in 1865.

"You young people of today can't possibly realize how crude were the Christmases 50 years ago, right at the end of the Civil War. There were no toy stores—most children had only homemade toys. There were no department stores as we know them today—no delivery systems—no pretty parcels. You didn't buy a new dress for Christmas parties—you simply bought yards of material and carried it home over your arm. And there were no tearooms to stop in after a hectic afternoon of shopping—except one little place over on Clark Street called the Maison Dore. Once in a while we would stop off there for ices and little cakes. And don't for-

Used with permission of Marshall Field's.

Under the Tree 1951

Baskin's was selling cuff links for between $3.50 and $5.95. Maurice L. Rothschild offered men's slippers from $5.95 to $9.95 and jersey checked women's dresses for $8.95. Mandel Brothers had glove and muffler sets for $3.99 and all wool sweaters for $5.00. Mach Importers was selling cuckoo clocks starting at $16.95.

The big family gift of 1951 might well have been a television set. Polk Brothers had seventeen-inch Motorola sets for $199.95. Console models cost $100.00 more.

Sports 1951

In sports, the University of Illinois football team was preparing to meet Stanford in the Rose Bowl. And there was a report that the Japanese baseball leagues had sent a scout to the United States in search of talent. The Japanese were said to be willing to pay up to $5,000 plus all expenses to ball players willing to spend one season in Japan.

On the Tube 1951

Chicago had four TV stations in 1951. Christmas Day programs included Breakfast with the O'Neils, *services from the National Cathedral in Washington,* The Dennis James Show, The Steve Allen Show, Garry Moore, Gabby Hayes, Kukla, Fran & Ollie, Captain Video, *and* The News with John Cameron Swayze.

Christmas night TV specials included Dickens' "A Christmas Carol" starring Sir Ralph Richardson, Arthur Treacher, and Melville Cooper. Boris Karloff starred in a special Suspense *program as a lighthouse keeper who gives refuge to a mother and child and recaptures his own boyhood for Christmas night; and Dinah Shore broadcasted her show from the living room of her home in California's San Fernando Valley.*

At the Movies 1951

On screen, Detective Story *opened Christmas Day at the Woods; it starred Kirk Douglas, Eleanor Parker and William Bendix. Gary Cooper starred in* Distant Drums *at the Roosevelt, and Audie Murphy played* The Cimarron Kid *at the RKO Grand on Clark near Randolph.*

get, the mud and snow were so deep around Christmas time that even the coaches were stuck most of the time; you risked being stranded when you came downtown for Christmas shopping." Thus goes the Christmas shopping account of one of Chicago's early citizens. . . .

CHRISTMAS BOXES

Many people have wondered how long Field's has had Christmas boxes. Our Archives Office dug around in old records, found a House Notice of December 18, 1907, which described the Christmas box for that year. As far as anybody seems to know, that marked the beginning of one of our famed Christmas traditions—the bright, sparkling Christmas box which today goes out by the hundreds of thousands to every part of the world, more than 17 nations by a count taken three years ago. That early House Notice urged section managers to try to use up all their Christmas boxes by Christmas Eve so that there would be very few "left over." That is no problem today!

1951: *Almost Three Feet of Snow*

Chicago's snowiest Christmas came in 1951. The snow started falling on Friday, December 14. By the twenty-first, it was twenty-two inches deep in the Loop, and there were thousands of stalled and abandoned cars littering the streets and hampering snow removal efforts.

Mayor Martin Kennelly declared a "dangerous emergency," urging all Chicagoans to get their cars off the streets. He ordered the police to ticket and tow cars found in violation of the 1947 snow ordinance. That law prohibited parking on arterial and through streets and streets used by buses and trolleys when the snowfall totaled an inch or more. Seven thousand tickets were issued, three thousand of them on the nineteenth and twentieth alone.

The city had 274 plows out trying to clear the snow, but Streets Commissioner Lloyd Johnson was forced to admit the sad fact that all side streets in Chicago were virtually impassable.

Then things got worse. On Saturday, December 22, the temperature plunged to four below zero and strong winds whipped the snow into mammoth drifts. On Monday, Christmas Eve, and Tuesday, Christmas

Day, another 8.5 inches of snow fell. That brought the grand total to 33.3 inches since the fourteenth. Thousands of families were unable to get together for the holiday—or else they found themselves stranded while trying. Midway Airport was closed for four hours on Christmas Eve. Streetcars and buses ran up to five hours late on Christmas Day.

All Chicago police cars were ordered into reserve at their stations at 4 A.M. on Christmas morning, but many were already out of service with burned-out clutches or other mechanical problems. Other cars were out of service because the city had not provided tire chains.

On the day after Christmas the fire department canceled all days off for firemen and made a desperate plea to the public to clear the snow

Used with permission of the Chicago Transit Authority

Top Songs 1951

The songs on Your Hit Parade on December 22, and the artists who made them popular included "Sin (It's No)" by Eddie Howard, the Four Aces, Savannah Churchill, and others; "Slow Poke" by Roberta Lee; "Down Yonder" by Del Wood and others; "Undecided" by the Ames Brothers, Ray Anthony, and Guy Lombardo; "Domino" by Tony Martin, Bing Crosby, and Doris Day; "Rudolph the Red-Nosed Reindeer" by Gene Autry; "Because of You" by Tony Bennett, Les Baxter, Gloria DeHaven with Guy Lombardo and others; "And So to Sleep Again" by Patti Page; "Cold, Cold Heart" by Tony Bennett and others; and "Charmaine" by Mantovani, Gordon Jenkins, and the Harmonicats.

On Stage 1951

On stage, Janet Blair and Richard Eastham starred in South Pacific at the Shubert Theater. Carol Channing had the top billing at the Palace, where the show was Gentlemen Prefer Blondes.

The Christmas turkey of 1951 cost 49¢ to 59¢ a pound at Hillman's. A dozen eggs were 57¢ to 63¢. A one-pound fruitcake cost 79¢. If you had $3.25 to spend, you could buy a gingerbread house.

Top Songs 1952

The songs on Your Hit Parade *just before Christmas and the artists who made them popular were "Why Don't You Believe Me" by Joni James, "Because You're Mine" by Mario Lanza and Nat "King" Cole, "Glow Worm" by the Mills Brothers, "I Went to Your Wedding" by Patti Page, "You Belong to Me" by Jo Stafford, "Jambalaya" by Jo Stafford, "Don't Let the Stars Get in Your Eyes" by Perry Como, "White Christmas" by Bing Crosby, "Lady of Spain" by Eddie Fisher and Les Paul, and "I Saw Mommy Kissing Santa Claus" by Jimmy Boyd.*

from around fire hydrants. Transportation officials said it would be days before anything moved again at anything approaching a normal rate. Officials appealed to citizens to clear walks and to help get stranded cars out of the way of plows.

Bad as it was for the people in Chicago, another kind of disaster made it a worse holiday for the families of 119 coal miners in southern Illinois. On the last work shift of the Friday before Christmas, an explosion and fire ripped through the New Orient Mine Number Two in West Frankfort. All through the pre-Christmas weekend, rescue workers pulled bodies from the shaft. Gov. Adlai Stevenson rushed to the scene, dropping plans to host thousands of children at a Christmas party at the Springfield armory. On Christmas Eve, the last of the bodies was recovered.

And on that day there was a Christmas miracle. One miner, Cecil Sanders, was found alive in an air pocket. He had been trapped in the mine for fifty-six hours. According to the *Chicago Sun-Times*, he told rescuers, "I just went to sleep and woke up a little while before they found me." When told that he'd been trapped in the mine for three days, he said: "This is a wonderful Christmas Eve."

The war continued in Korea and the news wasn't good. The Associated Press noted that the war entered its nineteenth month on Christmas Day "with prospects bleak of reaching an early armistice."

Chicago's New Highway

Five days before Christmas, there was a ribbon-cutting ceremony on the North Side. The man known as "the Father of Good Highways in Illinois," eighty-eight-year-old William Edens, snipped the ribbon opening the Edens Expressway. A motorcade of officialdom, preceded by a dozen snowplows, then made its way the length of the new highway.

Four days before Christmas a lawsuit was filed, challenging the Chicago Park District's authority to build an underground parking garage in Grant Park.

Illinois Bell was advising its customers to place their holiday calls to loved ones by giving out-of-town numbers to an operator, and making the calls before Christmas Eve if they wanted to be sure to get through. Forty-five hundred operators and supervisors were scheduled to be on duty during the holiday.

The U.S. Secretary of Labor was reporting that 45 percent of the nation's wage earners had failed to keep pace with the 10.1 percent increase in consumer prices from January 1950, to June 1951. The secretary said it was due largely to the twenty million unorganized workers in the labor force, most of whom were in white-collar jobs.

Lastly, from Washington came word that the Office of Price Stabilization (OPS) was exempting canned, fried worms from price controls. The Associated Press reported that the OPS gave no hint about who does what with fried worms or how much they cost, but the office did say that it found their price to have a trifling effect on the cost of living.

1952: Reds

Red was a suspicious color at Christmastime in 1952. On Capitol Hill, a special House committee was holding hearings on Communist attempts to gain control of the wealth of American philanthropic organizations. The committee heard from Maurice Malkin and Manning Johnson, both former Communists who had abandoned the American Communist Party. They testified that the attempted subversion had begun back in 1933, just after President Franklin D. Roosevelt had recognized the Russian government, and that the object was to use the wealth of foundations for the Communist cause.

In Los Angeles, the school board was debating loyalty oaths and textbook censorship. The board voted to appropriate $750 to have every school system employee investigated by the California State Senate Committee on Un-American Activities.

In Chicago, the board of the Chicago Housing Authority (CHA) had just voted three to two to reject a proposal that would have required loyalty oaths from the CHA's seven hundred employees. Residents of CHA buildings were required to take such oaths because of a mandate from

Under the Tree 1952

In 1952 Jimmy Boyd's "I Saw Mommy Kissing Santa Claus" reached the top of the record charts. You could buy a copy for $1.05 at the Wurlitzer Store on South Wabash. Lyon & Healy sold three-speed record players for $29.50. Marshall Field & Co. advertised Hamilton Beach mixettes for $19.75 and Salton hot trays for $11.95. Muntz advertised its twenty-inch television sets for $129.95, and L. Fish Furniture had Zenith TVs, with "the whitest white and the blackest black" ever seen on TV, for $329.95 for a twenty-one-inch model, or $599.95 for a TV radio phonograph console. Sears was selling Roy Rogers and Dale Evans wristwatches for $4.95.

On the Table 1952

The A&P had turkeys for 53¢ to 65¢ a pound. Eggs were 55¢ a dozen, milk was 45¢ for two quarts. In the Colonnade Room of the Edgewater Beach Hotel, Christmas dinner of turkey or goose cost $2.85. Prime rib was the most expensive entrée on the menu at $3.75.

Best-Sellers 1952

Thomas Costain's The Silver Chalice was the number one bestseller in Chicago's bookstores at Christmastime 1952. John Steinbeck's East of Eden was number one in the nation.

On the Tube 1952

The TV lineup for Christmas Eve included Captain Video, The Perry Como Show, Arthur Godfrey and His Friends, I Married Joan, *and* This Is Your Life.

On the Radio 1952

On the radio, you could hear Ma Perkins, Perry Mason, The Guiding Light, *and at 6:30* P.M. *Christmas Eve, WBBM broadcast Queen Elizabeth's Christmas message.*

At the Movies 1952

Movies of the season included The Happy Time *with Charles Boyer, Louis Jourdan, and Marsha Hunt;* Invasion, U.S.A. *starring Dan O'Herlihy, Gerald Mohr, and Peggie Castle;* Against All Flags *with Errol Flynn and Maureen O'Hara in a pirate swashbuckler; and* Tri Opticon, *which the Chicago Daily News described as a "three-dimensional film opening Thursday at the Telenews theater [that] will give Chicagoans the first look at one of several three-dimensional film processes that are bringing happy times back to theater box offices. Tri Opticon is a series of short film subjects, some in color. It is viewed through special spectacles provided by the theater."*

Washington. But the CHA's general counsel, Edward J. Fruchtman, told board members that requiring a loyalty oath from employees was an unconstitutional product of "hysterical times."

In New York, President-Elect Dwight D. Eisenhower told the annual meeting of the Freedoms Foundation that the U.S. needed to return to the fundamental religious convictions of the Founding Fathers if it were to be successful in its fight against world Communism: "I don't mean to be evangelical," he said, "but there is this basic doctrine to which we must always cling. We can stand before the world in our strength and let the leaders of other countries see we are not imperialists. We believe in the dignity of man."

In his Christmas message to the American people, outgoing President Harry Truman asked for prayer for our enemies: "As we pray for our loved ones far from home—as we pray for our men and women in Korea and all our servicemen and women, wherever they are—let us also pray for our enemies. Let us pray that the spirit of God shall enter their lives and prevail in their lands. Let us pray for a fulfillment of the brotherhood of man."

There was no Christmas joy on the battlefields of Korea. An Associated Press report from Seoul on Christmas Day began, "Jet battles,

artillery duels, and infantry attacks turned Christmas in Korea into a day of snarling fighting."

On the weekend before Christmas an Air Force *Globemaster* transport plane crashed near Moses Lake, Washington, killing eighty-four servicemen on their way home for the holidays. At the time, it was the world's worst air disaster.

Medical Advances

All through the Christmas period a life-or-death drama was unfolding at the University of Illinois Hospital. For more than twelve hours on December 17, a team of doctors labored to separate Rodney and Roger Brodie, fifteen-month-old twins conjoined at the head. Doctors gave the boys only a fifty-fifty chance for survival, but each day their struggle for life was front-page news in Chicago and across the nation.

On Christmas Day, the boys were still alive. Roger was in a deep coma, Rodney in critical condition. Roger would not survive, but Rodney would be in the news again at Christmastime 1953.

In another medical development, debate was raging over the value of the anticancer drug krebiozen. On December 22, the University of Illinois board of trustees voted unanimously to grant a six-month, unpaid leave of absence to Dr. Andrew C. Ivy, so he could travel to Argentina to study how the drug was produced from horses' blood. Ivy said he hoped "the substance can and will be removed from the category of a so-called secret drug."

Two Illinois lawmakers attended the board of trustees' meeting, and they threw it into turmoil when they demanded that the trustees pass a resolution commending Dr. Ivy for his service to humanity. State Rep. Charles Jenkins (R-Chicago) blamed what he called a "medical clique" for criticism of krebiozen. One day later, one of the nation's leading cancer specialists, Dr. Stanley P. Reimann, head of the Institute for Cancer Research at Lankenau Hospital in Philadelphia, issued a report calling krebiozen worthless.

In the fifties the American public was just getting used to the idea of dieting as a lifestyle. The author of *The Fat Boy's Diet* was in Chicago at Christmastime 1952. Elmer Wheeler spoke to a meeting of the National Association of Women's and Children's Apparel Salesmen. According to the *Daily News:* "The old calorie counter warned the salesmen to trim their waistlines if they want to put that extra sizzle in next spring's sales campaigns. . . . 'A hungry salesman is faster on his feet physically and mentally. . . . He'll be getting those orders,' " said Wheeler.

Among his suggestions: eat hard rolls because they crumble so fast that half the calories are left on the table; use soft butter because you get more spread mileage with less of it than with a frozen patty; and wear "fat boy" accessories like extra large shirt collars and belts that give the illusion of losing weight and "help keep up the courage to go on with dieting."

1953: Cold War Christmas

The weather forecast for the Friday Christmas of 1953 called for slushy, windy, and fair conditions. The temperature that day ranged between twenty-seven and thirty-eight degrees. This was a relief from the five degree readings of early Christmas Eve morning, but nothing compared to the icy walls thrown up between the Soviet Union and the United States.

Nevertheless, the Christmas of 1953 was one of hope. On the front page of the *Chicago Tribune,* under the banner headline "MERRY CHRISTMAS TO ALL!" was a picture of the painting *Virgin and Child* by Albertinelli.

An armistice had finally gone into effect in Korea, ending hostilities that had been raging there since 1950. American soldiers were still occupying Japan, and Walter Simmons wrote about celebrations in both lands in the *Tribune:*

U.S. SANTA GIVES KOREANS THEIR GREATEST YULE

by Walter Simmons

TOKYO, Dec. 24—Japan and Korea are celebrating the biggest Christmas in their thousands of years of history. Since 1945 when Christmas decorations went up outside Gen. MacArthur's headquarters in Tokyo the day has meant more to Japanese every year. For weeks "Silent Night" has been blared out deafeningly in shopping centers throughout the nation and gift shopping has run 30 per cent ahead of last year.

Although Christmas is not a holiday in Japan—where only one person out of 200 is a Christian—even Buddhist priests officiated at yule ceremonies this week.

GIFTS FROM *TRIBUNE* READERS

Across the water in Korea, big hearted GIs freed from combat worries by the armistice brought that battle scarred nation its biggest Christmas. Thousands of tons of gifts—sent from the United States in response to GI appeals—have arrived for distribution to needy Koreans.

War victims, orphans and refugees by the hundreds of thousands have benefited from this unprecedented generosity. Almost without exception military units have assumed responsibility for the communities near them.

In Japan the same thing has happened although needs are not so pressing and painful. Tens of thousands of Japanese children have been entertained at pre-Christmas parties by service men.

Chicagoland men in the Korea-Japan area were cheered for the fourth consecutive year by the timely arrival of big Christmas boxes from readers of the *Chicago Tribune* under the program sponsored by the *Chicago Tribune* Charities, Inc. (Copyright *Chicago Tribune.* Used by permission.)

At the White House, President Eisenhower expressed hope for America's future. Even Radio Moscow broadcasted a conciliatory message to the United States saying the New Year offered the prospect of mutual faith and friendship between the people of the United States and the Soviet Union.

This view was problematic in the days of the cold war and cold warriors. Josef Stalin had died of a stroke in March 1953, and Nikita Khrushchev was now the Communist Party Secretary, but party policy did not seem to have changed. In June, Soviet tanks had crushed a rebellion by workers in East Germany, killing at least twenty and wounding about two hundred others. The United States tried to send food supplies to the East Germans, but the Soviets demanded that it be stopped. On the day before Christmas, the news out of Moscow was that Lavrenti Beria, the head of the Soviet secret police, and six of his aides had just been executed by a firing squad after being convicted of high treason.

In this country, Ethel and Julius Rosenberg had been executed in June for passing atomic secrets to the Soviets. In November, Sen. Joseph McCarthy of Wisconsin went on TV to assert that the Truman administration had "crawled with Communists." The former president warned Americans to protect themselves against "the onslaught of fear and hysteria which are being manipulated in this country purely for political purposes." Thirty-five thousand teachers in New York were given booklets entitled "Permit Communist Conspirators to be Teachers?" General Electric pledged to dismiss all workers who were Communists. In Chicago, the city council decided to set aside $360,000 for a civil defense program.

At Union Station, a forty-foot Christmas tree was set up in the waiting room, and carolers provided a three-day program of holiday music for the increased loads of travelers. In Grant Park, two civil engineers went stamping in the snow, and when they were finished the words "Merry Christmas" appeared over a dormant tulip bed in script with letters up to seventy feet long.

In Maple Park in Kane County, it wasn't just snow that came swirling out of the sky that Christmas week:

Christmas tree on Michigan Avenue

Chicago Historical Society. ICHI 30902. Used with permission.

Top Songs 1953

The songs on Your Hit Parade *the night after Christmas and the artists who made them popular were* "Ricochet" *by Teresa Brewer,* "Ebb Tide" *by Frank Chacksfield and Vic Damone,* "You, You, You" *by the Ames Brothers,* "Rags to Riches" *by Tony Bennett,* "That's Amore" *by Dean Martin,* "Stranger in Paradise" *by Gordon McRae,* "Vaya Con Dios" *by Les Paul & Mary Ford,* "Changing Partners" *by Patti Page,* "Santa Claus Is Coming to Town" *by Bing Crosby & the Andrews Sisters, and* "The Christmas Song" *by Nat* "King" *Cole.*

On the Radio 1953

The Lone Ranger was on both radio and TV at Christmastime 1953. Other radio programs included The Romance of Helen Trent, Our Gal Sunday, *and* Guiding Light.

On the Tube 1953

TV programs included Dragnet, Captain Video, Boston Blackie, *and* Death Valley Days.

At the Movies 1953

Movies of the season included The Robe *starring Richard Burton, Victor Mature, and Michael Rennie at the State-Lake Theater;* Thunder Over the Plains *with Randolph Scott and Lex Barker at the Roosevelt;* How to Marry a Millionaire *with Marilyn Monroe, Betty Grable, and Lauren Bacall at the Oriental; and* The Man from Cairo *starring George Raft at the McVickers.*

Under the Tree 1953

Men's dress shirts were selling for $2.95 or $3.95 at Bond's at State and Jackson. Goldblatt's had RCA Victor table model radios for $19.95 (AM models) and $59.95 for both AM and FM.

Wieboldt's toy department was offered eighteen-inch-long steel semi-trailer trucks for $1.49. A winch truck with steam shovel was $2.49. Steel dolly bunk beds complete with mattresses and two fifteen-inch dolls were $17.95 a set.

it was money, $5, $10, and $20 bills to a total of $26,000. The money had been in a mail sack tossed off one commuter train and destined for a bank in town. When a second commuter train going in the opposite direction came racing through, the sack was drawn in under the wheels, the fastening strap was loosened, and the bills came tumbling out. Before Maple Park's postmistress and her assistant could pick up the money, a City of San Francisco streamliner came roaring through and the bills scattered into the air carried by a brisk northwest wind. Bills floated down on sidewalks, porches, roofs, and cornfields. Some people thought at first that they had been sent a special Christmas present from on high.

After it became generally known what had happened, a volunteer force of more than a hundred people went searching for the money, and all but $890 of it was recovered. The rest may have stuck to the streamliner and been scattered along the way, or it may still be hidden in obscure places in Maple Park.

Robert Burns of the University of Chicago's Industrial Relations Center told newsmen that there was no sound economic basis for compelling people to retire at the age of sixty-five. Burns said the age limit had been imposed during the Great Depression when there had been a surplus of manpower.

The University of Chicago's fact book reported that the average income of a Chicago family was $3,956 a year. The book noted a 54 percent increase in the number of children under age five who had entered the Chicago school system between 1940 and 1950.

It was just a few days before Christmas 1953, that Rodney Dee Brodie went home from the hospital for the first time. Rodney was almost two and a half years old. He had spent all but six weeks of that time at the University of Illinois Research and Educational Hospitals, where surgery had been performed on December 17, 1952, to separate him from his conjoined twin, Roger Lee, who had died in January. Rodney had undergone twenty major operations, and doctors still faced the problem of making a hard covering for his skull. But at this Christmas, the happy toddler called out to staff members as he left the hospital, clinging to his mother. He was able to stand by himself and was described as a "whiz" in his wheeled walker.

It was on Christmas Day 1953, that five-time Chicago mayor Carter Harrison II died. He collapsed in his hotel apartment at Lincoln Park West just as his daughter was about to serve Christmas dinner. Harrison was ninety-three. He had served as mayor from 1899 to 1905 and from 1911 to 1915.

Advent of Canned Laughter

Television was still a relatively new form of mass entertainment, and the *Tribune* carried a criticism about an addition to soundtracks that we take for granted today:

CANNED LAUGHS WRING GROANS IN MR. REMENIH

HOLLYWOOD DUBS IN FAKED
by Anton Remenih

PHONEY FUN: The TV program on the screen was a filmed situation comedy out of Hollywood. Every few seconds the loud speaker reverberated with hilarious bellowing, apparently provided by the studio audience present when the program was filmed. I looked around our family viewing circle.

The No. 1 boy, who laughs easily, didn't crack a smile. The No. 2 lad, who must pull his thumb out of his mouth to giggle, sucked placidly. The head of the family patched sox, and I waited patiently for a line good enough to use in my musings on TV.

The "studio audience" howled, yet nobody was laughing at our house. How can this be? This can be because the laughter is as phoney as the huckster giving away a car with every TV set.

Many Hollywood canned TV programs dub in laughter on the film's sound track after the show is recorded. This method has several advantages. For one thing it's good for writers' morale. Every precious yak line gets its yak. The practice also supports weak lines. The weaker the joke, the louder the laughter. This is why you so often turn to your viewing partner to inquire, "What was that? Did I miss something?"

I should think any self-respecting comedian or writer would deeply resent canned laughs just as much as a good plumber takes exception to the charge he installed a leaky faucet. (Copyright *Chicago Tribune*. Used by permission.)

On the Table 1953

At the A&P turkeys were 49¢ a pound. Canned hams were 79¢ a pound. Ninety-three-score butter was 70¢ cents a pound.

If you were planning to dine out, a full Christmas dinner at the Georgian Hotel in Evanston cost $2.95. It included soup, salad, entrée, two vegetables, rolls, dessert, and beverage.

Top Songs 1954

At Christmastime 1954, Lyon & Healy was selling hi-fi phonographs for $149.50. Twelve-inch, 33 1/3 rpm records cost 99¢ apiece. Titles included "The King and I," which also was on stage at the Schubert Theater, "South Pacific," and new releases by Sarah Vaughan, Dizzy Gillespie, and other jazz stars.

On the Table 1955

You could deck out your table for Christmas at the A&P, where tom turkeys were 43¢ a pound, yams were three pounds for 25¢, milk was 39¢ for a half gallon, and a one-and-a-half-pound fruitcake cost $1.39.

On the Radio 1955

On the radio 1955 you could have heard Gunsmoke, The Lone Ranger, Philo Vance, *Lionel Barrymore and his classic recreation of Scrooge in "A Christmas Carol,"* and a Christmas Sing with Bing.

1955:
The Montgomery Bus Boycott

Chicagoans could only dream of a white Christmas in 1955. The forecast for that Christmas Sunday called for partly cloudy skies, a chance of snow flurries, and temperatures in the upper twenties.

Bleak as that forecast was for Chicago, it was better than the weather being experienced by people living on the West Coast. In northern California and Oregon thousands were spending the holiday away from their homes, evacuated because of storms and flooding that President Eisenhower described as a major disaster.

The sounds of Christmas were everywhere. At Union Station, travelers were serenaded by the carol-ing of the Pennsylvania Railroaders, the Burlington Zephyr Chorus, or the Milwaukee Road Choral Club. Sixty workers at the Merchandise Mart formed a chorus and gave noontime concerts in the lobby of the building. At city hall, with Mayor Richard J. Daley and his staff looking on, it was the Lane Tech High School Boys' Chorus that provided the entertainment.

At the White House, President and Mrs. Eisenhower were serenaded by three of their four grandchildren. The fourth, Mary Jean, was a Christmas gift to the family, born four days before Christmas at Walter Reed Army Hospital.

On Christmas Day, the president planned to play Santa Claus to the children, handing out gifts from beneath the Christmas tree. The president himself was disregarding his doctors' advice that he head south to a warmer clime for a couple of weeks and get some

The Burlington Zephyr Chorus, Christmas 1955

Used with permission of the Burlington Northern and Santa Fe Railway Co.

outdoor exercise. Mr. Eisenhower had suffered a heart attack in September. While recuperating from it in a Denver hospital, he completed work on a painting of a Colorado outdoor scene. Copies of it were his Christmas gift to the seven hundred members of the White House staff.

The United States in the mid-1950s was marked by labor disputes and the seeds of the civil rights movement. It was on December 1, 1955, that Rosa Parks refused to give up her bus seat in Montgomery, Alabama, launching the civil rights movement into high gear. By Christmastime, the Montgomery bus boycott was well under way.

In Corpus Christi, Texas, there was a pointed example of the matter-of-fact racism that some people took for granted. The Nueces County chapter of the Texas Citizens Council objected to the town's decision to include black figures in downtown Christmas displays. Three blacks were in a children's choir display; one of the wise men in the Nativity scene was black. The manager of the Chamber of Commerce said he'd stand firm against the council's objections.

Two bitter labor disputes made the news. In Kohler, Wisconsin, members of the United Auto Workers (UAW) had been on strike against the Kohler plumbing ware company since April 1954. UAW president Walter Reuther came out with a "good will" message, noting that several thousand children in the area were about to observe their second Christmas with a parent on strike. Reuther offered to meet company president Herbert Kohler on Christmas day in face-to-face negotiations. Kohler, noting the wave of violence that had accompanied the walkout, called Reuther's message an "obvious publicity device."

The Union of Electrical Workers had been on strike for two months, forcing the closure of forty Westinghouse plants across the country. Negotiators for the Westinghouse Electric Corporation and the union did meet a few days before Christmas. But talks broke down when company negotiators accused the union of using language of "profane abuse." The union defended their language saying it was "common to all negotiations" and accused the company of "a childish excuse to walk out" of the talks. The company offered to make one hundred dollar no-interest loans

On Stage 1955

Duke Ellington was playing at Chicago's famous jazz spot, The Blue Note, at Christmastime 1955. The Hollywood Ice Revue was playing the Chicago Stadium. Box seats cost $4. Anastasia was on stage at the Blackstone; The Pajama Game was featured at the Shubert.

Top Songs 1955

The top tunes of the day included "Sixteen Tons" by Tennessee Ernie Ford, "Autumn Leaves" by Roger Williams, "Love Is a Many-Splendored Thing" by the Four Aces, "Moments to Remember" by the Four Lads, "I Hear You Knockin'" by Gale Storm, "Memories Are Made of This" by Dean Martin, "Great Pretender" by the Platters, and "Band of Gold" by Don Cherry.

At the Movies 1955

Movies in town included Guys and Dolls *with Marlon Brando, Frank Sinatra, Jean Simmons, and Vivian Blaine at the Chicago Theater;* I'll Cry Tomorrow *with Susan Hayward at the United Artists; and* Oklahoma, *which premiered the night after Christmas at the McVickers.*

On the Tube 1955

On TV there was Rin Tin Tin, Beat the Clock, Perry Como, The Honeymooners *with Jackie Gleason and Art Carney, and* Wrestling from Marigold *with Jack Brickhouse describing the action.*

Best-Sellers 1955

The Chicago Tribune's *list of best-selling books in the Midwest included the fiction* Andersonville *by MacKinlay Kantor,* Marjorie Morningstar *by Herman Wouk,* Cash McCall *by Cameron Hawley,* The Tontine *by Thomas B. Costain, and* Auntie Mame *by Patrick Dennis. Nonfiction best-sellers were* Gift from the Sea *by Anne Morrow Lindbergh,* The Power of Positive Thinking *by Norman Vincent Peale,* Inside Africa *by John Gunther, and* A Night to Remember *by Walter Lord.*

to all of its idle workers. More than twenty thousand workers took Westinghouse up on its offer.

The Labor Department reported that figures were good for the nation's factory workers. The cost of living rose only one tenth of one percent in November, while the average factory worker's pay rose 80¢ a week after taxes. The average pay was $72.85 a week for a worker with three dependents, $65.49 for a worker with no dependents. The Labor Department noted that take-home pay was $4.67 higher than a year earlier, representing the sharpest November to November increase in five years.

1956: Boldog Karacsony

"Santa Can't Use a Sleigh" was the way the *Chicago Tribune* described the weather for Christmas Eve. The forecast called for cloudy and colder conditions, with a low of about twenty-five degrees. The forecast for Christmas Day was partly cloudy with a high in the mid-thirties.

It was on Christmas Eve, 1956, that Vice President Richard Nixon arrived back in Washington from a four-day visit to the Austro-Hungarian border. He had been studying the problem posed by the thousands of Hungarian refugees who had fled their country as Soviet tanks violently suppressed the Hungarian revolution. "I am convinced," said Nixon, "as a result of firsthand study of the situation that the courageous peoples who fought for freedom in Hungary should be considered a problem only to the Soviet Union. As a result of their sacrifice, international communism has suffered a mortal blow from which it cannot recover."

Two days earlier, on December 22, the *Tribune* described the arrival of a group of refugees had arrived in Chicago.

REFUGEES ARRIVE IN TEARS, WONDER
THEY OFFER YULE GREETINGS AT CHURCH HERE
by Louise Hutchinson

They wept and cried "Boldog Karacsony" [Merry Christmas] as they stumbled from a chartered bus into a rain misted Chicago morning yesterday.

110

These 45 Hungarian refugees—first group of Protestant refugees to reach Chicago—arrived at the Southside Hungarian Evangelical Reformed church, 652 E. 92d st., after a long bus ride from Camp Kilmer, N.J. They carried only suitcases and boxes with their remaining possessions.

Some were dark-eyed with fatigue. Others seemed stunned. A former freedom fighter sat in a corner strumming a guitar.

GIRLS PLAY WITH DOLLS

Little girls played with dolls. But their parents sat quietly, looking at a tinsel wreathed Christmas tree, talking about harrowing days past, wondering what this new life would bring.

The group was sponsored by Church World service of the Church Federation of Greater Chicago, which hadn't expected the first group here until after Christmas. Their arrival yesterday was arranged for by the church's pastor, the Rev. Arpad George, who flew to Camp Kilmer last Thursday.

MANY OFFERS OF HOMES

"We could sponsor every one of them from among my own congregation," said the Rev. Mr. George. (Copyright *Chicago Tribune.* Used by permission.)

The *Chicago Daily News* reported that a tag day for Hungarian Relief raised $125,215 in Chicago shortly before Christmas.

In this country, a small step of progress had just been made toward ensuring the rights of some of our own citizens. On December 21, the Montgomery, Alabama, bus boycott ended under a federal order prohibiting segregation. Blacks were sitting anywhere they pleased on the city's buses, and without interference.

In Chicago, the head of the local chapter of the National Association for the Achievement of Colored People (NAACP), Willoughby Abner, called for the redrawing of public school boundaries so that more black and white students could go to school together. Abner planned to ask the Chicago School Board to adopt a definite policy on integration at its meeting later in December.

Under the Tree 1955

Among the things that money could buy were ladies' slipover sweaters, selling at Bond's for $2.00, men's shirts for $3.95 and $5.00 at Mandel Brothers. A brand new 1956 Pontiac could be had for $1,970.00.

Transistorized pocket radios were priced at $49.95. Portable tube model radios were $29.95. Most transistor radios didn't start coming down in price until 1958. That year, Walgreen's sold all-transistor portable radios for $18.88. At Polk Brothers, Zenith pocket radios with "all-transistor quality" cost $59.95, less your trade-in. By Christmastime of 1962, transistor pocket radios were selling for $8.47 at Walgreen's.

Da Bears 1956

Mayor Richard J. Daley had just proclaimed Sunday, December 30 as "Bear Down Chicago Bears Day." That was the day the Bears were scheduled to play the New York Giants in Yankee Stadium for pro football's title. The Bears would lose that contest 47-7.

Under the Tree 1956

The toy of the season in 1956 was Golfer Ike. It was a game sold by Abercrombie & Fitch:

> *Lay out 9 or 18 holes in your living room with shots played over or around hazards. That's "Golfer Ike" . . . the closet approach to real golf in-doors. Minatue [sic] ball is hit, chipped or putted with controllable club. Complete with book of rules, suggested courses, flags and greens.*

Golfer Ike cost $10.95 for a four-player set or $5.95 for a two-player set.

Top Songs 1956

Guy Mitchell's "Singing the Blues" was the top song on both Your Hit Parade *and the* Billboard *magazine survey. Elvis Presley's "Love Me Tender" was number two, Jim Lowe's "Green Door" was number three. Fats Domino's "Blueberry Hill" and Johnnie Ray's "Just Walking in the Rain" also made both surveys.*

On the Table 1956

Kroger's had turkeys for 39¢ a pound. Eggs were 43¢ a dozen, bread was 19¢ for a twenty-ounce loaf.

1957: Sputnik

Chicago's weather for the Wednesday Christmas of 1957 was nothing to write home about. It was cloudy with occasional rain. The predicted high temperature was forty-five degrees.

The top news of the day concerned the cold war. Just two days before Christmas, President Dwight Eisenhower made a nationally broadcast address appealing to the Kremlin for clear evidence of integrity and sincerity in promoting peace throughout the world. The cold war came home to America's teenagers in 1957: Elvis Presley got drafted. At Christmastime, Paramount Pictures was trying to get an eight-week stay of Elvis' induction into the army so that he could finish making a movie.

Americans were generally alarmed by one particular Soviet scientific advance of 1957. On October 4, the Soviets launched the first man-made satellite, *Sputnik 1*. On December 6, America's first attempt at launching a satellite blew up on the launch pad at Cape Canaveral, Florida.

Dr. Paul F. Klopsteg, the former director of Northwestern University's technological institute and at the time an associate director for the National Science Foundation, told the *Chicago Tribune* that Americans should be grateful because the launch of *Sputnik* had shaken Americans out of their sense of complacency. Very soon after *Sputnik* a push would be on in America's schools to increase interest in math and science.

Several Chicagoans thought they had spotted *Sputnik* in the southeast sky during Christmas week, but Argonne lab's moon watch team said no, they hadn't seen anything.

In other local news, Mayor Richard J. Daley announced that Chicago police officers would begin working a five-day week in January 1958. They had been working five-and-a-half days a week. Cook County assessor Frank Keenan said he would appeal his federal conviction on eight counts of income tax evasion.

A Chicago City Council committee had just voted down a proposal to spend $72,500 to rent a computer from the Remington Rand Univac division for traffic court for one year. The machine would have made a traffic offender's previous record available at the touch of a button, but the committee thought it would mean the loss of jobs.

1958: Our Lady of the Angels

In 1958 the Christmas season was darkened by the most tragic school fire in Chicago's history. On December 1 the Our Lady of the Angels School burned. More than ninety children and nuns were killed. The fire cast a pall on the season for most Chicagoans, who had watched or heard the

Manger scene on Carson Pirie Scott

Chicago Historical Society. ICHI 31248. Used with permission.

At the Movies 1956

At the movies, Dean Martin and Jerry Lewis starred in Hollywood or Bust *at the State-Lake. It was Yul Brynner and Ingrid Bergman in* Anastasia *at the Oriental Theater. The Mole People with Cynthia Patrick was playing at the Roosevelt.* Written on the Wind *with Rock Hudson and Dorothy Malone was at the United Artists. And* Giant *starring James Dean, Elizabeth Taylor, and Rock Hudson was winding up a run at the Chicago Theater. On Christmas Day* The Ten Commandments *was opening at the McVickers.*

On the Tube 1956

TV fare on Christmas Eve included Kukla, Fran and Ollie, Robin Hood *starring Richard Greene,* My Little Margie *starring Gale Storm,* The Danny Thomas Show, Burns and Allen, *Arthur Godfrey's* Talent Scouts, I Love Lucy, December Bride, *and* Great Gildersleeve *which had transplanted from radio.*

Best-Sellers 1956

The Tribune's *list of best-selling books in the Midwest included* Peyton Place *by Grace Metalious,* Don't Go Near the Water *by William Brinkley,* The Tribe That Lost Its Head *by Nicholas Monsarrat,* Merry Christmas, Mr. Baxter *by Edward Streeter, and in nonfiction* The Nun's Story *by Kathryn Hulme,* This Hallowed Ground *by Bruce Catton,* Much Ado About Me *by Fred Allen, and* Profiles in Courage *by John F. Kennedy.*

Top Songs 1957

American Bandstand made its debut on TV. Some of the songs you might have heard on the program at Christmastime included Pat Boone's "April Love," "At the Hop" by Danny and the Juniors, Presley's "Jailhouse Rock" and "Treat Me Nice," "Raunchy" by Bill Justis, and "You Send Me" by Sam Cooke.

On the Table 1957

If you were preparing Christmas dinner at home, turkeys cost 37¢ a pound at Hillman's, a half-gallon of ice cream was 69¢. A pound of coffee cost 89¢.

horror developing on live TV and radio broadcasts. All through that Christmas season, churches were filled with people praying for the victims and their families. The *Chicago Tribune* visited with some of them:

FIRE TRAGEDY HUSHES USUAL CHRISTMAS JOY
Neighborhood Grieves for Lost and Hurt
by Nancy McGill

They fondly remember Christmases past. They look hopefully toward Christmases to come. But in the neighborhood of Our Lady of the Angels school, there is no Christmas present.

Nightmarish memories of the Dec. 1 school fire which claimed 92 lives have smothered the spirit of joy that usually prevails during the yuletide season.

Crowd at Our Lady of the Angels fire

HUSH OVER AREA

"One would never know it's almost Christmas," said Mrs. Mary Vittallo of 3636 Chicago avenue. "There's an eerie hush over the entire area—a neighborhood that usually is gay and merry during the holidays."

There were no Christmas bells or carols heard in the area. Green wreaths were missing from most front doors. And only a few decorated trees could be seen in the front windows of homes.

"Try as I may, I find it very hard to feel the Christmas spirit," explained Mrs. Anne Brock of 906 N. Avers avenue. "Maybe it's because we live so close to the scene of the tragedy."

CHILD STILL UPSET

"She walked to her front living room window and looked outside. Directly across the street stood the dark, gloomy ruins of the school. My daughter, Mary, still gets nervous and upset every time she sees the school or anyone talks of the fire," she said. "I don't think she'll ever forget her experience in the hospital." Despite the heavy cloud that still lingers over the household, the Brocks will attempt to observe Christmas. "We have to carry on for the living, our grieving won't bring back the dead," Mrs. Brock added. (Copyright *Chicago Tribune*. Used by permission.)

A couple of days before Christmas, Chicago school superintendent Benjamin Willis reported to the school board that fireproofing the city's public schools would cost fifty million dollars. He said 130,000 youngsters were attending class in buildings or sections of buildings built before 1900. Willis estimated the cost of installing sprinkler systems in all city schools at eleven million. A few days earlier, Mayor Richard J. Daley had proposed an ordinance requiring sprinkler systems in all buildings with wooden floors that were two or more stories in height.

There is still no explanation of how the fire got started, though it is known that the fire began at the bottom of a stairwell where a stack of paper was illegally stored.

1959: *Peace on Earth*

Chicago found itself buried under eight inches of snow on the Friday, Christmas of 1959. A surprise storm snarled traffic the Wednesday and

Under the Tree 1957

By 1957 a twenty-two-piece Lionel train set sold for $37.50 at the West Town Hobby Shop. Sears had a transistor table AM radio for $46.88; an AM and FM model cost $10.00 more.

At the Movies 1957

And God Created Woman *starring Brigitte Bardot opened Christmas Day at the Loop Theater. The film had been given the okay by the Chicago police censor board, but only after several scenes were cut. Other movies of the season included* Legend of the Lost *with John Wayne and Sophia Loren, Marlon Brando in* Sayonara, *and the Disney movie* Old Yeller.

On Stage 1957

Duke Ellington was appearing at the Blue Note at Madison & Clark Streets at Christmastime. The Benny Goodman Orchestra was opening Christmas night at the Aragon Ballroom on the North Side.

Best-Sellers 1959

Books on the New York Time's *best-seller list included Allen Drury's* Advise and Consent, *James Michener's* Hawaii, *and Moss Hart's* Act One.

Top Songs 1959

The popular music at Christmastime included "Heartaches by the Number" by Guy Mitchell, "Mr. Blue" by the Fleetwoods, "Mack the Knife" by Bobby Darin, "In the Mood" by Ernie Fields, "Why" by Frankie Avalon, "El Paso" by Marty Robbins, "The Big Hurt" by Toni Fisher, "It's Time to Cry" by Paul Anka, and "Way Down Yonder in New Orleans" by Freddy Cannon.

Thursday before, but the forecast for Christmas Day promised sunshine with temperatures right around freezing.

A Chicago gangland murder made national news. Police were looking for the gunman who used big game ammunition to end the life of Roger "the Terrible" Touhy. He was gunned down eight days before Christmas, and just twenty-three days after being paroled from prison. He had spent twenty-five years behind bars for the 1933 gangland kidnaping of a swindler.

Touhy's murder made a runaway best-seller out of his just published biography. It was entitled *The Stolen Years*, and the *Chicago Daily News* reported that what Touhy had said in it might have provided a motive for his murder:

> "My hope is to live out the few years remaining to me in peace and quiet and freedom with those I love and respect."
> From Roger Touhy's book, *The Stolen Years*

. . .The book is a ringing indictment of Cook County justice in the 1930s.

It details Touhy's years in prison, his charge that he was railroaded in a prohibition conspiracy between the old Capone mob and some Cook County officials, and his fight for freedom.

The book tells how Touhy spent a quarter of a century behind bars for what he called "a crime that never happened," the kidnaping of John "Jake the Barber" Factor.

With Touhy's gangland death, *The Stolen Years*, at $4.50 a copy, has become a runaway best seller in Chicago book stores.

The chapter titles themselves give an inkling of the book's brisk, sometimes indignant, sometimes funny pace. A few of them: "Al Capone Didn't Like Me". . . "My Beer was Bootleg, But Good". . . "Over the Wall". . . "82 Days AWOL". . . "Jake the Barber Was KIDNAPED????" . . . "Alice in Factorland". . . "My Vindication in Court."

The book ends with a chapter called "A Great Judge's Opinion" and a tribute to the late Judge John P. Barnes who ruled that the kidnaping was a hoax.

Toward the end Touhy writes, "It was my privilege, thank God, under the American way of life, to tell my story." But the Touhy story goes on daily in headlines Touhy will never see. (Reprinted with permission of the *Chicago Sun-Times.*)

Four days before Christmas, 1959, the publishers of the *World Book Encyclopedia* announced plans in Chicago for a September 1960 expedition to the Himalaya Mountains to search for the Abominable Snowman. Mount Everest conqueror Sir Edmund Hillary would head up the two hundred thousand dollar expedition. Publisher Bailey Howard told reporters: "Hillary said to me, 'There's something up there. I know there's something up there.' I told Hillary, 'Go and bring it back.' " Howard said the only trouble was that if Hillary were to be successful, nobody was quite sure whether the creature should be taken to a zoo or to a hotel.

Controversy and the Church

Race relations were again making news in 1959. The planners of an integrated housing development sued the village of Deerfield because the village had condemned the proposed site and instead planned to turn it into a park.

This was a time when the terms "block busting," "panic peddling" and "white flight" were being coined. In Chicago, one of the most segregated of cities, the burgeoning black population was expanding into areas where they were not welcomed or wanted by many of the whites living there.

There was friction, anger, and hate.

But not from all corners. At Christmastime, seventeen southwest side ministers gave their support to the Reverend James Reed, the assistant pastor of the Trinity Methodist Church at Eighty-ninth and Winchester. The pastoral relations committee of the church was pressing Reed to either resign his post as assistant pastor or quit his membership in the Organization for the Southwest Community, a group made up of whites and blacks and whose avowed goal was to stop decay and obsolescence. Reverend Reed said that he, in good conscience, could not quit either post.

One supporter of the Reverend Mr. Reed wrote delicately and diplomatically about the racism involved, saying that the conflict had brought "into focus" similar controversies that had been troubling other churches "less sharply and clearly."

San Francisco's controversial Episcopal bishop James Pike was stirring religious controversy. Shortly before Christmas, *Time* magazine reported an overflow crowd at San Francisco's Grace Cathedral heard the bishop declare: "Responsible choice as to the number and spacing of children is simply one of the many areas of life in which people are called upon to make conscientious decisions under God." If a couple "ought to be having a child," any method of birth control—including abstinence from intercourse—is sinful. But if they should not be having a child—for economic, psychological, or physical reasons—they are under obligation to use the most effective methods to prevent it. "We are not permitted to use a chancy method like the rhythm method, which some have called 'Vatican roulette,' when a more medically-sound approach is available."

At the same time in Connecticut, the state supreme court upheld two laws banning the use of contraceptives and forbidding doctors from advising their use under any circumstances.

In the December issue of the *Walther League Messenger*, a publication of the Lutheran Church, the Reverend Alfred Klausler warned that religious novelties were flooding the market. They included such items as a switchblade knife imprinted "Jesus Never Fails," a ballpoint pen with a peephole on top through which one could read the Lord's Prayer, nail files inscribed "With God all things are possible," and head-of-Christ paperweights. The Reverend Mr. Klausler warned that "deliberately or not, they [dealers in religious articles] make suckers out of the pious."

President and Mrs. Eisenhower were planning a quiet Christmas at the White House. The president was just back from a nineteen-day trip to eleven nations in Asia, Europe, and North Africa. During the ceremonial lighting of the nation's Christmas tree, Mr. Eisenhower called on the Soviet Union to look beyond "bare co-existence, and to strive for peace in open partnership with all nations." The president declared that differing peoples and systems of government could exist in the world without the inevitability of conflict "in which one must triumph over the other."

At Langley Air Base in Virginia, America's astronauts were worried that the Soviets would be the first to successfully orbit a man in space. Capt. Virgil Grissom called on the United States to declare an out-and-out race with the Soviets. In April 1961 a cosmonaut would successfully orbit the Earth.

TV SETS

The big family gift you might have found under the Christmas tree in the late '40s and early '50s was a TV set. In 1948, a seven-inch table model sold for $179.95 or a ten-inch combined TV AM-and-FM radio with turntable in a fine wood cabinet sold for $595.00.

By 1951, Polk Brothers was selling seventeen-inch Motorola sets for $199.95. Console models cost $100.00 more. One year later, Muntz advertised its 20-inch TV set for $129.95. In 1952 L. Fish Furniture sold Zenith TVs, with "the whitest white and the blackest black" ever seen on TV, for $329.95 for a twenty-one-inch model, or $599.95 for a TV-radio-phonograph console. Color televisions soon became available. In 1950 a twenty-one-inch Muntz color TV cost $399.95. Network color services didn't fully come on the scene until 1965.

The effect TV had on the American lifestyle is reflected in a 1958 Wieboldt's ad for TV snack tray sets, five pieces for $12.95.

Marshall Field's bicycle display

1960-1969

1961: Christmas Daze

A Chicago Christmas street scene, from the *Chicago Daily News* on Friday, December 22, 1961, described the following:

LOOP CROWDS WANDER IN CHRISTMAS DAZE
Carols, Nativity Scenes and Santas Heighten Mood

It was a regular just-before-Christmas crowd at State and Madison, world's busiest corner.

A small girl in a wheelchair, braces on her legs, looked in a store window and seemed happy.

A woman with a white cane stood in a doorway, listening to the broadcast carols.

A lot of couples were holding hands—even persons over 25 years of age—as they walked along.

"THEY'RE preoccupied," said Patrolman Edward Smyth as he directed traffic there.

"They walk every which way . . . watch 'em awhile."

"They're a million miles away. It's a wonder they don't get killed."

But Smyth made sure the cars waited for the people.

A KINDLY looking man in a red suit and a white beard stood close by the northeast corner, ringing a bell near a portable chimney.

"The kids are great, but they can drive you nuts," he said.

"They say, 'Hi Santa,' and I say, 'Hi.'"

"They say, 'You're not the real Santa,' and I say, 'Okay, I'm Santa's helper.' "

To some, he is known as James Whelan, 44, of 735 N. Dearborn, a former railroad employee now working for Volunteers of America.

Under the Tree 1961

Polk Brothers had Royal portable typewriters for $79.95, Sunbeam electric blankets for $13.97, and Osterizer two-speed blenders for $44.95.

On the Table 1961

The Christmas turkey of 1961 cost 29¢ a pound at National. A two-pound can of coffee cost $1.25.

Top Songs 1961

The number one song of the day was the Tokens' "The Lion Sleeps Tonight." Other top tunes included "Please Mr. Postman" by the Marvlettes, "Run to Him" by Bobby Vee, "Walk On By" by Leroy Van Dyke, and "The Twist" by Chubby Checker.

The twist dance craze was sweeping the nation. Chicago's ballrooms were prepared to offer the twist at New Year's Eve parties. It was being said that the gentleman who didn't ask his lady to waltz or twist at New Year's just didn't have any romance in him at all.

Through some Christmas miracle and fancy footwork, Santa was making appearances in several big Loop stores.

There were also six nativity scenes in as many locations along State St.

Some 13,500,000 persons come to State St. for shopping and looking between Thanksgiving and Christmas, said Robert Johnson.

He is managing director of the State St. Council and can see the world's busiest corner from his window.

"And a looker is a shopper, eventually," he said.

There was plenty of activity in stores Friday. Letter carriers were busy, too. But in many offices little work was done, and early quitting times were the fashion of the day. (Reprinted with permission of the *Chicago Sun-Times*.)

The next day, Saturday the twenty-third, Chicago was hit by a surprise blizzard. Nine inches of snow fell on the city, assuring a white Christmas for 1961. The blizzard paralyzed much of the Midwest, from

Christmas Dream House

the Dakotas to Indiana. Hundreds of drivers found themselves stranded in the city or suburbs on that weekend before Christmas. Snow flurries and temperatures in the twenties were forecast for Christmas Day.

The nation's first family was preoccupied with the health of Joseph Kennedy, father of the president, who had just suffered a stroke and undergone surgery to relieve congestion in his throat and chest. He was in very serious condition in a Florida hospital.

The threat of nuclear war was a major concern. At this Christmastime, 459 midwestern scientists, doctors, and educators went on record, by sending an open letter to the president, asking him to de-emphasize fallout shelters and to instead push for a positive program of peace.

President John Kennedy and British prime minister Harold MacMillan had just concluded a series of talks in Bermuda. They agreed to go ahead with a new series of atmospheric atomic bomb tests in the wake of earlier testing.

A Northwestern University professor, Paul Witty, was urging parents to curb their childrens' addiction to television. Professor Witty noted that preschoolers were spending fifteen hours a week in front of the TV, grade-schoolers twenty-one hours. "Too much time in sedentary, passive, often stultifying pursuit," said the professor. Federal Communications Commission (FCC) chairman Newton Minow, meanwhile, told a Chicago audience that his efforts to goad the networks into improving their program standards should not be confused with censorship. It was in May of 1961 that Minow had referred to television as "a vast waste-land."

The finance committee of the Chicago City Council had just approved a controversial proposal to set up a six-member board to censor all films and to ban certain others to children under the age of seventeen. Scenes of lynching, the burning of a human being, and "depravity" would be outlawed. Fifth Ward alderman Leon Despres argued unsuccessfully that theater newsreels depicting real events ought to be exempted from the ordinance. "Not to make an exception for news film," he said, "would guarantee that the proposal would ultimately be judged constitutional."

On the Tube 1961

Among the programs on the tube on Christmas Eve were Topper, Death Valley Days, Bat Masterson, The Bullwinkle Show, Car 54, Where Are You? *and* The Ed Sullivan Show.

At the Movies 1961

Movies playing at Christmastime 1961 included King of Kings *playing at the Michael Todd Theater plus the* The Wonders of Aladdin *starring Donald O'Connor,* Mysterious Island, Pocketful of Miracles, Twist Around the Clock, Flower Drum Song, *and* Babes in Toyland.

Sports 1961

In sports, Chicago Bears' tight end Mike Ditka was just chosen the NFL's Rookie of the Year for 1961. Chicago had two basketball teams that winter, the Packers in the NBA and the Majors in Abe Saperstein's old American Basketball League. The Bulls were still in Chicago's future.

Transportation 1963

The nation's carmakers were predicting record sales in 1963, with even better prospects for 1964. Ford was ready to introduce its "dream car," the Mustang, at the New York World's Fair in April. At the same time Studebaker was announcing the layoffs of four thousand workers at its South Bend plant, with more bad news to come later.

Under the Tree 1963

Sears was selling power toothbrushes for $8.97. At Polk Brothers, you could buy a battery-powered six-inch "Little Miracle" micro TV for $169.95. Record albums cost $2.44 for monaural or $3.04 for stereo.

On the Table 1963

HighLow Foods had turkeys for 39¢ to 45¢ a pound. Large eggs were 49¢ a dozen.

A hamburger platter with french fries and coleslaw could be had at Woolworth's for 65¢.

Despres also attacked the wording of the proposal that allowed censors to ban any film for any reason deemed unsuitable for children. He said such an ordinance would make Chicago a "cultural wasteland." Several of the aldermen agreed that one of the current movies of the season, the biblical *King of Kings* at the Michael Todd Theater, would have to cut scenes of Roman depravity if the proposal were to be adopted by the entire city council.

The University of Illinois (U of I) issued a timetable for building its new Chicago campus, replacing the temporary one at Navy Pier. It was

Prudential Building in Christmas dress, 1962

predicted that seventy-six hundred students would attend what was then being called the U of I Congress Campus when it opened for the 1964-65 school year.

1962:
Christmas in Sunny South Vietnam

At Christmastime 1962, the lights in the rooms of the Prudential Building were so arranged that they depicted a cross to onlookers.

On the other side of the world, however, more than eleven thousand U.S. servicemen were stationed in South Vietnam as military advisers. When a helicopter was shot down on the weekend before Christmas, it was only the forty-second American death of the nearly fifty-eight thousand yet to come.

Vietnam was still a novelty to U.S. newsmen. At Christmastime, an Associated Press reporter's story read like a travelogue. He wrote that Vietnam was famous for its shellfish and other seafood. The local beer was a popular drink and the French rolls were crisp and tasty. It wouldn't be until March 1965 that American combat forces were committed to the war.

1963:
A Nation Torn by Grief

On Monday, December 23, an inch of snow fell on Chicago, and on the four hundred thousand shoppers who jammed the Loop. It was the first shopping day in two weeks in which the mercury climbed as high as the twenties. The forecast called for continuing temperatures in the twenties for the next two days, with a chance of snow flurries on Christmas Day.

To the east and south, it was much worse. Eight inches of snow fell on New York City. Parts of the South were experiencing their heaviest snowfalls in years: 14 inches in Memphis, Tennessee, 7 inches in Nashville, 8 to 12 inches across Arkansas, ice-glazed roadways from Virginia and the Carolinas in a wide swath down to Alabama, Mississippi, and Louisiana. More than fifty deaths were being blamed on the storm.

The Christmas of 1963 was one of subdued celebration, and perhaps a little contemplation, as the nation still mourned the assassination of President John F. Kennedy one month earlier. A Christmastime poll taken by the National Opinion Research Center at the University of Chicago found that most people had cried when they heard the news of the assassination. That included "a considerable majority of women" and "about half the men" questioned by the center, according to Peter Rossi, the center's director. A sizable minority was not touched at all by the shooting, saying that President Kennedy had it coming to him because of his stand on civil rights.

The American Friends Service Committee attempted to initiate a new Christmas shopping campaign. All across the Midwest the Quakers urged shoppers not to buy war toys or toys of violence for Christmas gifts. The campaign was dedicated to President Kennedy and launched because of concern over the acceptance of violence in American society.

Fairness for minorities was an issue in Chicago at Christmastime 1963. A nominating committee had just submitted a list of eight suggested nominees for the school board to Mayor Richard J. Daley. None were black. The Reverend Arthur Brazier, president of the Woodlawn Organization, called it unbelievable that the nominating committee should be so blind to the needs of the day. The Reverend Carl Fuqua, head of the Chicago branch of the NAACP, said he too was disappointed, but not surprised.

Albert Cardinal Meyer of Chicago had his own special way of spreading holiday joy. He took eighty-five poor youngsters with him when he went shopping on State Street. All of the lads came from Catholic schools in the poorest neighborhoods of Chicago. All were between the ages of six and fourteen.

The Cardinal picked up the tab at Bond's store, at State and Jackson, as the boys picked out exactly what they wanted, from flannel pajamas to button-down shirts to thick woolen coats. A store official estimated the cost for each boy at sixty to one hundred dollars.

After the shopping, the Cardinal treated his charges to a hot turkey dinner at Roma's Restaurant. "I've never seen a cardinal before and I'm afraid I won't be able to say anything . . . but I've got to thank him in person. This really means a lot to me," said one boy named Arquelio.

1964: Remembering the Forgotten

It didn't snow in Chicago on Christmas Eve, 1964, but nevertheless O'Hare International Airport was jammed with stranded holiday travelers. Heavy fog and low ceilings in the East had closed every airport from Boston to Baltimore, and it took until noon on Christmas Day before the backlog cleared at O'Hare. Then, as Chicagoans and their friends and families settled down Christmas evening after a day of festivities, snow started to fall. By midnight, there was a two-inch accumulation.

At Christmastime every year, a debate breaks out in newsrooms all across the country: "How do we cover Christmas *this* year? What groups should we highlight? We *always* seem to report on the same people!"

A familiar focus is the nation's poor, the city's down-and-outers. It was about a week before the Christmas of 1964 that the *Chicago Daily News* did what was perhaps the definitive study:

CHRISTMAS NO JOY ON SKID ROW
By M. W. Newman

Skid Row is declining in population but at Christmastime it's still a sick man etherized on a table.

The winds of another winter nag the old men hobbling on canes and batter the bottle gangs in the W. Madison St. back alleys.

At this holiday time, many of the homeless drunkies drink even more than usual, trying to stifle memories. They drift in a fog of cheap muscatel known as "sweet Lucy."

"Some of the men get very despondent," said Brig. Roland Quinn of the Salvation Army Harbor Light Corp, 654 W. Madison.

NOR IS THERE ANY LETUP in the violence of the W. Madison jackrollers who strongarm the old, the feeble and the drunk. Bloody trails in the snow bear witness to the casual cannibalism of the degraded.

"An old man going into a currency exchange to cash his welfare or pension check seems to be bait for the jackrollers," said Brig. Quinn.

These jackals strike boldly, in daylight or in darkness. They watch the currency exchanges and wait. That's one reason so many Skid Rowers cash their checks in taverns and spend there, too.

Some of the old men have been moved off the street by the county Public Aid Department. But a number have drifted back, too lonely to stay away.

Loneliness is one thing that everyone shares on Skid Row. To counter it, the Salvation Army center is planning a big Christmas Eve party and Christmas Day feeding. Other missions on the street also will have something extra for the men.

BRIG. QUINN DEFINES SKID ROW as that grimy mile of Madison Street between Canal (500 west) and Racine (1200 west).

He puts its flophouse population at 7,000. In depression days the figure may have been as high as 30,000. . . .

AS SKID ROW HAS SHRUNK, hope has risen that perhaps it has had its day and now will go away. But this is dreamstuff and not reality, according to Brig. Quinn.

He sees no magical evaporation of Skid Row, although progress is hemming it in, new office buildings to the east, expressways and housing to the west, the new University of Illinois campus to the south. In addi-

Top Songs 1964

The top songs on Billboard's charts at Christmastime included "I Feel Fine" by the Beatles, "Come See about Me" by the Supremes, "Mr. Lonely" by Bobby Vinton, "She's a Woman" by the Beatles, and "She's Not There" by the Zombies.

At the Movies 1964

Julie Andrews and Dick Van Dyke were starring in Mary Poppins at the State-Lake Theater. Opening Christmas Day at the United Artists was The Americanization of Emily with Miss Andrews and James Garner. Sean Connery's new James Bond movie, Goldfinger, had just opened at the Roosevelt. Cheyenne Autumn with Richard Widmark, Carroll Baker, and Karl Malden was playing at the McVickers.

On the Table 1964

The Christmas turkey of 1964 cost 33¢ a pound at Wieboldt's food department. A two-pound can of Hills Brothers coffee was $1.45.

Under the Tree 1964

You could buy a 1964 factory-equipped two-door Dart at West Side Dodge for $1,698.00, or you could take Olson Travel's twenty-one-day tour of Europe for $1,095.00.

tion, about five dozen buildings in the W. Madison St. area have been razed by the city Building Department.

"Skid Row won't go away by itself," Brig. Quinn said. "If it is uprooted it probably will move westward, that's all." (Reprinted with special permission from the *Chicago Sun-Times*, Inc. © 1999)

In other local news, Chicago police were a bit red-faced about a gambling raid they made during Christmas week 1964. Acting on an anonymous tip, they went to an apartment on Surf Street and arrested seven people: a sixty-nine-year-old optometrist, his wife, and five of her lady friends who had been playing poker. The police confiscated about eighty poker chips, a fifteen-year-old poker table, and three dollars and sixty cents. Police superintendent O. W. Wilson later issued a public apology for the raid.

The Chicago School Board was embroiled in a controversy over James Baldwin's book, *Another Country*, which was on the required reading list at Wright Junior College. Board member Edward Scheffler described it as "the filthiest one I have ever read." The book dealt with interracial sexual relations and homosexuality. At Christmastime, the board asked school superintendent Benjamin Willis to report on the matter.

In 1964 Dr. Martin Luther King Jr. won the Nobel Peace Prize for his campaign for civil rights for African Americans. On December 10, he accepted the prize and expressed an "abiding faith in America." At Christmastime, he told BBC interviewers that he thought it was possible for a black man to be elected president of the United States within the next twenty-five years, or sooner.

Some regions of America were still resisting the civil rights movement. Concern for the plight of poor blacks in Mississippi led comedian Dick Gregory, singer Sammy Davis Jr., and columnist Drew Pearson to organize a rally in Chicago to raise money to send twenty thousand turkeys to the poor in Mississippi. The drive was not well met by the prosegregation Ruleville, Mississippi, Citizens' Council, which sent two possums and a sack of sweet potatoes back to Chicago. The accompanying note accused drive organizers of using Mississippi as a whipping boy in a cheap publicity stunt.

There were twenty-two thousand American servicemen stationed in Vietnam at Christmastime 1964. On Christmas Day a terrorist bomb exploded in an officers' barracks in Saigon, killing two Americans and injuring more than a hundred other personnel from the U.S., South Vietnam, and Australia. A bit earlier, at the Bien Hoa Air Base northeast of Saigon, comedian Bob Hope and his sixty-member troupe had put on a show for twelve hundred American servicemen. Hope joked about the tighter than usual security, "I wasn't scared about the flight, but we had to blindfold the plane."

1965: Christmas in Vietnam

Chicago suffered a Christmas weather nightmare in 1965. On Friday, Christmas Eve, the city was hit by heavy rain, which turned to sleet during the day, and then snow—six-and-a-half inches of it—before the storm was over.

Many people, particularly in the western and southern suburbs, found themselves forced from their homes by flooding on Christmas Eve. As many as one hundred thousand families throughout the city and suburbs were without power—and in many cases heat—for thirty minutes to several hours. Several thousand homes were left without telephone service.

The bad weather made for dangerous driving conditions. Illinois recorded twenty-one traffic fatalities on the afternoon of Christmas Day.

By March 1965 American combat forces were directly involved in the war—no longer just military advisors. There was supposed to be a thirty-hour cease-fire over the Christmas holiday, but the U.S. command reported eighty-four of what it called significant Viet Cong actions during the period, including the chopping up of a U.S. marine patrol on Christmas Day. Just a few days before Christmas, the Viet Cong attacked Saigon with mortar and heavy automatic arms fire, marking the first such attack on the South Vietnamese capital city. At the United Nations, U.S. delegation chief Arthur Goldberg told reporters, "The use of atomic weapons in Vietnam is not conceivable."

Top Songs 1965

The top five songs on the Billboard *musical survey for the week of Christmas were "Over and Over" by the Dave Clark Five, "Turn! Turn! Turn!" by the Byrds, "I Got You (I Feel Good)" by James Brown, "Let's Hang On" by the Four Seasons, and "Sounds of Silence" by Simon & Garfunkel.*

On the Tube 1965

On Christmas night, you could have seen Death Valley Days, The Jackie Gleason Show, I Dream of Jeannie, Secret Agent, Get Smart, The Lawrence Welk Show, Gunsmoke, *or the "Hollywood Palace" with host Bing Crosby and guests Fred Waring and his Pennsylvanians, Dorothy Collins, Bob Crane and other leading players from the TV series* Hogan's Heroes.

On the Radio 1965

WBBM *Radio broadcast* Handel's Messiah *at* 8 *P.M.* Christmas Eve.

Photo by Laszlo Kondor. Used with the permission of the National Vietnam Veterans Art Museum.

Christmas in a bunker in Vietnam

At the Movies 1965

New movies of the season included Battle of the Bulge *starring Henry Fonda, Robert Shaw, and Robert Ryan, Federico Fellini's first color full-length film* Juliet of the Spirits, Never Too Late *starring Paul Ford and Maureen O'Sullivan,* The Tenth Victim *with Marcello Mastroianni and Ursula Andress,* The Agony and the Ecstasy *starring Charlton Heston and Rex Harrison, and the James Bond thriller* Thunderball *with Sean Connery.*

Under the Tree 1965

The Christmas gifts of 1965 might have included Lionel train sets, consisting of a steam locomotive, hopper car, log dumper car, gondola car, track, and transformer. They were selling for $10.87 at Shoppers World. E. J. Korvette's had Ideal's Tammy doll for 49¢ (one per customer). Her clothing outfits cost 66¢ or 99¢. Polk Brothers was selling palm-sized Sony AM-FM nine-transistor radios for $39.95. Goldblatt's had the RCA model for $10.00 less.

More manpower would be needed to fight the war, and that meant more young men could expect to receive draft notices. In December 1965, the ninety-eight draft boards in Chicago and Cook County had already drafted 2,415 men—either single or married without children. Their quota for January 1966 was 2,277.

The war and the draft spawned dissent and protest demonstrations. At Holy Name Cathedral there was a week-long sit-in at Christmastime to protest the censure of priests who spoke out. In particular, the sit-in focused on the punishment given to three East Coast clergymen, two of whom had voiced opposition to the war. One of them was the Reverend Daniel Berrigan, whose name would become synonymous with the anti-war movement. The third priest was punished because he devoted his time to working in a black slum in Albany, New York.

Figures of authority (mostly of an older generation) took a hard line against dissenters. Selective Service director Lt. Gen. Lewis Hershey, in a letter to House Judiciary Committee chairman Emanuel Celler (D-N.Y.), expressed the opinion that draft card burners should be given the opportunity to be inducted into the services instead of facing prosecution. Celler said Hershey's letter "confirms the allegation that the selective service law is being used to punish and as a sort of club to discourage and prevent political dissent."

At the Tan Son Nhut Air Field in Vietnam, comedian Bob Hope won roars of approval from ten thousand GIs as he aimed barbs at the protesters back home: "The student demonstrators back home have calmed down," he said. "They've run out of matches." And: "You've seen some of these demonstrators. Aren't you glad they aren't on our side?" A thundering "Yes" came from the audience.

For one American soldier in Vietnam, the Christmas of 1965 was very special. On Christmas morning, his story appearef in the *Chicago Tribune.*

CRIES OVER PHONE INTRODUCE GI IN VIET TO HIS SON
by David Halvorsen

Baby John Keith Lehman, 7 days old, softly cried last night into a telephone that carried his voice nearly halfway around the world to his father, an American soldier in South Viet Nam.

Little John will have to grow up a bit before he understands what it was all about. His father, Sgt. John Lehman, his voice tense with emotion, and the baby's mother, Margaret, tears running down her cheeks, will never forget it.

Sgt. Lehman, on duty with the 1st infantry division, was standing by at the international communications center in Saigon. It was 8 A.M. Christmas day for him. It was Christmas eve in Chicago.

GIVES HIM A PINCH

Mrs. Lehman held the baby close to the telephone receiver. She gave him a little pinch and he cried. At this age, it is the best he can do.

At first, the army sergeant could not hear his son over the 8,000-mile long circuit that relied upon radio from Manila to Saigon. The baby cried a little louder.

"Can you hear him, darling?" Mrs. Lehman asked.

"Yes, I can hear him. I can hear him. This is so wonderful. What does he look like?" Lehman asked. (Copyright *Chicago Tribune.* Used by permission.)

Angel Guardian Orphanage, 1965

Archdiocese of Chicago's Joseph Cardinal Bernardin Archives & Records Center.

On the Table 1965

Kroger's had turkeys for 32¢ a pound (14-to-18 pound birds). Two pounds of Hills Brothers coffee was $1.38. Ice cream was 59¢ for half-a-gallon.

Under the Tree 1966

Under the Christmas tree in 1966 you might have found a GE clock radio. They were on sale for $10.88. A transistor shirt pocket radio with earphone cost $7.00. A child's tricycle could be purchased for $8.88. Monopoly sets were $3.29, and a football, air pump and kicking tee set could be had for under four dollars. Long-playing phonograph records were selling for $1.79 monaural or $2.39 in stereo.

Top Songs 1966

The top tunes of the day included: "I'm a Believer" by the Monkees, "Snoopy vs. the Red Baron" by the Royal Guardsmen, "Winchester Cathedral" by the New Vaudeville Band, "That's Life" by Frank Sinatra; and "Sugar Town" by Sinatra's daughter Nancy.

On Stage 1966

The Eddie Higgins Trio was playing at the London House at Wacker and Michigan. Dan Dailey and Elliott Reid starred in The Odd Couple *at the Blackstone Theater.*

At the Movies 1966

Movies in town included Fantastic Voyage, After the Fox, *and the Dino DiLaurentis production of* The Bible.

On the Table 1966

You could treat yourself to Christmas dinner at Henrici's O'Hare Inn: a meal of roast turkey with corn bread stuffing cost $3.75. Filet mignon with bearnaise sauce was $6.95. Broiled New Zealand lobster tails were $5.95.

On the Radio 1966

WBBM was not yet Newsradio 78 in 1966. Personalities on the air included Jerry Williams, Mal Bellairs and Arthur Godfrey. Paul Gibson, a fixture on the station for twenty-four years and a man described as a "talking encyclopedia," died two days before Christmas in Passavant Hospital; he was fifty-three.

People who were teenagers in the mid-sixties will remember the deejays on rock-and-roll stations WLS: Clark Weber, Bernie Allen, Ron Riley and Art Roberts; and on WCFL: Joel Sebastian, Jim Stagg and Barney Pipp. Wally Phillips on WGN was the most-listened to personality on Chicago radio.

Lehman had been in Vietnam for five months at the time. He had received a commendation for helping an American who was wounded when a truck convoy hit land mines on the road to Lai Khe.

On Christmas Eve, President and Mrs. Lyndon Johnson announced the engagement of their daughter, Luci Baines, to twenty-two-year-old John Nugent of Waukegan. Nugent was a cadet in basic training at Lackland Air Force Base in San Antonio.

In other news, the Chicago School Board voted to spend $1.7 million more for textbooks in city schools, and to raise the pay of lunchroom workers, playground teachers, and teachers in the after-hours "lighted schoolhouse" program by 2 1/2 percent.

Chicago health commissioner Dr. Samuel L. Andelman reported that most contagious or epidemic diseases declined in Chicago during 1965. Dr. Andelman was particularly proud of the fact that no cases of polio had been reported in the city during the year. The board of health had begun giving the Sabin antipolio vaccine in 1964, and more than a million Chicagoans had so far received free immunizations.

Life magazine's year-end issue was out, and it contained a proposal to build Chicago's far western suburbs on platforms. Commuter trains and car traffic would run underneath buildings, clusters of which would be "urban spines" separated by man-made lakes. The idea was to prevent urban sprawl from destroying fields and forests near the Fox River. The proposal was the work of the urban design studio of the University of Illinois.

During Christmas week 1965, the *Tribune* printed a guest editorial from the *Raleigh News and Observer* which reminded us all that "Christmas is a day for children, but nothing their parents can give them now will be as precious as the stuff of memory they make for Christmases yet to come. The Christmas crown is the tender, the rejoicing, and the remembering spirit of those who count the years and not merely the packages under the tree."

1966: The War in Vietnam

Christmas fell on a Sunday in 1966. The forecast called for variable cloudiness with temperatures in the twenties and a chance of snow flurries.

The big news of the day was the war in Vietnam. The first contingent of a fresh American combat division, the Ninth Infantry, was just arriving in Vietnam, raising the number of American fighting men there to 370,000. For the first time in the war, North Vietnamese shore batteries had fired on a U.S. ship in the Gulf of Tonkin. Light casualties were reported aboard the USS *O'Brien,* a destroyer. At the United Nations, the United States was appealing to Secretary General U Thant to take the necessary steps to bring about a cease-fire in Vietnam.

In local news, Dr. Martin Luther King Jr. was in Chicago organizing a voter registration project and announcing plans to acquire and rehabilitate five hundred slum housing units in three Chicago neighborhoods. Dr. King told local black leaders although 65 percent of the Chicago Negro population was registered to vote, that figure was very misleading. Because of a lack of political education, only 45 percent of those regis-

Used with permission from the Chicago Defender, photo by Ted Bell, Chicago, Illinois.

On the Tube 1966

If you were watching TV on Christmas Eve, your choices included The Jackie Gleason Show, *on which the Poor Soul was to take a dreamy excursion through a land of make-believe and fairy tales;* Death Valley Days, The Buccaneers, Get Smart, Mission: Impossible, Gunsmoke, *and* Roller Derby *were also on.*

tered actually showed up on election days. Forty-five percent of the 65 percent translates into an actual voting force of about 30 percent of all those who could register and cast ballots.

The housing rehabilitation project involved Lawndale, East Garfield Park, and Kenwood-Oakland. Financing for the program was to come from a federal insured low-interest loan of four million dollars. It would be administered by cooperatives composed of Southern Christian Leadership Conference members, local community leaders, and local businessmen. "As I have said many times in recent months," stated Dr. King, "if urban renewal and redevelopment are to succeed in achieving their stated goals of uplifting the quality of urban life, then these same programs must be renewal of, by, and for the people."

There was the potential for violence when African Americans sought better housing for their families by moving into mostly white neighborhoods. In December 1966 alone, there were two illustrative incidents: the front, kitchen, and dining room windows of a black family's new home in Chicago Lawn were smashed by brick-throwers, and police recovered an unexploded Molotov cocktail from the front lawn of a home near Fifty-third and Lowe in what was the second arson attempt in three months.

On the Tuesday before Christmas, a committee of the Chicago School Board met with eleven representatives of civil rights groups in the first meeting of its kind to discuss how to integrate Chicago's public schools and provide a quality education for all pupils.

1967: The War at Home

By Christmastime 1967, American ground troop strength swelled to more than 474,000. On the home front, antiwar protests were becoming louder and more frequent. It was front-page news that a twenty-one-year-old named Dennis Riordan had been sentenced to three years in prison for refusing to be drafted.

At the University of Illinois in Urbana, trustees were startled during Christmas week when two young men, one a student and one a former student, interrupted their meeting by standing up and burning draft cards. They received a standing ovation from eighteen other students who were present. The protest came amidst a proposal from state officials that would require a code of conduct for university students forcing them to adhere to the Selective Service Act.

A Harris poll of 1,608 American homes was released. Among the findings:

—76 percent of Americans believed antiwar demonstrations encouraged the Communists to fight all the harder;

—70 percent believed demonstrations were hurting the antiwar movement;

—68 percent agreed that antiwar protests were acts of disloyalty to the men and women serving in Vietnam;

—Yet 53 percent agreed with Selective Service director Hershey that students who obstructed recruiting efforts should be punished by being drafted;

—40 percent were now having doubts about the right of peaceful protest against the war (up 10 points from six months earlier).

A retired commandant of the Marine Corps was having his own doubts about the war. It was about a week before Christmas that Gen. David Shoup, in a radio interview, said of the Johnson administration and the Pentagon: "They just keep trying to keep the people worried about the Communists crawling up the banks of Pearl Harbor, or crawling up the Palisades, or crawling up the beaches of Los Angeles, which of course is a bunch of pure, unadulterated poppycock."

Christmas decorations at State and Lake, 1964

Chicago Historical Society. ICHI 24305 Used with permission.

Transportation 1968

The fare on the CTA was the highest in the nation at 40¢ a ride.

On the Radio 1968

On the Friday after Christmas, a thirty-five-and-a-half-year radio tradition was coming to an end. Don McNeill's Breakfast Club *would sign off ABC Radio for the last time.*

On the Table 1968

At Hillman's the Christmas turkey was selling for 45¢ a pound fresh, 27¢ a pound frozen. Two pounds of Maxwell House coffee cost $1.19. You could get a dozen large eggs for 68¢. Milk was 89¢ a gallon.

On the Tube 1968

On television, Illinois senator Everett Dirksen was a guest host on The Red Skelton Hour *on CBS on Christmas Eve. Steve Allen's guests on channel 9 included Louis Nye, Mother Hubbard, Frankie Randall, and Al Goshman the magician. Joey Bishop's guests on ABC included the Johnny Mann Singers, Sammy Davis Jr., and Stu Gilliam. At midnight, channel 9 broadcast midnight mass from St. Patrick's Church, Cardinal Cody celebrating. Channel 2 aired the 1951 version of the movie* A Christmas Carol, *with Alastair Sim, Kathleen Harrison, and Jack Warner.*

At the Movies 1968

The Odd Couple starring Jack Lemmon and Walter Matthau opened Christmas Day at Chicago movie theaters. The Shoes of the Fishermen was playing at the McVickers. Funny Girl was at the United Artists, and Bullitt with Steve McQueen was at the State-Lake.

Top Songs 1968

Billboard's top music hits at Christmastime were Marvin Gaye's "I Heard It Through the Grapevine," Diana Ross & the Supremes' "Love Child," Stevie Wonder's "For Once in My Life," Dion's "Abraham, Martin and John," and Johnnie Taylor's "Who's Making Love."

President Lyndon Johnson was just back at the White House following a whirlwind round-the-world trip in which he met President Nguyen Van Thieu of South Vietnam in Australia, visited with American pilots in Thailand, and discussed the war with Pope Paul VI at the Vatican. The president told reporters he and the Pope had agreed that "an honorable settlement was still possible" in Vietnam.

In Vietnam, efforts were being made to make it at least seem like Christmas:

DA NANG, Vietnam (UPI)—The Air Force is wrestling with a monumental logistics problem in South Vietnam's northern quarter—how to get 1,000 Christmas trees to the troops in the field.

Nobody is complaining. By helicopter or giant cargo plane, the Air Force is determined to make "operation Christmas tree" a success.

When Airman 2-c Ron Key, 21, of Mount Vernon, Wash., wrote Gov. Daniel Evans of Washington, asking for one giant Christmas tree for the Da Nang air base, he got 1,000 small ones and the Air Force got a problem.

Monsoon rains now blanketing the area have cut into operations at the giant supply base, grounding planes occasionally and keeping priority lists tight. Ammunition and food go first, in that order.

The same transportation network that resupplies the troops will be used to deliver the trees—everything from helicopters and C-47s to truck convoys, an Air Force spokesman said. "We are going to get them delivered."

It began innocently with Key's letter to the governor in early October.

"Morale is important to everyone here," he said, "and without good morale we could all be in trouble. With December only a few months away, I was wondering if you could help improve things for us at Da Nang air base by sending us a giant-sized Christmas tree from my home state."

In an interview Key said the plan was to put the tree on top of the passenger terminal at the base, where everyone could see it. Then he got the answer from the governor.

"Obtaining a giant-sized tree was easy enough but getting it to you was a problem," the letter said. "Experts advise that such a tree would be too large to airlift and susceptible to damage and undue delay if shipped by surface transport.

"So that you and the men at Da Nang would not be disappointed entirely, I am making arrangements to ship you some smaller trees—1,000 to be exact." (Copyright United Press International. Used by permission.)

1968: And to All On Earth

The tormented and tumultuous year of 1968 was almost over. It had been a year of assassination and riot, of protest and politics. On the last day of March, President Lyndon Johnson stunned the nation with his announcement that he would not seek another term in the White House. April brought the assassination of Dr. Martin Luther King Jr. in Memphis and rioting in several cities, including Chicago, where four people were killed and 162 buildings were destroyed. June brought the assassination of presidential candidate Robert F. Kennedy. In August, it was the Democratic National Convention in Chicago, with nearly a full week of nightsticks and tear gas, marches and taunts, beatings and arrests, as thousands of anti-war demonstrators tried to influence the outcome of the convention in the International Amphitheater while the whole world watched on TV.

Hubert Humphrey had received his party's nomination at the Democratic convention. He made a close race of the presidential election, but in the end it was Richard M. Nixon and the Republicans who stood triumphant.

Now, at Christmastime, the country's attention was focused on the future. On Christmas Eve, 1968, there occurred something that had never happened before: the Earth heard a radio broadcast from a quarter of a

million miles away. The astronauts aboard *Apollo 8*—Frank Borman, James Lovell, and William Anders—had achieved orbit around the moon. That evening, listeners in Chicago and around the world heard Colonel Borman's voice in the crackly ether, offering a prayer from the first ten verses of Genesis:

In the beginning, God created the heaven and the earth. And the earth was without form, and void; and darkness was upon the face of the deep. And the Spirit of God moved upon the face of the waters.

And God said, Let there by light: and there was light.

And God saw the light, that it was good: and God divided the light from the darkness.

And God called the light Day and the darkness He called Night. And the evening and the morning were the first day.

And God said, Let there be a firmament in the midst of the waters; and let it divide the waters from the waters.

And God made the firmament, and divided the waters which were under the firmament from the waters which were above the firmament; and it was so.

And God called the firmament Heaven, And the evening and the morning were the second day.

And God said, Let the waters under the heaven be gathered together unto one place, and let the dry land appear; and it was so.

And God called the dry land Earth; and the gathering together of the waters called He seas; and God saw that it was good.

And from the crew of *Apollo 8*, good night, good luck, a Merry Christmas, and God bless all of you, all of you on the good Earth.

Transportation 1969

Ten days before Christmas, a Pan American Airways Boeing 747 jetliner became the first jumbo passenger plane to land at O'Hare. The Chicago Tribune's Richard Joseph got a ride on one of the new planes: "This is truly a gee whiz airplane. Four-and-a-half times the length of a railway car and more than twice as wide. . . . The cabin of this aircraft is unlike that of any plane ever built. It's more like a six-room apartment, each decorated in different colors."

On the Table 1969

The A&P had turkeys for 35¢ a pound. Navel oranges were 59¢ a dozen, an eight-inch pumpkin pie cost 55¢.

Under the Tree 1969

Goldblatt's was selling Royal Mercury manual portable typewriters for $39.99.

Goldblatt's also had a music sale: long-playing records were marked down to $3.77 apiece, 8-track cartridge tapes were $4.89.

Peace Talks

In Paris, peace talks aimed at ending the war in Vietnam had been underway with little effect until October. That's when Hanoi signaled its willingness to recognize the South Vietnamese government. Saigon at first agreed to join the Paris talks, then balked, refusing to be placed on an equal footing with the National Liberation Front, which was the political organization of the Viet Cong. As a result, much of the remaining time before Christmas was spent haggling over the shape of the bargaining table.

It all moved Peter Lisagor, in his *Chicago Daily News* column, to write a Christmas rhyme:

Tis the season to be jolly and clout all grumps with boughs of holly.
Drag Clifford, Marshal Ky and Ho to tables neath the mistletoe,
Add Kissinger, McGovern too, and set a place for Nguyen Van Thieu.
Give LBJ a four-jet sleigh and let him soar up, up away to Saigon,
Paris, Moscow, Rome to say adieu, Ahm going home.
Ah give to you this olive branch, come reason with me at the ranch.
Close the gaps and open doors, scrape the losers off the floors.
St. Nixon's coming with tax rebates, to rebuild slums at bargain rates.
To cool the nation's fevered brow, and light a lamp for Brezhnev, Mao.

And if it fails, this college try, Mel Laird will keep the powder dry.
(Reprinted with special permission from the Chicago *Sun-Times*, Inc., © 1999)

It was two days before Christmas, 1968, when the eighty-two surviving crew members of the USS *Pueblo* walked through a snowstorm and out of captivity in North Korea. They had been held for eleven months, enduring torture and malnutrition. The North Koreans had seized the *Pueblo* and its crew, accusing them of spying in North Korean waters.

A Sign of the Times

Woodstock was still eight months in the future, but a precursor occurred one week before Christmas in London:

STUDENTS STRIP AT 'HAPPENING'

LONDON (UPI)—American student Elizabeth Marsh tossed back her hair, slipped out of her long, black dress, and sat stark naked in the third row of the Royal Albert Hall Wednesday night. A band of pleading policemen looked on.

Beatle John Lennon and his girlfriend Yoko Ono took it in stride. They climbed into a huge bag on stage and writhed lyrically to the lilting melody of a flute.

Red-faced police posted at the "Hippy Happening" began to make a timid approach toward Elizabeth, of Texas, who sat nude and serene.

But some of the 600-strong audience at "An Alchemical Wedding," rose up and formed a human shield around her. Several men stripped in sympathy.

Hall officials pleaded with the bespectacled Elizabeth to get dressed. The audience booed and jeered.

Looking up State Street, 1967

The management finally switched off the electricity and threatened to stop the show if Elizabeth didn't put on some clothes.

She eventually pulled a coat around her shoulders.

"I don't know why I did it, but at the time I had some good reasons," Elizabeth said later.

"I did it all without realizing it was happening. It was the music, I wasn't at all embarrassed," she said.

The "happening" consisted of Indian music, underground poetry, music, psychedelic lights and impromptu acts.

Elizabeth's English boyfriend, Peter Evans, 24, said he wasn't in the least embarrassed. "I've seen her in the nude before, but never in public," he admitted. (Copyright United Press International. Used by permission.)

A group of doctors and social workers were accusing Cook County Juvenile Court of sending severely beaten children back to their parents—and possible death. Said one social worker: "Lawyers and judges just don't want to believe some parents could destroy their children."

Chicago police believed, and they also believed that hippie women were unfit mothers. A twenty-one-year-old mom who called herself Duffy had just gotten her three-year-old daughter Missy back from a foster home. Police had seized the child and jailed Duffy because they disapproved of her living in a communal apartment behind an Old Town poster store. Duffy spent six hours in the lockup before being bailed out and getting her child back.

And lastly, at the University of Chicago, Dr. Anthony Amarose discovered a method for accurately determining the sex of an unborn baby. Now couples wouldn't have to wait to find out if they were having a boy or a girl.

1969: An Unsettled Christmas

Chicago's Christmas Eve, 1969, was cold and snowy. Ten inches of snow had fallen two days before, with two more inches to accumulate as hundreds of worshippers gathered on the steps of the newly renovated Holy Name Cathedral for midnight mass. The cathedral had been closed for twenty months for a three million dollar renovation. Those attending the reopening would find the inside shining with a new red-black altar made of granite quarried in Argentina. Other additions included new shrines, new lighting, a new floor, new pews, new stained glass windows, and a new air conditioning system.

Seventeen hundred parishioners and guests had tickets for the reopening, but by the time the front door opened at 11 P.M., many more were waiting to get in. Only one door was opened—work on the others hadn't been completed—and only one or two people could enter at a time. There was some shoving and pushing, and Chicago police were called to restore order to the process. They soon decided that it was hopeless; that the only thing to do was to allow those nearest the door to enter, whether they had tickets or not. A thousand people were turned away.

Meanwhile, about two dozen demonstrators marched outside the cathedral. They called themselves Seminarians Organized for Racial Justice, and they were unhappy that the archdiocese had spent so much money renovating the church rather than meeting the needs of the poor.

Inside the cathedral, a group of demonstrators disrupted the midnight mass by standing up and marching out while the congregation was singing "Adeste Fidelis."

Days of Rage

This was indeed a winter of discontent, not only in Chicago, but all across the nation. Traditional institutions were under fire, society was riven along various lines, and the war in Vietnam continued to fracture the American public.

In October, the Illinois National Guard had been called to the streets of Chicago to quell the violent "Days of Rage" antiwar demonstrations led by the radical Weatherman faction of the Students for a Democratic Society.

One week later, many people, in all walks of life, participated in a peaceful national Vietnam Moratorium protest, a day when "business as usual" was somehow changed, whether it be with the wearing of a black armband, the participation in an antiwar march, or the distribution of

On the Tube 1969

On television, millions watched Johnny Carson's Tonight Show *on December 17 to see Herb Khaury, otherwise known as "Tiny Tim," marry Vicki Budinger, otherwise known as "Miss Vicki." TV fare on Christmas Eve included* The Beverly Hillbillies, Kraft Music Hall, The Virginian, The Flying Nun, *and* Hawaii Five-O.

Da Bears 1969

On the Sunday after Christmas, the Bears would end their worst season in fifty years with a 20-3 loss to Detroit in a game played at Wrigley Field. The Bears record for the season was 1-13.

antiwar leaflets at places like O'Hare Airport. On that day, the presidents of seventy-nine American universities appealed to President Nixon to step up his timetable for the withdrawal of American troops from Vietnam. Gov. Francis Sargent of Massachusetts, himself a World War II combat veteran, said, "This war is costing America its soul." Meanwhile, rumors and allegations about Lt. William Calley and the massacre of 567 civilians at My Lai, Vietnam, were just beginning to make an impression on the American public.

Throughout the year and across the nation, including Chicago, police had been involved in a series of gun battles with members of the Black Panther party, who took a militant view of ways to settle the racial inequities and injustices in American society. On the other hand, the Panthers also were responsible for setting up breakfast centers where poor children could get a good meal, and they were working to get medical clinics located in poor neighborhoods.

It was on December 4 that a detail of fourteen Chicago police officers assigned to Cook County state's attorney Edward Hanrahan raided the Black Panthers' headquarters at 2337 West Monroe Street. Panther leaders Fred Hampton and Mark Clark were killed. Four other Panthers were wounded, three others arrested. The police claimed the Panthers had fired first, but survivors of the raid vehemently denied it.

The raid sparked outrage. Three thousand people, including blacks, whites, and Latinos jammed the Church of the Epiphany on Ashland Avenue for a memorial service for Hampton and Clark. Hundreds more were turned away. Leonard Chabala, the mayor of Maywood where Hampton was raised and lived,

quickly called for the indictment of the fourteen officers.

At first there was confusion: was the police department's Internal Investigations Division (IID) looking into the raid or not? Richard Jolovec, head of the state's attorney's special prosecutions unit, told the *Daily Defender* that IID was investigating, but the head of IID, Capt. Harry Ervanian, told the same newspaper that it was not. Finally, a few days later, police superintendent James Conlisk said that all shootings involving Chicago police officers are investigated, as this one would be.

The Afro-American Patrolmen's League was conducting its own investigation. League vice president, Officer Howard Saffold, asked, "If the idea was to confiscate illegal weapons, why was tear gas not used, instead of bullets?"

Emotions ran so high that some in the black community were calling for a 6 P.M. to 6 A.M. curfew that would bar all white people from "black areas." Most black leaders disagreed; even Black Panther party defense minister Bobby Rush thought it was a bad idea that "played into the hands of white bigots."

On Thursday, December 18, U.S. attorney general John Mitchell announced that a federal grand jury would be impaneled to investigate the Hampton raid. Two days later, five black congressmen held their own hearing on the killings in Chicago. One of them, Adam Clayton Powell of New York, said he had no faith in the Justice Department. Jay Miller, head of the Chicago American Civil Liberties Union, put it more strongly. "An investigation by the Justice Department is like asking the wolf to investigate the lamb," he said. The five congressmen received little help in their inquiry. First assistant state's attorney James Murray would answer no questions because the hearing wasn't authorized by Congress, but neither would Kermit Coleman, the attorney for Rush.

Eleven days before Christmas five hundred people, most of them white, jammed a Unitarian Church near Deerfield for a memorial service for Hampton. That same day four dozen teachers and students from Northern Illinois University in DeKalb visited the Monroe Street apartment to see for themselves where it had happened.

Subsequently, it would be shown that the Panther survivors were right: they had fired no shots. The killings of Hampton and Clark might well be considered, as the Afro-American Patrolman's League's Saffold had put it, "obviously political assassinations."

In addition to all this chaos, the Chicago Seven trial was taking place in federal court. The prosecution of seven men accused of organizing the disruptive demonstrations during the 1968 Democratic National Convention in Chicago was, for many, as much theater as it was legal proceeding. On the Monday before Christmas, the Seven asked Judge Julius Hoffman for a longer-than-usual recess on Christmas Eve so they could participate in a march protesting the Hampton-Clark shootings and in what was being called a "citizens' arrest" of State's Attorney Hanrahan. Judge Hoffman denied their request.

On Christmas Eve, the trial adjourned early anyway. Defendant Abbie Hoffman was in the hospital. His doctor said he had bronchial pneumonia. Judge Hoffman appointed a court doctor to examine the Yippie leader and to report to the court on the day after Christmas.

The fourteen jurors hearing the case had to spend Christmas away from their families. They were sequestered in a Loop hotel, so they held their own Christmas party and bought gifts for each other, drawn by lot. The Christmas shopping was carried out by four U.S. marshals.

In other local news, a city council committee gave its okay for the sale of one block of Quincy Street. Sears, Roebuck and Company would pay $2.7 million for the land, and begin building what would become Sears Tower.

Christmas Eve
Hear Handel's
Messiah

WBBM Radio [780] 8 p.m.

1970 - 1979

1970: Christmastime Reunion

Christmas came on a Friday in 1970. The weather forecast read: mostly cloudy with some light snow or flurries likely; highs in the mid-twenties.

At Christmastime, 340,000 American soldiers were still in Vietnam. The year had been one of upheaval. On April 30, President Richard Nixon had ordered an incursion into Cambodia to destroy enemy sanctuaries. America's college campuses erupted in a storm of protest. There was violence. National Guardsmen shot and killed four students at Kent State University in Ohio; police killed two students during a protest at Jackson State College in Mississippi.

But on Christmas Eve, a front-page story in the *Chicago Tribune* was not about the war or protests. It was about the joy of a reunion:

VIET GI VISITS BRING KIN JOY
by Charles Mount

Barbara Lemley was sitting in her trailer yesterday afternoon wearing a bathrobe with her hair rolled up in curlers. She looked out the window and there was her husband.

Staff Sgt. Daniel Lemley, 30, had made it home for Christmas, the time soldiers most want to be with loved ones. For the three-tour veteran of the Viet Nam jungle, the holiday season, at least, would be a joyous one.

Transportation 1970

CTA fares were 45¢ at Christmastime 1970. Transfers cost a dime.

At the Movies 1970

Love Story—*the movie—was opening Christmas Day at the Chicago Theater. The book was already number one on Chicago's best-seller list. Other movies playing in town included* Ryan's Daughter *at the Michael Todd Theater and* The Owl and the Pussycat, *opening Christmas Day at the State-Lake.*

On Stage 1970

Disney on Parade *was the big attraction at the Chicago Amphitheater. Neil Simon's* Promises *was playing at the Shubert Theater. Myrna Loy and Jerome Kelty were starring in* Dear Love *at the Studebaker.*

On the Table 1970

The Christmas turkey of 1970 cost 31¢ to 49¢ a pound at Jewel. A sixteen-ounce can of cranberry sauce was 18¢. You could buy a two-pound can of Folger's coffee for $1.60.

"I'LL CLOBBER YOU!"

Lemley was one of about 200 Army and Air Force men who arrived at O'Hare International Airport on a "Project Reunion" flight from Saigon, but unlike most of the other men, Lemley had not told his wife and 9-year old daughter who live in the trailer on the military side of O'Hare.

"I'm going to clobber you!" his wife yelled. Seconds later they were in each other's arms for the first time in six months.

"It feels darn good not to be in the field this time," said the career soldier, who was unable to get home during his first two tours.

Lemley and about 2,500 others in the Chicago area will be home this time thru the efforts of the United Service Club, Pan American World Airways and Trans International Airlines. (Copyright *Chicago Tribune.* Used by permission.).

Two days before Christmas Mayor Richard J. Daley filed his nominating petitions to run for a fifth term in office. The mayor was predicting his biggest victory ever, over Republican Richard Friedman.

The returning soldier

Illinois Attorney General William Scott, meanwhile, vowed to go to federal court to make it easier for an independent candidate—Jesse Jackson—to get his name on the ballot in April. As things stood, the Democratic candidate for mayor needed four thousand names to be nominated, the Republican two thousand, but any independent needed fifty-eight thousand.

On December 21, 1970, the U.S. Supreme Court upheld the 1970 Voting Rights Act which extended the right to vote in federal elections to eighteen year olds. Illinois was one of several states which opposed the move. Attorney General Scott urged the state's 102 county clerks to keep separate registration lists for would-be voters under the age of twenty-one.

At a federal court in Newark, New Jersey, the ACLU filed suit at Christmastime alleging that New Jersey state troopers were pulling over motorists because they wore their hair long. Thirty-seven motorists were party to the suit, including four lawyers, eight law students, and several teachers. The suit charged that the practice was so common that a British travel guide published in London was advising young people with long hair not to drive on the turnpike between New York and Philadelphia.

Plans were being firmed up at Christmastime to expand the Chicago Art Institute and the Goodman Theater over the Illinois Central tracks between Michigan Avenue and Columbus Drive.

The Plight of the Panama Limited

The people who boarded the Illinois Central's Panama Limited train in New Orleans on December 23 made it home to Chicago in time for Christmas, but just barely. Shortly after leaving New Orleans the train hit a tractor-trailer in Arcola, Louisiana, heavily damaging the locomotive. It took ninety minutes to get a freight engine in place to pull the train to McComb, Mississippi, where another diesel engine was added. But that locomotive's steam heat generator broke down near Brookhaven, Mississippi. The train had to wait to take a locomotive from a southbound train. That locomotive's generators broke down near Grenada, Mississippi.

Under the Tree 1970

Levi's corduroy bell-bottom trousers were selling for $8.88 at S&S Men's Wear. True Value hardware stores had portable typewriters for $39.99, electric portables for $85.00.

Sports 1970

A special mayoral committee was studying the feasibility of constructing a new sports stadium to be used by all of the city's pro teams. Cubs owner Philip K. Wrigley was not in favor, saying he thought it would be great if there were a new stadium for amateur athletics only. Wrigley said, "We are happy where we are and if the team keeps going like it has been, Wrigley Field in a few years will be the star of all ball parks."

Top Songs 1970

The most popular songs of the day were "My Sweet Lord/Isn't It a Pity" by George Harrison, "One Less Bell to Answer" by the Fifth Dimension, "The Tears of a Clown" by Smokey Robinson & the Miracles, "Knock Three Times" by Dawn, and "Black Magic Woman" by Santana.

The Panama Limited was running nearly eight hours late when workmen finished repairs and the train pulled out of Memphis, Tennessee. That's where it hit a garbage truck, causing another thirty-minute delay.

Near Elkville, Illinois, trouble developed in the train's air-pressure brake system, stopping the train for forty-five minutes in the middle of nowhere. A new engine was added in Carbondale, but there was another delay as the Panama had to wait for a freight train to clear a crossing near Odin, Illinois.

When the Panama limped into Union Station at 6:45 P.M. Christmas Eve, it was nine hours overdue, and there was not a lot of Christmas spirit left among the passengers. "Sometimes there was kind of a lynch mob mood, but there was no one to lynch," said passenger Daniel Grassman.

1972: "Peace Is at Hand"...or Is It?

The Christmas Monday of 1972 came eight weeks after Secretary of State Henry Kissinger made the famous pronouncement: "Peace is at hand."

He was wrong.

One week before Christmas, with the Paris peace talks stalled, President Richard Nixon ordered a full-scale resumption of B-52 bombing raids over North Vietnam. It was some of the heaviest bombing of the war. The North Vietnamese responded by refusing to continue the peace talks until the bombing stopped.

It did, temporarily, on Christmas Day.

American servicemen in the war zone were demoralized, or so reported William Mullen from Bien Hoa in the *Chicago Tribune*: "Christmas has become a glum joke to the U.S. Army's last fighting units in the Vietnam War." Soldiers had been sending personal gear home to avoid the rush; maintenance had begun to lapse; but the fighting continued and many of the men were wishing they hadn't sent their radios and extra underwear home so soon. Capt. Pete Runnels of the Eighth Cavalry Troop told Mullen: "It's got everybody down. . . . Everybody had so many plans and now morale is lower than I've ever seen it."

Morale would pick up about a month later. On January 27, 1973, U.S. and North Vietnamese representatives at the Paris peace talks signed a cease-fire agreement, ending the United States's role in the Vietnam war.

The last American to die in combat was Lt. Col. William Nolde of Michigan, killed by an artillery shell at An Loc.

Two major news stories were developing in Latin America on Christmas Day. A major earthquake had just leveled three quarters of all the buildings in Managua, Nicaragua. Ten thousand people were dead. On the Saturday before Christmas, survivors told a tale of a city decorated for the holiday that turned into a scene of devastation: rubble, huge fires, the cries of wounded and trapped children, people walking the debris-strewn streets like cadavers, drained of emotion.

From Chile details were just emerging about sixteen people who had survived for two months in the Andes Mountains after their plane had crashed twelve thousand feet up. Twenty-nine were dead, twenty-one immediately from the crash, eight others from the ordeal on the mountaintop. The survivors told of using melted snow and chocolate bars, and making a kind of lichen soup. Only later would the reports of cannibalism come out.

In Chicago, a blind spot on a radar screen was being blamed for the collision of two jets on a fog-shrouded runway at O'Hare Airport on the night of Wednesday, December 20. Nine people were killed in the incident, fifteen others injured. The authorities said that a North Central Airlines DC-9 was just reaching a takeoff speed of 140 miles an hour when it sheared off the tail of a Delta Convair 880 that had just landed. The Delta plane was on a taxiway where it should not have been. Investigators weren't able to question the ground controller in charge. When the accident occurred, he had collapsed.

Earlier in December, a United Airlines jet had crashed just short of a runway at Midway Airport, killing forty-five people, including reporter Michelle Clark and the wife of Watergate figure E. Howard Hunt.

It was at Christmastime 1972, that the American Medical Association and the National Academy of Science's National Research Council issued a statement warning that a link had been discovered

Best-Sellers 1972

Best-selling books in Chicago were Jonathan Livingston Seagull *and* The Best and the Brightest.

Da Bears 1972

Football fans remember the weekend before Christmas, 1972, for a play that was dubbed "The Immaculate Reception." Trailing 7-6 with just twenty-six seconds to play and facing fourth down and 40, Pittsburgh quarterback Terry Bradshaw fired a pass at running back John Fuqua. But Oakland's Jack Tatum smashed into him, and the ball went flying—right into the arms of Franco Harris, who ran for the winning touchdown. There was pandemonium as hundreds of fans poured out onto the field to celebrate.

At the Movies 1973

The movies in town included Day of the Dolphin *at the Carnegie,* Cleopatra Jones *at the Chicago,* Papillon *at the State-Lake, and* The Sting *at the Loop Theater.*

On the Table 1973

Jewel had turkeys for 59¢ to 79¢ a pound. Lettuce was 18¢ a head. You could get a forty-ounce can of yams for 49¢.

between coronary heart disease and the cholesterol level of the blood. The groups urged Americans to start changing their diets by eating less fatty foods.

1973:
Oil I want for Christmas . . .

Chicago's Christmas Tuesday of 1973 was a sloppy one. Freezing rain early the morning of Christmas Eve snapped power lines throughout the area. The forecast called for fog and more freezing rain on Christmas Eve, changing to snow on Christmas Day.

Driving was hazardous throughout the Midwest, but there were fewer cars on the road than usual that Christmas because of events in the Middle East. There had been fuel shortages in the United States during the summer, and when the United States resupplied Israel during the October Middle East war, the Arab states clamped an oil embargo on the Western world's oil supplies. Of the 17 million barrels of oil the U.S. consumed daily, 1.1 million came from Arab states.

By Christmastime, the pinch was really beginning to hurt. There were long lines at gas stations, and the government asked all stations to voluntarily shut down on Sundays. December 23 was the fourth such gasless Sunday in Chicago. The Chicago Motor Club estimated that only 40 percent of the area's stations were pumping gas on Monday, Christmas Eve. Twenty percent of gas stations were expected to run completely dry by January 1.

In Washington, Congress went home for the holiday following a bitter, marathon session in which it failed to approve legislation that would have given

Chicago Historical Society. ICHI 31249. Used with permission.

Overdecorated house at 8523 S. Damen Avenue

President Nixon emergency powers to deal with the gas crisis. The House, the Senate, and the White House were blaming each other over the impasse, which was caused by disagreement over a proposal to curb the windfall profits of oil corporations. With no legislation in place, the Federal Energy Office was debating the details of several possible gasoline rationing systems. The Nixon administration appealed to all Americans to limit consumption of gasoline to ten gallons a week.

Meanwhile, six Persian Gulf nations and Venezuela announced a price increase for oil. On January 1, 1974, the price of a barrel would more than double to $11.65. At the beginning of 1973, the price of oil had been $3.11 a barrel.

Because of the war in the Middle East there was fear of terrorist attacks like the December 17 attack at the Rome airport that claimed more than thirty lives. This made for an unsettled Christmas in the Holy Land, according to the Associated Press on Christmas Eve:

> The little town of Bethlehem prepared for Christmas as usual this weekend, but city fathers and merchants were worried that the Middle East conflict and fears of hijacking might keep visitors away.
>
> Hoteliers in Bethlehem counted only 50 visitors over the weekend in the town where Christmas began with the birth of Jesus nearly 2,000 years ago.
>
> "At first we thought they were not coming because the fighting continued after the cease-fire that was supposed to end the war," said an Arab guide. "But now it is fear of hijacking or the outbreak of a new war. The tourists are simply scared."
>
> Workers dangled holiday lights around the Christmas shrines of Bethlehem, erected a 30-foot

yule tree and topped it with a neon star.

> The town fathers of Bethlehem expect an influx for the carols and midnight mass at Manger square. But they don't expect the crowds to reach the 5,000 or more who trooped in last year.
>
> Bethlehem and the rest of Israeli-occupied West Jordan generally were peaceful during the October war. But Arab guerrilla bombs and grenades have exploded frequently in the last few weeks and Israeli security is tight.

President Nixon had a lot more on his mind than peace in the Middle East and the energy crisis. At Christmastime, the Watergate affair was unraveling, and the House Judiciary Committee was talking about impeachment proceedings. Vice President Ford told reporters the American public wouldn't stand for it. He said the committee would need more evidence linking President Nixon to the Watergate burglary.

Evangelist Billy Graham accused the president of using poor judgment, saying he ought to admit his mistakes. Peter Lisagor of the *Chicago Daily News* wrote a wonderful column in which he put the matter into perspective:

> A WONDROUS NIXON DREAM
> WASHINGTON—On Christmas Eve a year ago, according to his own melancholy recollections, President Nixon sat down just before midnight and wrote out "some of my goals for my second term as President."
>
> He recalled that moment in his address to the nation on April 30, 1973, when the temple began to crumble and when he announced the resignation from his White House staff of "two of the finest public servants it has been my privilege to know," Bob Haldeman and John Erlichman.

Top Songs 1973

The top songs on Billboard's *survey just before Christmas included "The Most Beautiful Girl" by Charlie Rich, "Goodbye Yellow Brick Road" by Elton John, "Top of the World" by the Carpenters, "Just You 'n' Me" by Chicago, and "Time in a Bottle" by Jim Croce.*

On Stage 1973

Ramsey Lewis was appearing at the London House. The Impressions were at Mr. Kelly's. On stage Grease *was at the Shubert Theater. On Thursday, December 20, the Chicago Symphony Orchestra presented the world premier of Dmitri Shostakovich's Fifteenth Symphony.*

Under the Tree 1974

Montgomery Ward's was selling H-O gauge Cannonball diesel train sets for $19.99 at Christmastime 1974. A seventeen-inch Rub-a-Dub Dolly was $8.99. Monopoly board games were $3.99.

Remember leisure suits? Goldblatt's was selling them for $25.00. Record albums were $4.44 at TurnStyle stores.

On the Table 1974

Treasure Island stores had turkeys for 39¢ a pound; self-basters were 85¢ a pound.

He also announced the resignation of Attorney General Richard Kleindienst and the appointment of Eliot Richardson to succeed him. Richardson, the President said, will be "both fair and he will be fearless in pursuing this case wherever it leads. I am confident that with him in charge, justice will be done."

The speech was Mr. Nixon's first tortured account of the Watergate investigation, and he revealed a mind-set then that spoke volumes about his outlook on the whole sordid affair. "I will not place blame on subordinates—on people whose zeal exceeded their judgment, and who may have done wrong in a cause they deeply believed to be right," he said. He added that the "responsibility" was his: "I accept it."

He went on to praise a system that exposed Watergate, a system that included "a determined grand jury, honest prosecutors, a courageous judge, John Sirica, and a vigorous free press." It was essential to place faith in the judicial system, he said, promising to "do everything in my power to insure that the guilty are brought to justice."

It was essential, too, he said, to get on with "the larger duties of this office," the vital work of peace and prosperity.

Then the President spoke of writing out his goals on Christmas Eve, "during my terrible personal ordeal of the renewed bombing of North Vietnam, which after 12 years of war, finally helped to bring America peace with honor."

The goals were conventional ones, taken from any standard test of political platitudes, a world of peace for our children and their children, full and equal opportunity for every American, jobs for all who can work and generous help for those who can't, a "climate of decency, and civility, in which each person respects the feelings and the dignity and the God-given rights of his neighbor," and a land in which "each person can dare to dream, can live his dreams—not in fear, but in hope—proud of his community, proud of his country, proud of what America has meant to himself and to the world."

None of these goals, Mr. Nixon said, could be achieved unless the nation dedicated itself to another goal.

"We must maintain the integrity of the White House, and that integrity must be real, not transparent. There can be no whitewash at the White House."

The bravura of that speech is now a haunting memory, one Christmas later. The "honest prosecutors" have been reviled. White House spokesmen have slyly condemned "a determined grand jury" as predominantly black, poor and anti-Nixon, whispers about Judge Sirica's penchant for publicity and his reversible record echo about the White House and the "vigorous free press" is the object of a special contempt and aversion surpassing anything experienced by the oldest journalists in the field. Eliot Richardson, and the man he chose to prosecute the case, Archibald Cox, have pursued the case into temporary unemployment. And the President has chosen, in Sen. Barry Goldwater's phrase, to "dibble and dabble" instead of doing everything in his power to expedite justice.

One year of Mr. Nixon's second term has been spent in stubborn retreat. The words that marched across his yellow legal pad with bold and burnished promise a year ago limp now through the rubble of his hopes. The gods cackle and mock. This lonely man's vision is overcast, and the rumble is ominous..." (Reprinted with special permission from the *Chicago Sun-Times,* Inc. © 1999)

Chicago had its own scandals. Mayor Daley was maintaining that he was shocked and stunned by the disclosure that a real estate firm in which his neighbor and protégé, Matthew Danaher, was a partner, had allegedly received a payoff of three hundred thousand dollars.

Police were investigating the gangland style murder of a former chief investigator in the Cook County Sheriff's Department. Richard Cain was gunned down by two men wearing ski masks in a sandwich shop on West Grand Avenue on the Thursday before Christmas. The speculation was that an attractive lady in blue may have set Cain up.

John Cardinal Cody, the head of the Roman Catholic archdiocese of Chicago, took note of the Middle East war, the political scandals, and the energy crisis in his Christmas message: "If there be a Christmas challenge yet unanswered, it is the question of how to make the short day of Christmas extend into the long year of 1974," said the Cardinal. In an interview with WBBM-TV, the Cardinal said he was horrified by the Watergate scandal. But he also said that if Christ were to come back and visit Chicago, "He would be pleased to find peace and harmony."

The peace and harmony of Christmastime could be found in a variety of locations and in various ways in 1973. There was a Christmas Eve Nativity pageant for children at Rockefeller Chapel at the University of Chicago. Carolers gathered under the Picasso in the Civic Center at 5 P.M. on Christmas Eve. In Pullman on the South Side, one of the few remaining pipe organs in the United States accompanied worshippers at the Pullman United Methodist Church. Characters from the "Peanuts" comic strip explained Christmas to family groups at the Hope Presbyterian Church in Wheaton. The multitude of ethnic celebrations around the area included an Afro-American brass quartet, Spanish carols played by a mariachi group, Italian carols accompanied by accordion, and Filipino, Japanese, and Chinese Christmas music.

Peace and harmony did not reign everywhere in the city. On the Friday before Christmas, the Chicago City Council approved a three-dollar-a-month head tax on employees of Chicago businesses. It was esti-

Top Songs 1974

The top songs of the day included "Cat's in the Cradle" by Harry Chapin, "Kung Fu Fighting" by Carl Douglas, "Angie Baby" by Helen Reddy, "When Will I See You Again" by Three Degrees, and "You're the First, the Last, My Everything" by Barry White.

At the Movies 1974

Movies of the season included Airport 1975, The Godfather Part 2, *Mel Brooks'* Young Frankenstein, The Towering Inferno, *Roger Moore as James Bond in* The Man *with the Golden Gun, and Jack Lemmon and Walter Matthau in* The Front Page.

Da Bears 1974

Chicago architect Salvator Balsamo proposed that an eighty-thousand seat underground sports arena be built for the Bears at an unused quarry at Halsted Street and the Stevenson Expressway. Only a retractable dome would protrude above the ground. Balsamo said he had a lot of support for the project, and hoped to take his plan to Mayor Daley.

mated that the tax would raise forty million dollars each year for the city. Opponents said it was illegal, and they promised to fight it.

The Chicago Police Department was looking for horses: four- to eight-year-old mixed breed geldings to be exact. The city had budgeted funds in 1974 to re-establish the mounted police patrols in parks. There had been no mounted police since 1947.

And energy crisis or not, Rudolph the reindeer's red nose was glowing bright that Christmas. Robert May, creator of the most famous reindeer of all for a Montgomery Ward promotion back in 1939, had for years kept a nine-foot-tall Rudolph lit up as a Christmas display in the front yard of his home on Avers Avenue in Skokie. When the *Daily News* reported that Rudolph would be dark in 1973 because of the energy crisis, May was deluged with calls from children and grown-ups.

He changed his mind and, using a single one hundred-watt red bulb instead of the usual multicolored string of lights, lit up Rudolph's nose once more.

Robert L. May, the man who wrote the story and song about Rudolph the Red-Nosed Reindeer

1974: All the King's Men

Chicago's weather forecast for the Wednesday Christmas of 1974 called for cloudy skies, a chance of snow, and a high in the lower thirties.

Politics was also in the air. It was one week before the Christmas of 1974 when Mayor Richard J. Daley filed thousands of petitions nominating him for a sixth term of office. Forty-third Ward Alderman William Singer also filed, and State Senator Richard Newhouse and former State's Attorney Edward Hanrahan were expected to join the Democratic field.

As for the Republicans, the *Chicago Tribune* put it this way in an editorial entitled "The G.O.P.'s Chosen Victim:"

The Chicago Republican Central Committee [yes, there is one], has chosen its victim for the mayoral election, that horrid sacrificial rite the party goes thru every four years. After a long, mildly amusing show of seeking volunteers to run against Mayor Daley in February [it asked practically every Chicagoan who breathes regularly], the committee settled on one of its own: Ald. John J. Hoellen [47th] the only self-confessed Republican in the 50-member City Council.

Mr. Hoellen has our condolences. (Copyright *Chicago Tribune.* Used by permission.)

Politics was also in season nationally. Closing arguments were under way in the Watergate cover-up case. On January 1, 1975, John Mitchell, H. R. Haldeman, John Erlichman, and Robert Mardian would be convicted of covering up the Watergate burglary, the attempt at sabotaging the Democrats' 1972 presidential campaign which ultimately led to President Richard Nixon and his eventual downfall. He resigned during the summer of 1974.

Now, at Christmastime, Nixon was in seclusion at his estate in San Clemente, California. The *Tribune* painted a picture of the place, calling it:

SAN CLEMENTE: A STUDY IN MELANCHOLY
By Aldo Beckman
Chicago Tribune Press Service

SAN CLEMENTE, Cal.—A trawler, its decks circled with anxious fishermen, rolls lazily in the Southern California surf. A year ago, a Coast Guard cutter was anchored near the same spot to shoo away intruders, such as fishermen, and guarantee privacy on the seaward side of the western White House.

A volleyball net is stretched across a concrete court that a year ago was a helicopter pad for the President of the United States. Tall weeds grow on a four-hole golf course, once the pride of a President.

Inside the nearby office complex, in an office still marked Executive Dining Room, a middle-aged woman volunteer from a local Republican club, sorts thru part of the one million pieces of mail that has arrived at Richard Nixon's San Clemente home since he resigned as President on Aug. 9. About 25 boxes of letters are in a corner of the room that a year ago was so exclusive that a ticket to eat there was a coveted status symbol.

AT THE residence next door, the former President is resting in his study, unlit pipe in hand, with a phlebitis-wracked leg elevated in the recliner chair bought for him by Mrs. Nixon to put in front of his television set.

He has been in seclusion here since returning Nov. 14 from a Long Beach hospital, where he nearly died after going into shock following an operation on his left leg.

In the yard outside, Manola Sanchez, Nixon's personal valet, scurries about, chopping wood for the always burning fireplace in his boss' study, and dragging water hoses around to make sure the grass and the shrubs stay green.

It is not a happy place. "Melancholy" is a word that inevitably tumbles from the lips of anyone who has been there.

NIXON IS convinced that his poor physical condition is a direct result of the trauma he went thru at resignation. Looking to the future, he anticipates continued poor health.

His staff denies that he has even lost the will to live. One aide insisted that a strong will to live is all that saved Nixon from death on Oct. 29.

A man who suffered from insomnia thruout his Presidency, seldom sleeping more than two or three hours at a stretch, Nixon now gets from 10 to 11 hours of sleep each night. He is incredulous that he can sleep so well for so long. His voice is weak and his hair much grayer than it was three months ago.

He is always in bed by 9:30, and sometimes as early as 8. He wakes up about 7:30 or 8 A.M.

Those who see him regularly say that Nixon has aged "at least 10 years" since Aug. 9, and he has not regained any of the 10 to 15 pounds he lost during his hospital stay. (Copyright *Chicago Tribune*. Used by permission.)

Nixon's successor, Gerald Ford, spent the holiday much differently, enjoying a ski vacation in Colorado. The new vice president, Nelson Rockefeller, took his oath of office on the Thursday before Christmas.

"Win"

The biggest problem facing the new administration was the economy. The cost of living was going up: 11.6

percent in the Chicago area during the twelve months leading up to December 1974. The administration had a plan: "Whip Inflation Now," the WIN program as it was called, came complete with buttons and forms pledging the signer to be an inflation fighter and energy saver. But as the Associated Press reported:

> A lot of people were asking whether Mr. Ford wasn't fighting the wrong battle. With six million people out of work, and the total growing daily, the nation clearly had slipped into a recession during 1974, although the Administration was slow in admitting it. Virtually all business indicators were falling sharply.

Even with rising unemployment and inflation, there was talk of putting a tax on gasoline in order to cut America's energy dependence on foreign sources. Illinois Senator Charles Percy was proposing a twenty-cent-a-gallon tax. A Harris poll found that 51

percent of Americans favored a ten-cent-a-gallon tax, provided it were tax deductible.

In Chicago, discontent with economic conditions manifested itself among Chicago Transit Authority (CTA) bus drivers and rapid transit workers. On the Friday before Christmas they rejected a proposed three-year contract that would have made them the highest paid in the nation, with cost of living benefits boosting the top scale to nearly ten dollars an hour by September 1, 1977. The workers union leadership had recommended approval of the contract.

There was controversy on the small screen in Chicago. Because of hundreds of letters from angry viewers, the management of Channel 2 decided to bring back popular weatherman John Coughlin. He had been replaced for a time by model Melody Rogers, whose previous claim to fame was the TV car ads she had done with Bears' coach Abe Gibron.

On the Friday before Christmas, seventy-five-year-old widower Umberto Tust collected his first forty-nine thousand dollar check from the Illinois state lottery. It came just in time since Tust's pension plan was about to expire. Tust was the third one million dollar winner in the lottery's short history.

1976: The Death of a Mayor

On Saturday morning, Christmas Day, Chicagoans awoke to news of a deadly fire. On Christmas Eve, twelve people, ten of them children, were killed in a fire in a three-story building at 1811 West Seventeenth Street. As many as fifty children had been attending a Christmas party there. Witnesses saw a person running down a hallway carrying a pan of flaming grease or oil. The stuff splattered, the wooden stairway burst into flames, and the stairwell acted like a chimney, spreading smoke and fire to the upper floors. "The whole building was in flames in a matter of minutes," said a neighbor.

This calamity added to a heavy emotional burden Chicagoans were already carrying. They had just laid to rest the man who probably was the most popular mayor in the city's history, Richard J. Daley.

On the Table 1976

The Christmas turkey of 1976 cost 39¢ a pound at Jewel. Eggnog was 69¢ a quart.

Under the Tree 1976

Perhaps the gift of the season was a citizens band radio. Radio Shack was selling a set for $60 off its regular price of $179.95.

Montgomery Ward's was selling one of the first TV video games. It was commonly known as Pong, and after you attached it to the back of your TV, you could use it to play a sort of electronic ping-pong, handball, or hockey.

At the Movies 1976

A film about the TV industry was one of the movies of the season. Network *starred Faye Dunaway, William Holden, and Peter Finch, who as anchorman Howard Beale made famous the line "I'm mad as hell, and not going to take it any more." Other movies in the theaters included* The Seven Percent Solution, The Enforcer *with Clint Eastwood,* Rocky *with Sylvester Stallone, and* Silver Streak.

It had all begun on Monday, the 20 of December. Mayor Daley had had a typically busy morning, which included a trip to the South Side to dedicate a new park district gymnasium. The mayor had even impressed the crowd on hand by shooting—and making—a basket.

During the return ride to city hall, however, he suffered chest pains, and directed his driver to take him to the Michigan Avenue office of his doctor, Thomas Coogan, Jr. Coogan took an electrocardiogram but could not find anything abnormal. He suggested that the mayor check into Rush Presbyterian St. Luke's Medical Center for more tests, and went into another room to make the arrangements. While he was out of the room, Daley suffered a massive heart attack.

When Coogan returned to the examining room at about 2:10 P.M. he found the mayor slumped over. He, his colleague Dr. Robert Reid, and three other doctors and two paramedics all tried to revive the mayor, but to no avail. Thus, the mayor who had led the city since 1955 was pronounced dead at 3:40 P.M. His death left the city, and the nation, in a state of shock.

President Ford and President-elect Carter were among the first to make personal calls of condolence to the Daley family. Governor Walker declared a state of mourning throughout Illinois, and ordered flags flown at half-staff for thirty days. John Cardinal Cody, the Roman Catholic archbishop of Chicago, said Daley was a man of the people who never forgot his origins. "In our memory he will always be 'the mayor,'" said Cody. A. Robert Abboud, the chairman of the First National Bank of Chicago, said Daley made him feel "like an adopted member of the family, and so the loss, of course, is deep and personal." Comedian Bob

Hope recalled the previous Saturday night he had spent with Daley at a benefit for St. Ignatius College Prep school. Hope had told the mayor that he was looking great. He praised Daley for making Chicago a model for the whole nation: "He was able to keep this city humming." Another of the mayor's favorite entertainers, Frank Sinatra, was reported to have burst into tears when he heard of Daley's passing.

On Tuesday, the twenty-first, the people of the city of Chicago got their chance to pay their last respects to the mayor. Thousands of people turned out for the wake in bitterly cold and windy weather.

The *Chicago Tribune* report was poignant:

> The lines stretched for more than a block outside the Nativity of Our Lord Catholic Church at 37th Street and Union Avenue, whee Daley's body lay in state.
>
> And if the people of Chicago showed respect for their mayor, the grieving Daley family more than returned that respect to the people.
>
> The Daleys remained at the church hour after hour, welcoming each person as a particular friend, shaking every hand though they numbered in the thousands, and extending condolences as often as they received them.
>
> It was a neighborhood event in which all Chicagoans were regarded as neighbors by the Daleys. (Copyright *Chicago Tribune*. Used by permission.)

The next morning the bells tolled at all Catholic churches, hospitals, and convents throughout the archdiocese. The great and the powerful mingled with the common citizen at the funeral mass for the mayor. President-elect Carter was there. So was Vice President Rockefeller, Governor-elect Jim Thompson,

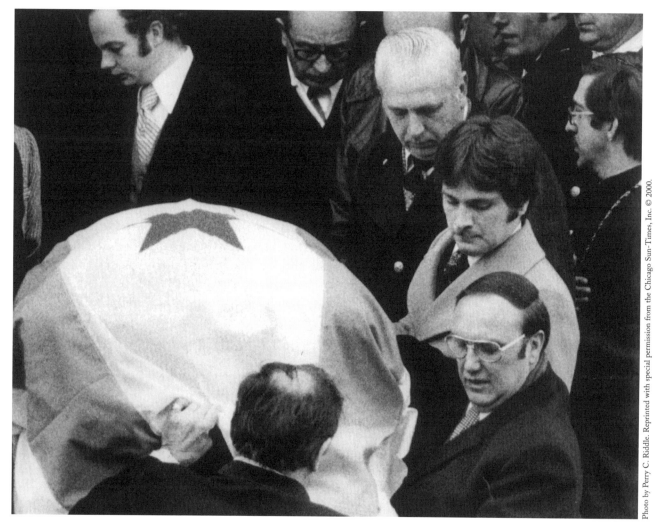

Pallbearers carry the mayor's casket covered by the Chicago flag

Defense Secretary Donald Rumsfeld, Senator Edward Kennedy, and hundreds of other people whose names would not be familiar.

The Reverend Gilbert Graham told the mourners that the Daley family wished no formal eulogy: "It wasn't his style. The quality of his life and actions are enough eulogy. That is a far more eloquent testimony for this man."

Two thousand other people lined 111th Street in Worth to watch the funeral procession into Holy

At the Movies 1977

On the entertainment scene, Star Wars, Close Encounters of the Third Kind, *and* Saturday Night Fever *were among the big box-office attractions at area movie houses.*

On Stage 1977

Zoot Sims, Steve Goodman, and James Brown were among the musicians performing on stage in town.

On the Tube 1977

Popular TV programs again included All in the Family, The Carol Burnett Show, Bob Newhart, Kojak, *and* The Love Boat.

Top Songs 1977

Popular songs on the Billboard *survey included "How Deep Is Your Love" by the Bee Gees, "You Light Up My Life" by Debby Boone, "Blue Bayou" by Linda Ronstadt, "Back in Love Again" by LTD, and "It's So Easy" by Linda Ronstadt.*

On the Table 1977

Fresh turkeys were 89¢ a pound at Hillman's, or 59¢ to 69¢ a pound frozen. Cranberry sauce was 29¢ for a sixteen-ounce can.

Sepulchre Cemetery. One little girl held a hand-printed sign that spoke for all Chicagoans. "We will miss you, Mayor Daley," it said.

After Mayor Daley was laid to rest, the headlines in the *Tribune* and the *Daily News* began to tell a different sort of story: "Battle to Succeed Daley" blasted the *Trib*, "Bilandic reported gaining support" and "Ald. Frost asserts he's acting mayor." "How four hatched deal to halt City Hall chaos" was the lead headline in the *Daily News* on Christmas Eve.

Ald. Michael Bilandic would emerge as the new leader of the city after all the bickering stopped and all the deals were brokered. But as Christmas rolled around most Chicagoans, still mourning the loss of their mayor, felt confused and disillusioned by the unclear and unsatisfactory transition.

In other local news, two Chicago psychologists conducted an experiment and concluded that the joy that comes from sending and receiving Christmas cards is contagious. The psychologists, Kenneth Wessel of Roosevelt University and John Trybula of the Family Services Mental Health Center in Chicago Heights, together sent Christmas cards to 470 strangers, most of them people whose names they took out of telephone books.

Within a few weeks, they had received in return forty-eight Christmas cards, nine telephone calls, and an invitation to a party. Wessel called the 12 percent return "astonishing," considering that 13 percent of the cards were returned because the addressee had moved and left no forwarding address. Wessel told the *Daily News* that he and Trybula had concluded that "at least during the holiday season, people are more open to one another and more in the mood to communicate with others and show a kindness."

1977: Ask the Mayor?

Christmas came on a Sunday in 1977, and a cold one it was. Following a high temperature of thirty-nine degrees on Christmas Eve, cold Canadian winds blew into the city, and on Christmas Day there was a windchill of minus twenty-seven degrees.

The big news of the day was coming out of the Middle East. A little more than a month had passed since President Anwar Sadat of Egypt had made his historic visit to Israel, addressed the Knesset, Israel's Parliament, and pledged "no more war." Now, on Christmas Day, Sadat and Prime Minister Menachem Begin of Israel were holding a summit meeting in Ismailia, Egypt. The talks were going so well that they were being extended for another day. Both leaders spoke optimistically about negotiating a peace treaty between their two countries.

During Christmas week, 1977, Bilandic submitted to questioning on an hour-long "Ask the Mayor" program on television. But he did not have much to say about his firing of Jane Byrne, the city's Consumer Affairs Commissioner (Byrne would defeat Bilandic in his bid for election in 1979), nor about a Federal Trade Commission investigation that was under way into the alleged Yellow and Checker monopoly of Chicago's taxicabs. "I'll say plenty after it's over," he promised. Bilandic did tell the interviewers that he considered "keeping the citizens of Chicago working together" the single greatest accomplishment during his first year in office.

Chicago Transit Authority bus drivers had again overwhelmingly rejected a new contract proposal. Charles Hall, the secretary-treasurer of Amalgamated Transit Union Local 241 was saying the drivers deserved more money because their jobs were hazardous: "You know about assaults and crimes and accidents. It's getting to be a very unsafe occupation." As if to underscore his words, two days later, on December 21, two gunmen shot and fatally wounded a fourteen-year veteran bus driver, Donald Sucilla, during a robbery.

Two convicted felons got five-day holiday furloughs from prison over Christmas. Former Chicago alderman Thomas Keane had already done twenty months of his sentence for mail fraud and the purchase of tax delinquent property for resale to public agencies. John Erlichman was part-way through his eighteen-month term resulting from the Watergate cover-up.

Under the Tree 1977

Long-play record albums were on sale for $5.49 at Montgomery Ward's. Cassette tapes were going for $2.99. Gadgets of the season included the computerized Chess Challenger—on sale for $149.00, or the upgraded version with three levels of play for $225.00. Designer telephones were on sale for from $45.00 to $70.00. And Goldblatt's was advertising the Atari video computer system for $170.00, claiming: "This is not a toy," but "a fascinating game to play 100 ways. You'll never get bored."

Da Bears 1977

Chicago Park Board president Patrick O'Malley was advising Mayor Bilandic to demolish Soldier Field, leaving the created space as open park land, and to build a new sports stadium elsewhere, perhaps on Madison Street near the Chicago Stadium.

Under the Tree 1979

General Motors was announcing an average price increase of $138.00 on its 1980 models. That meant you could buy a brand new Buick Riviera coupe for $12,151, or an Olds Cutlass Supreme for $6,895, or a Chevy Citation coupe for $4,665, or a Cadillac Seville for $19,978.

Skunk Christmas

It was at Christmastime that Chicagoans were following the fortunes of Wishbone the skunk, whom the *Chicago Sun-Times* was calling "the skunk that stumped the state."

The skunk had taken up residence in Bill Stanton's garage near 113th and Hamlin, and for more than a month Hamlin had been haggling with animal control officials, trying everything he could think of to get rid of the skunk. Under various state regulations it was against the law for him to kill, de-scent, or release the animal.

Finally, on December 21, in the presence of a lawyer, TV cameras, and microphones, an agreement was reached. Stanton won his demands that the animal not be put to sleep nor released into an area where it could be hunted. A state conservation officer led Wishbone off camera to "live a proper skunk's life." On that day, the Stantons' seven children even stayed home from school so they could say good-bye to their skunk friend.

How did it get the name Wishbone? Because of its penchant for Thanksgiving turkey.

1979:

Ayatollah Khomeini and Jane

On the night before Christmas, high winds swept through the city breaking windows, flooding the Drive, and knocking down power lines. The forecast for Christmas Day was somewhat more pleasing: partly cloudy skies with temperatures slightly above freezing.

Mr. & Mrs. Mouse shopping at Field's

Christmas Day, 1979, marked the fifty-second day of captivity for fifty-two Americans being held hostage by revolutionaries who had overthrown the Shah of Iran. In a Christmastime broadcast, the new leader of Iran, the Ayatolla Ruhollah Khomeini, addressed the American people: "Do know that our youths are treating the spies in such a way as to please God, since Islam calls for kindness to prisoners, even if they are cruel and spies. . . . American nation: Demand of [President] Carter that he return the deposed and criminal Shah to Iran, since the key to the release of the spies is in his hands."

At the same time the United States was calling for economic sanctions against the new government of Iran. On Christmas Day, three American clergymen and a French archbishop were allowed into Tehran to hold religious services for the hostages.

The hostages were very much on the minds of the American people. For Chicagoans, that meant writing and sending a quarter of a million Christmas cards and letters to the hostages, to let them know they were not forgotten. The post office said Chicago's mail to Iran weighed in at three tons. Busy Christmas shoppers even stood in line on State Street to write greetings on preaddressed Christmas cards that were made available by the State Street Council.

Chicago's public school teachers went without pay on the Friday before Christmas. It was the third time in six weeks that the school board had flirted with such a possibility. Twice before, emergency state aid had helped the board meet its $41.5 million payroll. This time, Gov. Jim Thompson was not willing to bail out the system without a commitment from the local school board. He wanted the board to issue state-aid anticipation warrants, with the state, the city of Chicago, and Chicago banks buying them. Mayor Jane Byrne wanted the state to buy all of them.

While the governor and the mayor pointed fingers at each other, members of the Chicago Teachers Union were reacting with shock, anger, and outrage. Union chief Robert Healey urged teachers to request that they be laid off. That way they could at least receive unemployment compensation.

At the Movies 1979

Star Trek, the Motion Picture *was playing in Chicago at Christmastime 1979. So were the movies* 10, Kramer versus Kramer, 1941, *and* The Electric Horseman.

On Stage 1979

On stage, The Elephant Man *was at the Blackstone.* They're Playing Our Song *was at the Shubert. Tom Stoppard's* Travesties *was on the stage of Wisdom Bridge Theater.*

Top Songs 1979

The top tunes on the Billboard *survey that week were "Escape (Pina Colada Song)" by Rupert Holmes, "Please Don't Go" by K. C. & the Sunshine Band, "Babe" by Styx, "Send One Your Love" by Stevie Wonder, and "Still" by the Commodores.*

Sports 1979

In sports, the Bears lost their wild-card playoff game to Philadelphia on the day before Christmas. The Blackhawks were in second place in the Smythe Division of the NHL, the Bulls were fourth in the Midwest Division of the NBA, and the Chicago Hustle was in third place in the Midwest Division of the Women's Professional Basketball League.

The CTA's proposed rapid transit line extension to O'Hare Airport was in trouble. The project was already a year behind schedule, and the expected cost was as much as $35 million over the original estimate. The federal government was balking at coming up with the extra money.

The Friday before Christmas marked the end of a brief strike by CTA bus drivers and motormen. Circuit Court Judge Donald O'Brien ordered an end to the work stoppage. He also ordered a twenty-four-cent-an-hour pay raise for the workers, plus contract arbitration.

Mayor Byrne took time out from her city hall duties to appear on the *Phil Donahue* television talk show. The *Tribune* noted that "the politics of confrontation that have become the hallmark of her eight months in office were very much a part of her hour before the cameras." Changing his usual format, Donahue asked the mayor some difficult questions such as how she dealt with the CTA strike, the school board's problems, her leadership style, and her endorsement of Senator Edward Kennedy over incumbent President Jimmy Carter for the 1980 Democratic nomination. When Donahue pointed out that her popularity in the most recent public opinion polls had fallen dramatically, Byrne said the figures were being misinterpreted. When Donahue suggested that some were calling the mayor "Ayatollah Jane," her comeback was that she'd just read about the woman from Britain (Prime Minister Margaret Thatcher) who was known as "Attila the Hen."

It was just a few days before Christmas that the Illinois Supreme Court ruled, five to two, that a divorced woman could not live with a boyfriend and continue to keep custody of her children. The court said, "Conduct of that nature, when it is open, not only violates the statutorily expressed moral standards of the state, but also encourages others to violate those standards and debases public morality." Divorce lawyers called the ruling a landmark victory for divorced men who wanted custody of their children.

In another ruling, the high court said that Illinois communities could order their residents to clean their sidewalks after a snowstorm. Because of recently enacted legislation, the drinking age in Illinois would be going back up to twenty-one on January 1, 1980.

From the collection of Laurel and Stu Heiss

Cost of Living

The cost of living was on everybody's mind as 1979 came to a close. Consumer prices were up more than 12.5 percent over the past twelve months, up 1.8 percent in Chicago for just November. The *Chicago Tribune* carried a chart comparing the cost of various items showing the huge difference between 1959 and 1979 prices:

Set of children's blocks	$2.00	$6.50
Lincoln Logs	$3.80	$16.00
Coaster wagon	$9.90	$23.70
3-speed bicycle	$57.00	$122.00
Barbie doll	$3.50	$8.50
Woman's lamb's wool sweater	$19.00	$25.00
1 oz. French perfume	$32.50	$65.00
Man's permanent press shirt	$6.00	$15.00
Stereo record	$5.00	$6.50
17" black-and-white TV set	$190.00	$150.00
Basic calculator	$125.00	$10.00
1 theater ticket	$6.60	$22.50
Chicago-to-New York airplane ticket, one-way, coach		
	$64.60	$155.00
3-minute Chicago-to-New York phone call, holiday rate		
	$1.15	$0.76
2-lb. fruitcake	$3.00	$8.00
1 qt. eggnog	$0.49	$0.99
2-lb. assorted chocolates	$3.80	$9.00

(Copyright *Chicago Tribune*. Used by permission.)

1980 - 1989

1981: Daring to Hope

On Thursday, Christmas Eve, 1981, candles burned in the windows of thousands of homes in the Chicago area and millions of homes nationwide. President Ronald Reagan had asked Americans to place the candles there as a "beacon of our solidarity with the Polish people." Less than two weeks before Christmas, Polish leader Gen. Wojciech Jaruzelski had declared martial law. Members of the Solidarity labor organization were being rounded up and arrested. Troops broke up strikes in steel mills and coal mines.

Two nights before Christmas, President Reagan addressed the American people. He accused the Polish government of making "war against its own people," and he said this "crime will cost them dearly in their future dealings with America." Mr. Reagan announced the suspension of major economic ties with Poland, including the shipment of farm and dairy products, the twenty-five million dollar line of credit Warsaw had with the Export-Import Bank for the purchase of Western goods, aviation privileges, and fishing rights. Mr. Reagan threatened further action if the repression continued.

Time magazine, in its January 4, 1982, issue, declared Solidarity leader Lech Walesa its "Man of the Year," saying, "He dared to hope."

By the end of 1981, the U.S. economy was in a recession. Unemployment was up to nearly 9 percent. At the same time, the cost of living had climbed 9.6 percent nationally in the twelve months leading up to December, 6.6 percent in the Chicago area alone.

The Reagan administration was proposing a 1982 budget with a $109 billion deficit. Many in Congress, including Republicans, were urging the president to go easy on spending cuts for social programs. Just before Christmas, President Reagan announced plans to distribute 560 million pounds of surplus cheese to poor people.

Because of fears about the nation's economy, most retailers cut down on the number of part-time sales clerks they usually hired for the Christmas shopping season. This caused a lot of frustration among shoppers, who often had a difficult time finding somebody to take their money for a purchase, or who had to wait in long lines to make their purchases.

Despite fears about the economy, the *Chicago Tribune* noted:

CRUNCH CAN'T STEAL CHRISTMAS FOR TOY LOVERS
By Patricia Leeds

If there's a recession you'd never know it by the way toys are selling in the Loop department stores. Practically all of the toy departments sell out of the most expensive electronic toys as soon as they get them in. The same is true of a line of costly dolls.

"We just can't keep them in stock," said Debbie Meier, toy department manager for Marshall Field & Co.'s State Street store. Managers at Wieboldt's and Carson Pirie Scott & Company agreed.

Atari and Intellivision are the top electronic toys. The Madam Alexander storybook dolls are the other hot item.

However, it's nice to know many of the traditional favorite toys are still as popular today as in the days when the children's parents were wide-eyed kids.

Teddy bears and trucks, games and dolls are still among the most loved toys.

But only the games remain the same—Monopoly, Sorry, Clue, Payday and Life, which are among the favorites.

"The others have become a lot more sophisticated," said Lurri Edwards, toy manager at Carsons' State Street store. "Rag dolls have been replaced by Tippy Toes, who pushes a stroller, and it seems every little girl wants the doll named Strawberry Shortcake, among the younger ones. The older ones still want Barbie."

Even Barbie has a new look. She's gone ethnic. Now you can get a Black Barbie, a Hispanic, Italian, Parisian and Western Barbie (the most popular this season) to mention a few. Also, Barbie has acquired a few more curves and looks sexier.

Teddy Bear has gone modern, too. There is now a preppy version in which he is outfitted in the most collegiate clothes. Not to be outdone, there is a preppy alligator with the figure of a man stitched on his shirt, a takeoff on the popular shirts with the alligator on the pocket. (Copyright *Chicago Tribune*. Used by permission.)

Tales of Terror

At Christmastime 1981, NASA aerospace engineer-on-leave Herman Regusters and his wife were insisting that they had seen a brontosaurus-like creature during an expedition along the Congo River in Africa. They told reporters at the Los Angeles Museum of Science and Industry that the creature was "brownish and about the size of two hippos," having a "serpent-like head on a neck some two feet thick." They said about two dozen other people on the month-long expedition had also seen the creature. Other witnesses included officials from the governments of the Republic of the Congo and Ghana.

The Regusters were forced to admit to the skeptical reporters, however, that they had no solid evidence of the beast, not even a photograph. Regusters maintained that stories of the mysterious creature, called "moke'e mbembe" or "one who eats the tops of palm trees," had been circulating in the Lake Tele region for more than two hundred years. A University of Chicago expedition led by zoologist Roy Mackal was also just back from the region, having failed to find the creature.

Weirdness was not only the fashion among scientific sightings at Christmastime 1981. Some of America's teenagers were, well, becoming very different. The *Tribune's* Ronald Yates reported from Los Angeles:

> Tina Terror leaned against a car in front of the Starwood nightclub and took a long drag from a cigarette.
> "Yeah, man, that's my real name, Tina Terror," she said, running a hand through her hair, which was dyed in blond and black splotches.

At the Movies 1981

Movies playing around the area included George C. Scott in Taps, Chariots of Fire, *John Belushi and Dan Ackroyd in* Neighbors, Raiders of the Lost Ark, Ragtime, Pennies from Heaven, *and* Reds.

Top Songs 1981

The top pop singles, according to the Billboard *survey, included "Physical" by Olivia Newton-John; "Waiting for a Girl like You" by Foreigner; "Let's Groove" by Earth, Wind & Fire; "Oh No" by the Commodores; "Young Turks" by Rod Stewart; "I Can't Go for That" by Daryl Hall & John Oates; "Why Do Fools Fall in Love" by Diana Ross; "Harden My Heart" by Quarterflash; "Don't Stop Believin'" by Journey; and "Leather and Lace" by Stevie Nicks with Don Henley.*

Top Songs 1983

The top tunes on the Billboard *survey were "Say, Say, Say" by Paul McCartney and Michael Jackson; "All Night Long" by Lionel Ritchie; "Uptown Girl" by Billy Joel, "Say It Isn't So" by Hall & Oates, and "Love Is a Battlefield" by Pat Benatar.*

Under the Tree 1983

Because of the cold, sweaters were a popular Christmas gift in 1983. Carson Pirie Scott & Co. was having a sale: men's orlon acrylic sweaters for $19.99, wool polyester shetlands for $5.00 more; women's silk, acrylic, angora, or nylon pullovers for $17.99, Icelandic woolen sweaters for $49.99.

Polk Brothers was selling Sony's popular Betamax videocassette recorders for $488.88. You could buy a Commodore 64K RAM home computer at Sears for $199.99. An Apple II was $1,495.00.

At the Movies 1983

Movies of the season included Scarface *with Al Pacino,* The Right Stuff, *the James Bond thriller* Never Say Never Again, *Barbra Streisand in* Yentl, *Clint Eastwood as Dirty Harry in* Sudden Impact, *and William Hurt and Lee Marvin starring in* Gorky Park.

"What do my parents think?" she said, repeating a reporter's question. "Who cares what they think? I'm a punker, man. That's where it's at, you know. Punking and slamming. That's the world."

Tina Terror took one last drag from her cigarette and crushed it out in the palm of her hand. Then she turned and walked over to her boyfriend, whose bleached blond hair was cut Mohawk style and whose left earlobe was pierced with a giant paper clip. (Copyright *Chicago Tribune.* Used by permission.)

A new Illinois law about to take effect on January 1 allowed Illinois residents, for the first time since Prohibition, to own machine guns. But one federal official noted that it would not be very easy to acquire such weapons.

1983: Cold to the Bone

Like the song, Chicagoans for the most part can only dream of a white Christmas. The records indicate that there is only a one-in-three chance of an inch or more of snow on the ground on December 25.

Chicago's Christmas weather is in fact remarkably variable. There might be huge amounts of snow on the ground. Or it might be green and

Photo by Terry Wheeler

springlike. Or super frigid. Or foggy. Or gloomy under a leaden sky. Or it might even be so warm that the steamed-up kitchen windows have to be opened.

Chicago's warmest Christmas came in 1982, when the mercury shot up to sixty-four degrees. Even though the Lake Michigan water temperature was a mere forty-two degrees, a few hardy sailors spent part of their Christmas Day on the lake. The record of 1982 surpassed the previous fifty-six degree mark set in 1936.

Chicago's coldest Christmas came in 1983. It was so cold that chimney smoke seemed to freeze in the sky and noses tingled from the bracing chill. At 7 A.M. on Saturday, Christmas Eve, it was twenty-five degrees below zero. The windchill was minus eighty degrees. On Christmas Day the temperature warmed to minus seventeen degrees. That was as high as it got all day!

At the Cabrini-Green public housing development conditions were miserable. Because of a broken water pipe, there was no heat for 140 families. It took fourteen hours for workmen to make repairs, and in the meantime the Chicago Housing Authority (CHA) handed out electric heaters to help stave off the cold. But they did not help those poor residents whose electricity also had gone out.

The frigid temperatures were a contributing factor in five major fires that left sixty people out in the cold. Firefighters found themselves battling frozen hydrants, high winds, and frostbite as well as the flames. The Cook County Medical Examiner's Office counted at least ten people dead from hypothermia.

Going over the river and through the woods to grandma's house was a holiday nightmare. The cold and high winds forced the authorities to close several major interstate highways in Illinois and Indiana. The Chicago Motor Club averaged two hundred calls per hour from motorists needing assistance. The Illinois Department of Transportation reported it was so cold that salt was no longer effective on slick roadways.

Even the postal service threw in the towel and canceled mail delivery in six Illinois cities. Rock Island postmaster John Bromley told the *Chicago Tribune:* "It just isn't possible to send our carriers and jeopardize

On the Table 1983

Turkey was 59¢ to 69¢ a pound at Jewel or Dominicks. A two-pound can of Folger's coffee was $3.69. Milk was 99¢ for a sixty-four-ounce carton.

Best-Sellers 1983

The best-selling books included James Michener's Poland *and* Stephen King's Pet Sematary.

The Bulls 1984

The Bulls did not play on Christmas Eve or Christmas Day, 1984. Their last game before the holiday was a 110-85 victory over the Boston Celtics at the Chicago Stadium on Saturday night, December 22. In that game, Michael Jordan scored 32 points. He was the Bulls' leading scorer with a 24.8 average. Jordan was a rookie celebrating his first Christmas as a Chicago Bull in 1984, and it was clear that he was a basketball star. When the Chicago Tribune Magazine *published a short article on December 23 asking noted Chicagoans what Christmas delights they remembered from childhood, MJ was among the handful in the selection. He was identified, however, as merely "Guard, Chicago Bulls."

On the Tube 1985

Christmas was very much in evidence on Chicago TV Christmas Eve, 1985. Not only was there Kennedy-King College's production of The Messiah *on Channel 20, but the* Do-It-Yourself Messiah *was on Channel 11 a few hours later.*

There were broadcasts of Christmas services from the Chicago Methodist Temple, from St. Peter's Lutheran Church in New York, from St. Peter's Basilica at the Vatican with the Pope presiding, and there was midnight mass from Holy Name Cathedral, Joseph Cardinal Bernardin officiating.

Silent Night, Lonely Night was one of the movies to be seen, as was the longtime favorite, It's a Wonderful Life.

Regular series on the air that night included The A-Team, Riptide, Moonlighting, *Remington Steele, and* Stir Crazy.

their health today. We hope our customers understand."

What made it all the worse was the fact that the extreme cold had been lingering for most of the week: a record eleven below on the Sunday before Christmas, a record minus fourteen the next day, eighteen below on the Friday before Christmas.

War at Home and Abroad

It was not the cold, but the Irish Republican Army (IRA) that caused Christmas misery for one Chicago family. Kenneth Salveson of Chicago was one of five people killed by an IRA bomb that exploded in Harrod's Department Store in London on the weekend before Christmas. The IRA apologized for the civilian casualties and promised that it wouldn't happen again.

Bombs and fears of bombs were much in the news at the end of 1983. In October, 216 American marines were killed by a car bomb in Lebanon. During Christmas week, President Ronald Reagan renewed his pledge to keep the marines in Lebanon. He also explained the new concrete barriers being erected at the front gate of the White House as "normal" security precautions.

Chicago's famous "city council wars" were raging at Christmastime 1983. Members of the majority bloc had just scuttled a proposed compromise budget that had been worked out in laborious negotiations between Mayor Washington and Finance Committee chairman Ed Burke.

Chicago Transit Authority (CTA) chairman Michael Cardilli told reporters that opposition from senior citizen and community groups had forced him to change his mind: he was now opposed to a proposal to cut the basic bus and train fare while at the same time eliminating transfers. It was estimated that more than half of the CTA's riders would wind up paying more to ride if the proposal were approved.

On the weekend before Christmas, one hundred Illinois State Police set up roadblocks on seventeen roads leading from Wisconsin into Illinois. Forty-seven drivers were arrested for drunk driving in what was called "Operation R-A-I-D," for Remove Ale-Impaired Drivers.

1985: The Super Bowl Shuffle

Christmas Eve was cold and snowy with temperatures in the teens, getting down to five degrees that night. The Christmas spirit was really in the air in 1985. The *Tribune* went so far as to say that the holiday spirit had struck the city "with a vengeance of kindness." On the eve of Christmas Eve more than ten thousand people jammed the hotel Hyatt Regency for the fourth annual World's Largest Office Party. The benefit provided cash and toys for the Neediest Kids Fund and the Toys for Adoptable Kids campaign. There were celebrity bartenders, star look-alikes, and two stages of entertainment. Gov. Jim Edgar was there, and according to the *Trib*, denying that he was the loneliest guy at the party because of his tea-totaling habit. Then there was the reconditioned fur giveaway sponsored by a State Street furrier. Sixty-three senior citizens in the Second Ward won the coats at a drawing. And finally, there was the mysterious Santa Claus who, for the fifth year in a row, anonymously dropped gold coins into a Salvation Army kettle. The five gold Canadian maple leafs were worth $1,650.

Mayor Washington, Chicago's first black mayor, and the city council, dominated by old-line white aldermen, often did not see eye-to-eye in those days of "council wars." During the Christmas season of 1985, the

Photo by Mark Busch. Courtesy of the Press Republican Newspapers

The gold coins

Top Songs 1985

The top hits on Billboard's chart included "Broken Wings" by Mr. Mister, "Separate Lives" by Phil Collins and Marilyn Martin, "We Built This City" by Starship, "Never" by Heart, "Say You, Say Me" by Lionel Ritchie, "Party All the Time" by Eddie Murphy, and "Alive and Kicking" by Simple Minds.

Under the Tree 1985

One of the hottest Christmas gift ideas of 1985 was a telescope. Stores across the country were selling them faster than their shelves could be restocked. The reason was the return of Halley's Comet to the skies; it would be visible until May of 1986.

Cabbage Patch dolls were among the most popular of toys in the early 1980s. In 1985, the spin-offs were available. Sears was selling Cabbage Patch Kids twins for $70.00 and Cabbage Patch Kids world travelers in their costumes for $40.00.

An HO gauge train and battle set cost $50.00 at Toys R Us.

On the Table 1985

Jewel was selling the Christmas turkey for 79¢ a pound. Sweet potatoes were four for $1.00.

At the Movies 1985

Movies showing around town included Jewel of the Nile, A Chorus Line, 101 Dalmations, White Nights, The Color Purple, Out of Africa, *and* Rocky IV.

On Stage 1985

On stage, the selections included Cats, Hello Dolly, Pump Boys and Dinettes, Rap Master Ronnie, *and* The Wind in the Willows.

The Bulls 1985

By Christmas, 1985, Coach Stan Albeck was thinking about having Michael Jordan play forward. The team was struggling, 11-20, and in fifth place in the division. But they again won their last game before Christmas, 117-104 over Utah on Saturday, December 21. What would happen later that season would catapult the Bulls into the national TV spotlight on or around Christmas for years to come. What happened was that the Bulls crept into the playoffs and MJ put on quite a show in their final game. He scored 63 points, an NBA playoff record, on April 20, 1986, as the Bulls lost to Boston in double overtime.

Chicago Tribune reported that Mayor Washington often put those troubles aside, snuck out of his office, and spent many an afternoon visiting sick children and veterans in Chicago hospitals, trying to cheer up people who wouldn't be going home for the holiday. And he tried to do it without any publicity. Two years later the city would mourn his passing on November 25, 1987, the day before Thanksgiving.

The ornaments on Chicago's Christmas tree in 1985 ought to have been shaped like footballs. On the Sunday before the Wednesday Christmas, the Bears beat the Detroit Lions 37-17 to finish the regular season with a record of 15-1.

Just about everybody in town was singing or humming "The Super Bowl Shuffle," that ditty that had the Bears strutting their stuff. Everybody, that is, except for Coach Mike Ditka, who professed to be terrified that the team's 15-1 record would wind up on the scrap heap of history if the Bears played in the playoffs the way they finished the regular season: "We'll be the underdogs, no question about it," said Ditka. "Maybe we're doing too many 'Super Bowl Shuffles.'"

"Heck, we won," said the spunky quarterback, Jim McMahon. "I don't put any weight on that. It has nothing to do with our play." The Bears would go on to win the Super Bowl, 46-10, against the New England Patriots on the last Sunday in January.

While the Bears were filling Soldier Field, the White Sox were worried about the condition of Comiskey Park and wishing for a new stadium. The team's owners had even bought land in Addison with a view to build there. On the Friday before Christmas, Mayor Harold Washington commissioned two downtown developers to hammer out a plan for building an open-air baseball park for the Sox by 1989, at a cost of $125 million. The city favored a site along the east bank of the Chicago River just south of Roosevelt Road.

The city was also making big plans for O'Hare International Airport, looking to provide Nautilus equipment, showers, business facilities, ethnic restaurants, and an Art Institute shop for the 120,000 daily travelers at the world's busiest airport.

Capone's Vault

A ghost from Chicago's past was in the news: Al Capone. A TV crew was at work in the basement of the old Lexington Hotel at Michigan Avenue and Cermak Road, which used to be Capone's headquarters. In the basement was an eight-by-eight-foot concrete wall or vault. Plans were being made to break through the concrete and see what was inside during a live TV special. Rufus Taylor, the son of the man who used to be Capone's electrician, speculated that anything could be there, even "a body or two." When the TV lights went on and the wall was finally cracked in April, there was nothing on the other side.

On Christmas Eve, 1985, Anglican church envoy Terry Waite left Beirut, Lebanon, without the four American hostages he had hoped to free from the clutches of Shiite Muslim extremists. Among the hostages was Father Lawrence Martin Jenco of Joliet. Upon his arrival in London, Waite told reporters that there could be major developments within days. About a month later, Waite was back in Beirut on another mediation mission. However, he himself would be taken hostage during that visit.

1987: Controvery over the Crèche

Surely there is a lesson to be learned from the scene at Daley Center Plaza on Thursday, Christmas Eve, 1987. It is a lesson about freedom of religion in America, the First Amendment's freedom of expression, and the doctrine of the separation of church and state. On that day one group of people sang Christmas carols near a Nativity scene that was surrounded by an orange snow fence. Another group admired an eighteen-foot aluminum menorah. A third group of about a hundred people frequently drowned out the carolers with chants such as "Peace and justice go hand in hand. Stop the killing in the Holy Land!" They were protesting Israel's use of force in the Gaza Strip and the West Bank.

On Friday, December 18, Lubavitch Chabad of Illinois had erected the Hanukkah menorah after posting a one hundred thousand dollar bond with the Public Building Commission of Chicago. The commission required the bond to cover legal expenses in the event it was sued

The Bulls 1986

On Christmas Day, 1986, the Bulls were in the NBA's showcase game against the Knicks in New York's Madison Square Garden. One CBS-TV spokesperson called it "the Michael Jordan showcase." One producer told the Tribune, *"He's Air Jordan. He's happy, healthy, talented, and a superstar." The NBA's Entertainment division even made a commercial for the league featuring Jordan.*

The game itself was dramatic. Patrick Ewing hit a shot at the buzzer to give the Knicks an 86-85 win. That left the Bulls with an even record, 13-13, and in fourth place in their division.

The Bulls 1987

The Bulls and Knicks again were matched up on Christmas Eve in 1987. And again, it was Ewing's shot late in the game that gave New York a close victory, 90-89. That left the Bulls at 15-10 and in third place.

Top Songs 1987

The soundtrack from the Patrick Swayze film Dirty Dancing *was the number one pop LP in the nation. Michael Jackson's* Bad *was number two. George Michael's "Faith" was the top pop single, followed by Whitney Houston's "So Emotional" and Whitesnake's "Is This Love?"*

over a religious display on public grounds. On Sunday, the twentieth, the Nativity Scene Committee erected its crèche, but it didn't have money for the bond. On Monday, city workers began using crowbars to tear down the stable that formed part of the Nativity scene, and by Tuesday supporters of the crèche were there to protect the figurines, as the matter received the highest public attention.

Joseph Cardinal Bernardin, the Roman Catholic Archbishop of Chicago, said he was "dismayed" at the way the crèche was dismantled. He also spoke out against vandalism toward both Christian and Jewish holiday displays saying, "Disrespect for religious symbols is not merely offensive; it is reprehensible." On Tuesday afternoon, Federal Judge James Parsons worked out a compromise. It allowed the Nativity

© Chicago Tribune 2000

Ald. Louis Farina joins other visitors at the controversial crèche

Scene Committee to re-erect its display without posting bond, but only from the morning of Christmas Eve until the day after Christmas. The committee would also have to post a notice reading: "Religious exhibits on display at Daley Center Plaza are not sponsored or endorsed by any governmental entity."

The compromise did not please everybody. The lawyer for Lubavitch Chabad argued that it was unfair to require a hundred thousand dollar bond from his group but not from the Nativity Scene Committee. On Wednesday, a Cook County judge assured Lubavitch Chabad that it would get its money back. That same day the Chicago City Council debated the matter and finally voted 36-8 to approve a resolution recommending that free expression, including religious displays, be allowed on all public lands.

Meanwhile, on Tuesday, as all the arguing over religious displays was going on, statues of the three wise men, Mary and Joseph, the head of the baby Jesus, three lambs and two shepherds disappeared from the nativity scene at Holy Name Cathedral. They were found a day later at a Near North Side pizza restaurant. The restaurant's manager told police that on Monday evening she had given a bowl of soup to a thirty-something down-and-out man who collected cans for a living. He had promised to give her a Christmas present to show his gratitude. She joked that he'd better hurry, since Christmas was only a couple of days away. Then he started showing up with the statues.

Police questioned the man and reported that the Christ child was not broken out of any malice. The statue was wired down, and the head came off as the thief pulled on it.

Scientists at the U.S. Department of Agriculture's Human Nutrition Research Center at Tufts University in Boston came out with a report containing Santa Claus's secrets for living to a ripe old age. The scientists concluded that Santa has plenty of high-density lipoprotein in his blood, protecting him from the high cholesterol effects of all those milk-and-cookie snacks. They also noted that he must eat a lot of oranges because his vision for spotting house numbers is so keen, and that living at the North Pole and out of the sun so much of the year contributed to his healthy and relatively smooth skin.

Under the Tree 1987

The people at Marshall Field's predicted they'd use 146,000 feet of gift wrap during the 1987 Christmas shopping season.

At Toys R Us, the Sega Master and INTV video game systems were big sellers. So were the talking toys Big Bird of Sesame Street and Alf of the TV show of the same name.

At the Movies 1988

Movies of the season included Talk Radio, Mississippi Burning, *Bill Murray in* Scrooged, Twins *with Arnold Schwarzenegger and Danny DeVito, and* Working Girl *with Melanie Griffith and Harrison Ford.*

Under the Tree 1988

Children might have found a California Dream Barbie and Ken ($8.99 each) and a Barbie Hot Dog Stand ($14.99), or a Lionel six-unit heavy iron train set ($189.99), or a twenty-eight-inch wagon ($21.99).

One of the most heavily advertised techno gifts of the season was the mobile cellular telephone. But it was the kind that could only plug into your car's battery. Sets cost between $400.00 and $500.00.

Radio Shack was advertising its Tandy 1000 TL computer with "fast 286 performance" for $1,099.00. The Tandy HX with an MS-DOS operating system was down to $499.00.

On the Table 1988

The Christmas turkey cost 69¢ a pound for a ten to fourteen pounder at Dominicks. Bigger birds were cheaper. You could buy a twenty-six-ounce can of Maxwell House coffee for $2.99.

WHERE TO GET YOUR HANDS ON THE TIMEX SINCLAIR 1000.

Reproduced with the permission of the Timex Corporation

Due to unprecedented demand, our 800 number has been ringing off the hook. That's why we're providing the names of these fine stores that sell the Timex Sinclair 1000, the first home computer for under $100.*

1988: Pan Am Flight 103

Snow was in the forecast for Chicago for the Christmas holiday weekend of December 24-25, 1988. But it didn't happen. The snowstorm dumped its load on New England instead, and Chicago Christmas travelers had a smooth go of it, with partly cloudy skies and high temperatures around thirty degrees.

No doubt there was some trepidation among the travelers who passed through O'Hare and Midway on the Thursday, Friday, and Saturday before Christmas. That's because on the Wednesday night before Christmas, December 21, Pan Am flight 103 exploded in the sky and came crashing down on the small town of Lockerbie in Scotland. Two hundred fifty-eight people died in the air, seventeen on the ground.

The plane gouged a deep trough in the ground, wiped out forty homes, and scattered burning debris across an area ten miles wide. Bodies, some still strapped in their seats, landed in yards and on rooftops. Holiday gifts were scattered amid the debris.

By Christmas Day, the flight data and voice recorders from the plane had been recovered. They provided no clue. It wouldn't be until a few days after Christmas that investigators would confirm that a terrorist bomb had brought down flight 103.

Earlier in the month, the U.S. government informed airlines, airports, and embassies that the U.S. embassy in Helsinki had received a call, warning that a flight from Frankfurt to the U.S. would be a bomb target within two weeks. Pan Am 103 originated in Frankfurt.

A New Kind of Poor

A stuffed animal left too close to an electric baseboard heater may have caused a fire that very nearly ruined Christmas for poor children in Uptown. The fire at the Uptown People's Community Service Center on Wilson Avenue destroyed a thousand toys on the Wednesday before Christmas. Volunteers had been collecting them for months. The toys had already been wrapped and tagged with the names of needy children.

As news of the fire spread, people began dropping off new toy donations and cash gifts. Volunteers vowed to stay open round the clock, if necessary, to make Christmas joyous for children, just as the center had been doing for twenty years.

Chickens, stuffing, and cranberry sauce were only part of what went into food bags that the Chicago Housing Authority (CHA) was passing out to families in nineteen CHA developments. It was CHA's second annual food drive, and between December 16 and 22, the agency filled fifteen hundred bags of food and collected ten thousand articles of clothing for the poor.

At Operation PUSH on the South Side, a thousand parcels of food were being given away. The food had been collected by students at twenty-five Chicago schools. PUSH executive director Rev. Willie Barrow told the *Chicago Tribune* that there was a new hunger in the land, and a new type of person accepting food charity: "I think people reached

The Bulls 1988

On Christmas Day, 1988, the Chicago Bulls' record was 13-11. The team was fifth out of six teams in the NBA's Eastern Conference Central Division. Nonetheless, a sellout crowd of 23,388 at the Charlotte Coliseum gave Michael Jordan a standing ovation on the Friday night before Christmas. The Bulls lost that one 103-101.

Top Songs 1989

Top Pop Singles: "Another Day in Paradise," Phil Collins; "Don't Know Much," Linda Ronstadt; "We Didn't Start the Fire," Billy Joel; "Rhythm Nation," Janet Jackson; "With Every Beat of My Heart," Taylor Dayne; "Back to Life," Soul II Soul; "Pump Up the Jam," Technotronic; "Just Like Jesse James," Cher; "This One's for the Children," New Kids on the Block; "Living in Sin," Bon Jovi.

People lining up for a meal

Courtesy of the JPUSA Archives

out this year because they know this was a year with so many people unemployed, due to plant closings, and all of that."

The Labor Department's unemployment figure for December 1988 was 5.3 percent. However, earlier in the year a census bureau study had found a growing gap between the nation's richest and poorest families. Among the top fifth of families, the average income was then $76,300, an increase of $6,040 since the last survey. Among the bottom fifth, the average income had fallen from $8,761 to $8,033. The study also noted a new and growing class of worker: temporaries, who didn't get job benefits.

It was on the Thursday before Christmas that President Ronald Reagan told ABC News interviewer David Brinkley that it was the choice of some homeless people to sleep on sidewalk grates or on the grass. "There are shelters in virtually every city and shelters here, and those people still prefer out there on the

grates or the lawn to going into one of those shelters," said Mr. Reagan.

Mitch Snyder, a nationally acknowledged advocate for the homeless and the operator of a shelter in Washington, had reported that during bitterly cold weather earlier in December his shelter had been filled to capacity. Some estimates at the time had put the number of homeless Americans at three million.

At the Calvary-St. George's Episcopal Church in Manhattan, Rev. Thomas Pike planned to make a Christmas statement about homelessness. The Mary and Joseph participating in a Nativity service would be portrayed as a homeless couple seeking shelter. "The growing callousness and willingness of people to live side-by-side with this tragedy affects everyone," said the Reverend Pike. "What we see is the erosion of the worth of life, of the dignity of the human person."

In Chicago, there was much ado about politics in December 1988. The nineteenth of the month was the file deadline for candidates wishing to run in the special mayoral primary in February to finish out the remaining two years of the late Harold Washington's term. At the deadline, seven Democrats and eleven Republicans were counted in the field. Former mayor Jane Byrne and former alderman Edward Vrdolyak did not seek election. Among the Democrats was Cook County State's Attorney Richard M. Daley.

In the week before Christmas, the Chicago City Council approved Mayor Eugene Sawyer's gay rights ordinance. The human rights bill prohibited discrimination in housing, employment, and public accommodation based on sexual orientation, age, disability, and other factors. Shortly after approval, the Roman Catholic Archdiocese of Chicago criticized the action, saying it was concerned that the wording of the ordinance might be construed to provide acceptance and approval of homo-sexual acts.

In north suburban Winnetka, two hundred residents turned out for a public hearing on a proposal to ban handguns from the community. Seven months earlier Laurie Dann had gone on a rampage, entering a school first and then a home, shooting six children, one of them fatally, before ending her own life.

1989: Dominoes

The forecast for Chicago's Monday Christmas of 1989 called for clouds, snow flurries, and temperatures in the twenties. That was a relief. Four days before, on Thursday, December 21, the mercury had plunged to thirteen below. The wind chill was minus fifty-four. By Christmas Eve, the extreme cold had gone south—to Florida, to be exact. A wind chill of minus five in the Orlando area prompted the declaration of a state of emergency. Florida's citrus crop was in danger. In the Carolinas, snow piled up in eight-foot drifts.

In Chicago on Christmas Eve, with temperatures in the bitter teens, about five hundred ethnic Romanians attended a rally at Daley Center Plaza. They were there to show their support for the democratic forces then engaged in violent struggles with the crumbling Ceausescu regime on the streets of Bucharest and other Romanian cities. Those in attendance expressed confidence in the final outcome, hope for the future, but fear of what price in human lives it would all cost.

Reports from Romania spoke of a "savage war" and the "fiercest street fighting in Europe since World War II." It included secret police sniper fire that emptied streets and filled morgues with its victims, of citizen roadblocks set up to capture any members of the hated regime who were trying to escape, and of tense and dangerous Christmas celebrations in the city of Timisoara, where the revolution had started on December 15, and where, on Christmas Eve, Christmas trees had been set up at some roadblocks.

The Ceausescu regime was in its last days. In fact, as demonstrators gathered on Daley Plaza in Chicago, dictator Nicolae Ceausescu and his

Under the Tree 1989

Gifts of the season might have included the Sweet Roses Barbie doll ($19.99 at Toys R Us), Radio Flyer Trav-Ler wagons ($49.99), or Milton Bradley's Scattergories board game ($19.99).

Polk Brothers was advertising Brother electric typewriters for $119.95 and Sega video game systems for $79.95.

Radio Shack had just cut its Tandy 286 personal computer $300.00 to $999.00.

At the Movies 1989

Movies of the season included Tom Cruise in Born on the Fourth of July, Tango and Cash, Back to the Future Part 2, The War of the Roses, *and Disney's* The Little Mermaid.

The Bulls 1989

Philadelphia pounded the Bulls 131-104 on Saturday, December 23, 1989. Despite the loss, the Bulls were in first place in the Central Division, 16-9, half a game ahead of Atlanta and Detroit, and one game up on Indiana.

wife Elena were already in the hands of their democratic opponents. An "extraordinary military tribunal" would summarily try them and execute them by firing squad on Christmas Day.

Romania was one in a series of Communist bloc countries that experienced revolution in 1989 as their people threw off the yoke of Communism. The repressive regimes in Poland, East Germany, Czechoslovakia, Hungary, and Romania had toppled like dominoes.

Government reform had already taken place in Poland and Hungary. Perhaps the most symbolic moment came on November 9 when the East German government of just-installed Premier Egon Krenz threw out travel restrictions for its citizens, and holes began to open in the Berlin Wall.

For some, however, the Friday before Christmas was even more significant. It was on that day that the Brandenburg Gate, separating East and West Berlin, was finally opened. Thousands of Germans streamed through from either side, some finally being reunited with family separated by the cold war. There was singing, dancing, and champagne celebrations.

Czechoslovakia's moment came on December 10 after President Gustav Husak resigned and a new coalition cabinet was sworn in. Street demonstrations by more than one hundred thousand Czech citizens had preceded this turn of events which was dubbed "The Velvet Revolution" because of its relative lack of bloodshed.

In Panama the United States had issued a million dollar bounty for Gen. Manuel Noriega. Five days before Christmas, thousands of American soldiers invaded Panama with the intent of ousting the dicta-

tor. The search for Noriega was violent and frantic. Finally, he turned up on Christmas Eve, inside the Vatican embassy in Panama City, where he had asked for political asylum.

Christmas in America

At Christmastime 1989, country-western star Kenny Rogers was out with a new song, entitled "Christmas in America." It included this spoken prayer:

> Dear Lord, we pray, this Christmas Day
> Your love will lift us all.
> And help us see our brothers' needs
> Before we deck our hall.
> And teach us how to give the greatest gift
> we can hand out
> (Song begins.) "Love is what America and
> Christmas is about."

Heeding the message of that song, whether or not actually hearing it, somebody—an anonymous donor—provided five hundred pairs of new shoes for Chicago's disadvantaged children. The shoes and fifty live Christmas trees were distributed Christmas Eve at Holy Angels Parish on the South Side. People showed up at the church after hearing about the gift on radio stations WBBM and WGCI.

A few miles away and a few days earlier, a similar story had played to its happy conclusion. On Monday, December 18, somebody had broken into the trunk of Cynthia Davis's car as it was parked outside the Beale Elementary School at sixtieth and Englewood. The $175 worth of toys for Davis's Head Start preschoolers had been stolen.

The story got a lot of publicity, and as a result individuals and corporations all contributed to make

Christmas happy for Ms. Davis's preschoolers. Jay's Potato Chips provided 150 hot dogs and buns and 150 bags of potato chips. The United Auto Workers union provided apples and oranges. People from all over the area made donations that added up to nearly twelve hundred dollars. The Head Start kids at Beale Elementary had one of their happiest Christmases ever.

For those with the money, there were other gifts, according to the Associated Press:

> For the kid who has almost everything, there's a half-scale Ferrari Testarossa that reaches a maximum speed of 30 miles an hour. It goes out the door for $15,000 and change, and it has a trunk to store the youngster's Nintendo games.
>
> Youngsters accustomed to getting everything on a platinum platter can join their socially correct little pals in winter fun with a minimum of strain. The Hammacher Schlemmer catalog offers a $20 hands-free snowball maker that "helps eliminate wet gloves and cold hands for safer, more comfortable winter fun."

On the day after Christmas, the fifth day of Hanukah, history was made. About a hundred members of Lubavitch Chabad, an international education and social service agency, gathered at Daley Plaza to light the fifth candle of the huge menorah on display there, and to join in Hannukah festivities taking place in Jerusalem, New York, London, Paris, and Moscow via a special worldwide satellite broadcast.

The decade of the 1980s was filled with upheaval and change, and nothing demonstrates this more than the story of Jiang Xue-bing. At the City Colleges of Chicago, the winner of the $100 prize for Christmas card design was Jiang Xue-bing. That was exactly $100 more than he had received for some of his earlier works, which included Mao Tse-Tung's mausoleum and the first subway station in Beijing. City College officials were surprised to find Jiang taking art classes at Truman College in Uptown. Jiang, age forty-seven, had been in the United States five years. He was hoping to be allowed to stay and to become a commercial artist.

LIONEL TRAINS

It was Christmastime 1993, and my wife, Andi, had gone upstairs to retrieve our little, eleven-month-old boy, Jamie, who was just getting up from his nap. While he had been asleep, I had been busy setting up a ring of three-rail track around our newly decorated Christmas tree. On that track, a big, heavy O-gauge Lionel steam engine was chugging around, pulling a tender and various freight cars. It was the train set my father had bought when I was born, way back in 1947.

When Jamie saw the train, his little face lit up with a look of joy and ecstasy that I'll never forget. Talk about making a child happy! And talk about the warm feeling it produces in an adult heart.

Since that Christmas, of course, we have always had a train chugging around the tree, and more often than not the builder of the "layout" has been a Little Boy who loves trains.

I often surmise that that original Lionel set produced the same feelings of warmth and love in my dad when he brought out the set each year for, first, his older son, me, and then for his two little boys. I also often reflect on that old adage about toy trains being as much intended for the fathers as for the sons. Toy trains allow Dad to get down on the floor with his sons and tinker with the track and the couplers and all the equipment.

Joshua Lionel Cowen's first trains were simple, something like a motorized cigar box that ran around a track in a store display window in 1901. But they very quickly captured the American public's fancy.

By 1902, Cowen was out with his first toy train catalogue, which included his first accessory, a bridge. Cowen's Lionel trains were expensive; they cost about a week's pay for the average American worker back then. Through the years Lionels were always expensive, yet always of high quality and always the top-selling brand.

Train whistles were added in the mid-1930s, smoking steam engines in the mid-1940s, and in 1947, Lionel's most popular operating car: the white milk car with the little man who comes out and tosses little metal milk cans onto a platform. Ours still operates occasionally, much to the joy of now six-year-old Jamie.

My wife says she used to complain, as a girl, that she too wanted a toy train. She was always met with the response that they were for boys, not girls. Lionel made an ill-fated attempt to lure girls into the market in 1957 when it produced a pink locomotive and pastel-colored cars. It was a flop then, but probably worth a lot of money now as a collector's item. In any event, my wife's wish was fulfilled a few years before our son was born, when one of our friends presented her with her very own HO gauge train set one Christmas.

By the 1960s train travel and toy trains were falling out of favor, replaced by air travel and toy racing cars. Television replaced the time needed to set up toy train layouts, and "newer" toys caught the fancy and fascination of America's youth.

The Lionel Corporation itself went through several changes in management. The quality of equipment it produced in the 1960s wasn't the same as it had been. By 1967, Roger Miller was singing a Christmas song, remembering the toy trains of earlier times:

Old toy trains, little toy tracks
Little boy toys, comin' from a sack
Carried by a man, dressed in white and red
Little boy, don't you think it's time you
were in bed.

But the Lionel Corporation survived, and if you go to a train store these days you'll find an assortment of very expensive rolling stock lining the shelves. These are for the collectors whose layouts can be seen in an assortment of videos produced in recent years, either to fan the flame of nostalgia or to spark new interest in model electric trains.

The toy train as toy, I'm happy to report, is not dead. This past Christmas, three or four manufacturers, including Lionel, had train sets available, complete with rolling stock, track, and transformer, at an expensive, but not outlandish, price. Some even came with computerized train sounds, producing a lot more noise than you can make with just a simple whistle. These new models offer steam locomotives, not diesels, which is ironic since the only time one can see a steamer these days is on special occasions. The kids still love them (Dads too).

Only a Lionel Electric Train will satisfy your boy!

Because only Lionel trains are realistic in appearance and performance. They are instructive as well as entertaining for every boy!

1990-1999

1991: A Whole New World

Chicago's weather forecast for Christmas Day seemed as if it could be applied to the whole world: mostly sunny and thawing.

The world changed on Christmas Day, 1991. In Moscow on that Wednesday, Mikhail Gorbachev gave a twelve-minute speech that was televised around the world. In it, he resigned as president of the Union of Soviet Socialist Republics. The red flag with the hammer and sickle came down from over the Kremlin. In its place rose the tricolor of Russia. The Soviet Union ceased to exist.

Boris Yeltsin was the new president of the new Commonwealth of Independent States, comprised of eleven of the twelve former Soviet republics. The cold war was officially over.

The U.S. economy was in a recession. Unemployment stood at 6.8 percent of the work force, but the number of payroll jobs had fallen by 241,000 in November. People were worried about their financial future. As a result, they were giving less than usual to charities.

In Chicago, donations to the Salvation Army were down 10 percent from 1990. This was despite the good news on Christmas Eve that an anonymous donor had dropped six more gold coins into a kettle in Crystal Lake, bringing the seasonal total areawide to eighteen. Because of the shortfall, the Salvation Army decided for the first time to extend its kettle campaign. Instead of ending on Christmas Eve, it would end on the Sunday after Christmas.

On the Tube 1991

On TV Christmas Eve you could have seen the 1946 Frank Capra film, It's a Wonderful Life. *In fact, it was hard to miss it. The movie was on nine different times on eight different channels, four over-the-air and four on cable. The 1951 film version of Charles Dickens's* A Christmas Carol *was on twice, once in the original black-and-white and once in the colorized format. Regular network series included* Rescue 911, Home Improvement, Roseanne, *and* The Homefront.

Sports 1991

The Sox got their new stadium in 1991, located at Thirty-fifth & Shields, right across from where the old Comiskey Park once stood.

The Bulls 1991

On Christmas Day, 1991, the champs clobbered Boston 121-99, giving them a record of 21-4 enroute to their second straight championship.

The Salvation Army also planned to provide Christmas dinner for about 3,000 poor people at its two centers in Chicago. The Chicago Christian Industrial League prepared dinners for 1,100 on the West Side. Operation PUSH was readying a thousand food baskets for the needy. Chicago-area food pantries were not short of food; they were the beneficiaries of the U.S. military, which donated millions of dollars worth of food stockpiled during the brief Persian Gulf War.

On the campaign trail, Republican challenger Patrick Buchanan told reporters in Washington that he thought chronically homeless people ought to be locked up as vagrants. "I don't think we should have to have them wandering the streets frightening women and people," he said. Buchanan was hoping to wrest the 1992 GOP nomination away from incumbent president George Bush.

The Chicago Coalition for the Homeless was battling the developers of Presidential Towers just west of the Loop. There was a heated confrontation just before Christmas over the developers' request for tax-exempt state bonds to subsidize their debt. The Coalition used the occasion to dramatize the difficulties low-income people were having in finding affordable housing.

Even the newly deceased were having a difficult time. Workers at twenty-six Chicago-area cemeteries were on strike at Christmastime. The dispute was over wages and health-care costs. It meant that families grieving the loss of a loved one would also have to bear the burden of not being able to bury the deceased, of having to keep the body in storage at some funeral home.

1992: Homes for the Homeless

Chicago's Friday Christmas of 1992 was a cold one. The forecast called for strong winds, a high temperature of twenty-six degrees, with snow likely.

The message being sent from Chicago's churches and synagogues was to remember the poor and oppressed, both in Chicago and around the world. American military forces were just in the initial stages of

Operation Restore Hope, the intervention to end the famine that was devastating people in Somalia. On the Wednesday before Christmas, the U.S. suffered its first casualty of the intervention, when an army civilian employee's vehicle hit a land mine. Rabbi Louis Tuchman of the Chicago Board of Rabbis said that the American intervention in Somalia was "in the true spirit of Hanukkah, raising the standards of people and struggling against repression and tyrants."

In southern Europe, about eight thousand United Nations troops were in Bosnia-Hercegovina to protect convoys bringing aid to refugees. In April, Bosnia-Hercegovina had been recognized as an independent state by the European Community, a condition that radicals in the neighboring and rival states of Serbia and Croatia could not countenance. By December, a campaign of murder, rape, and propaganda was well underway, primarily by Serb paramilitaries, to wrest control of Bosnian towns and drive the Muslim population out. The term "ethnic cleansing" was beginning to be heard.

At midnight mass at Holy Name Cathedral, Joseph Cardinal Bernardin told worshippers the world "is made up of individuals and will change only when each of us changes. . . . Little will be accomplished if we spend most of our time looking for others to blame but refuse to put our own houses in order."

Photo courtesy of the JPUSA archives

Woman and baby at a Chicago shelter

Best-Sellers 1992

Best-sellers on the Chicago Tribune's list at Christmastime included The Tale of the Body Thief *by Anne Rice and* Dolores Claiborne *by Stephen King, and the nonfiction books* Hang Time *by Bob Greene and* Above Chicago *by Robert Cameron.*

At the Movies 1992

Movies of the Christmas season in 1992 included Scent of a Woman *starring Al Pacino,* Toys *with Robin Williams,* Hoffa *starring Jack Nicholson and Danny DeVito, Disney's* Aladdin, The Muppet Christmas Carol, Home Alone 2, *and Eddie Murphy in* The Distinguished Gentleman.

On the Tube 1992

The movie It's a Wonderful Life *was on only five times, three on over-the-air and two on cable. Regularly scheduled TV series included* Cheers, L.A. Law, Room for Two, *and* Homefront.

The Bulls 1992

Christmas Day, 1992, found the Bulls beating New York 89-77 as MJ scored 42 points. That was nearly 10 points more than his league-leading 32.2 ppg scoring average. The Bulls were first in the Central at 18-7. New York was first in the Atlantic division, 16-8 after the loss.

In America thousands were homeless. Incoming president Bill Clinton was just putting his cabinet together, but advocates for the homeless were expecting him to address the issue with a national conference within six months of his inauguration. The actual number of homeless people was in dispute. In 1990, the Census Bureau had set it at 49,793 with another 178,828 living in emergency shelters. But advocates suggested those numbers were flawed because they didn't include people who had received shelter from friends and relatives. One expert at the University of Chicago counted 3,000 people in Chicago's shelters on any given night.

For the poor young people who attended the Schiller Elementary School near the Cabrini-Green housing development, it looked like a mean Christmas. On the Wednesday before the holiday, brightly wrapped presents were to be given to each of the students, handed out by parent volunteers. But, as it happened, some of the volunteers took the presents for themselves, and two hundred children were left with nothing but empty wrapping. For many of these children, those gifts were to have been the only ones they would receive. Montgomery Ward, which had donated many of the original gifts, stepped in again on Wednesday evening replacing the stolen toys.

A Cup of Joe at the Superstore

The Internet existed in 1992, but then it still was the near private preserve of academics, defense officials, and those with computer expertise. At Christmastime newspapers were carrying ads that began:

HEY! MODEM OWNERS!
Get On-line for Free

The ad was for Chicago On-line, a precursor of America On-line. Computer store ads, meanwhile, were touting machines with a 486 chip, and little if any mention was being made of modems.

At the same time, the specialty coffee craze was building steam as it swept the country. Howard Schultz, the president of Starbucks, was one of *INC.* magazine's entrepreneurs of the year in 1992. Starbucks had a presence in Chicago, but was only then plotting an invasion of the East

Coast. Specialty coffees accounted for 20 percent of U.S. coffee sales in 1992, up from 11 percent eight years before. Schultz was predicting 30 percent of the market by 1994.

Another trend, noted primarily in business magazines, was the growth of giant super bookstores, where customers could enjoy a cup of specialty coffee while browsing books and magazines.

If business was good for coffee bars and bookstores, it wasn't so good at Sears. On the Monday before Christmas, the Chicago-based retailer announced plans to close one hundred stores around the country.

According to a Harris poll conducted at Christmastime, 77 percent of adults planned to give children clothing for Christmas. The poll allowed respondents to name more than one gift, and 70 percent said they'd give games or puzzles, 69 percent mentioned books, 48 percent said dolls, 29 percent electronic games. The top gifts for adults were clothing, money, and perfume or cologne.

On the Monday before Christmas, the citizens' group Common Cause called for a House Ethics Committee investigation into one of the nation's best-known congressmen, Dan Rostenkowski of Chicago. Rostenkowski was being accused of using campaign funds to rent space in a building that he himself owned, a violation of House ethics rules. He was the chairman of the Ways and Means Committee, and broadcast reports usually prefixed his title with the adjective "powerful." Within a few years, Rostenkowski would be defeated for re-election by a relatively unknown and unheralded Republican, and spend months in a federal prison.

1994: Yule by the Pool

"Yule by the Pool?" was the headline atop the *Chicago Sun-Times* on the morning of Saturday, Christmas Eve, 1994. That Christmas holiday weekend would be balmy by Chicago standards. The mercury hit a high of fifty-two degrees on Christmas Day. It was only the ninth time since 1871 that the thermometer registered fifty degrees or better on Christmas Day in Chicago.

A few days earlier another weather phenomenon combined with a new city law to cause confusion, near panic, and then anger among Chicago's firefighters and paramedics. On the night of Wednesday,

Under the Tree 1994

What was number one on the Christmas shopping lists of mid-westerners? Clothing, according to a survey by Deloitte and Touche. Sixty-three percent of midwestern shoppers put wearing apparel at the top of their lists. Toys were the second most popular category (56 percent), followed by jewelry (33 percent), electronics and sporting goods (23 percent each).

The biggest selling toy was sets of Mighty Morphin Power Rangers action figures. Spotty shortages were reported throughout North America, as the manufacturer could not keep up with demand. Barbie dolls were also popular, as were Talking Baby Simba and Storytelling Pooh dolls.

Top Songs 1994

Kenny G's Miracles: the Holiday Album *was the top-selling album at Christmastime 1994. It sold more than seven hundred thousand copies within eight weeks of its release.*

The most popular singles, according to Billboard *magazine, were "Here Comes the Hotstepper" by Ini Kamoze, "On Bended Knee" by Boyz II Men, "Another Night" by Real McCoy, "Always" by Bon Jovi, and "Creep" by TLC.*

At the Movies 1994

The new movies of the season included Little Women *with* Winona Ryder, Gabriel Byrne, Trini Alvarado, *and* Susan Sarandon; Mixed Nuts *with Steve Martin;* Richie Rich *with Macaulay Culkin;* Disclosure *with Michael Douglas and Demi Moore; and* Dumb and Dumber *with Jim Carrey and Jeff Daniels.*

The Bulls 1994

On Christmas Day, 1994, it was Scottie Pippen's 36 points leading the Bulls to a tough 107-104 overtime victory over the Knicks. But the team was only a mediocre 13-12 and in fourth place in the Central Division. The Bull's leading scorer, Michael Jordan, had decided to retire from basketball in 1993. They sure wished Michael Jordan would come back from retirement.

December 21, a thermal inversion trapped warm air over the city, and with it the carbon monoxide exhausts from cars, trucks, buses, and other sources. It was the first time in seven years that outdoor levels of the gas had exceeded the federal standard in Chicago. It was also the first time that this condition had occurred since the city had ordered all homes and apartment buildings to install carbon monoxide detectors. That law went into effect October 1, 1994. The result was a staggering 1,852 emergency calls to the fire department as home carbon monoxide detectors kept going off all through the night. Only one call turned out to be a real emergency.

The next morning fire commissioner Raymond Orozco appealed to citizens not to call for help unless somebody in the household was actually experiencing symptoms of carbon monoxide poisoning. There was some finger-pointing at the company that made most of the detectors, and complaints that they were defective or too sensitive. The company agreed to offer refunds, the inversion dissipated, and by Christmas Eve, everything was back to normal except for the unusually warm temperatures.

Not back to normal by a long shot was the world of baseball. In 1994, for the first time in ninety years, the owners of the teams were forced to cancel the World Series. That was because the players had gone on strike on August 12. It was a preemptive move designed to stop the owners from imposing their own system of doing things, including a cap on how much of baseball's revenue could be used for player salaries. On the Thursday before Christmas, with no progress toward a negotiated settlement, the owners unilaterally imposed their system, salary cap and all.

Jerry McMorris, the owner of the Colorado Rockies, in what the *Chicago Tribune* called a "stunning" statement, admitted that the owners needed help in controlling their own spending habits. He said he felt it was the players' duty to help because the owners were too "fiercely competitive" to do it themselves. Players union chief Donald Fehr reacted: "What has been said is that, left to their own devices, the owners can't stop themselves. They are going to make sure that the industry is shut down until the union agrees to stop management."

It all made for a bitter Christmas for baseball fans. It was a bitterness that lasted into 1995, when attendance was down for a shortened baseball season.

If the Christmas spirit was not alive and well in the world of baseball, it certainly was in the heart of Chicago cab driver Clarence Williams. When Williams found a wallet containing $1,025 in the back of his cab, instead of pocketing the money he took it to the Monroe District police station. Two hours later the cash was reunited with its owner, army sergeant Stanton Walker, who had lost it on the trip to his West Side home. The money was for Christmas presents for his family. "I'm glad there's still someone out there honest enough to think about someone else's Christmas and return something vitally important to me," said Walker. "I wanted this guy to remember this Christmas," said cabbie Williams.

Also giving special thanks on the Christmas of 1994 was Wheaton insurance executive Donald Merkel. He was just back home at Christmastime, after spending nine days in a Raleigh, North Carolina, hospital, one of five survivors rescued from the crash of an American Eagle commuter plane. Fifteen other people died in the crash.

When Merkel was asked what he thought about being among the few survivors, he referred to the guardian angel in the classic Christmas movie *It's a Wonderful Life:* "I guess Clarence was on my shoulder."

Following brain surgery a few days before Christmas, Chicory the gorilla was back at Brookfield Zoo and recovering nicely. It was the first time doctors at Loyola Medical Center had ever removed a tumor from a gorilla's brain. A sign that it was successful, according to the *Sun-Times,* was that back at the zoo Chicory tried to take a bite out of his veterinarian's arm.

1995: Christmas in Sarajevo

The Christmas of 1995 was not a white one. The ground was barren of snow in Chicago on that Monday, despite mostly cloudy skies, gusty winds, and an occasional snow flurry. The high temperature was in the low thirties.

Da Bears 1995

Bears' owner Michael McCaskey was dissatisfied with the city's plan for revamping Soldier Field when the team's lease expired in 1999. He was looking closely at an offer from a northwest Indiana group to build a new stadium, Planet Park, in Gary.

This came amid the backdrop of the Browns moving out of Cleveland for Baltimore, and the Oilers abandoning Houston for Nashville. Mayor Daley was incensed; he accused McCaskey and other NFL owners of being greedy. Bears' management accused the mayor of trying to negotiate a stadium deal through the news media.

The Chicago area did have a football team it could applaud loudly at Christmastime 1995. The Northwestern Wildcats were in southern California, preparing for their first Rose Bowl appearance since 1949. Theirs had been a surprising Cinderella season, with victories over powerhouses Notre Dame, Michigan, and Penn State.

It was a grim Christmas for 280,000 federal workers nationwide, including thousands in Chicago. The federal government was in partial shutdown, and "inessential" workers were without work—and without pay—because of a budget fight between Congress and President Bill Clinton. The Republican-controlled Congress wanted a working plan to balance the federal budget by the year 2002 before it would approve any funding measure; Democrat Clinton had agreed to that idea, provided it did not cut too deeply into social programs, like Medicare and Medicaid. It would be the first weekend of the new year before a deal was struck to send workers back to their jobs, with no balanced budget plan yet in sight.

It was a very different kind of Christmas for American soldiers moving into Bosnia, where ethnic differences were tearing that country apart. The *Chicago Sun-Times* carried this story on Christmas Day:

BOSNIA FOES SWAP 200 PRISONERS
by Kurt Schork

REUTERS, SARAJEVO—Serb and Muslim armies swapped more than 200 prisoners of war Sunday in a Christmas Eve gesture.

In Sarajevo, the Muslim-led government army left some of its most fiercely contested front-line positions in the Bosnian capital in compliance with NATO demands to pull back from military trouble spots throughout the city.

The two events highlighted the slow arrival of peace after 43 months of war. Europe's worst conflict in a half century killed 200,000 people and displaced as many as 3 million.

The commander of the NATO force, U.S. Adm. Leighton Smith, said he foresees little more than isolated resistance that would be dealt with swiftly.

"There may be pockets of resistance and localized skirmishes but they will be of very short duration," he said.

Across the country, units of the NATO force, which will be 60,000-strong at its height, improvised Christmas with tinsel and turkey in the billets and barracks where they are based to keep Muslim, Croat and Bosnian Serbs apart.

Thousands of turkeys and Christmas puddings have been flown in to boost morale for homesick soldiers in a potentially dangerous place.

For the 20,000 U.S. soldiers participating—including those still in Hungary, Croatia or Germany—the Pentagon menu includes 28,500 pounds of turkey, 23,250 pounds of ham, 2,520 cans of cranberry sauce, 10,530 pounds of corn, and 1,125 cans of olives.

The NATO Implementation Force took over from the United Nations last Wednesday. Its only setbacks so far have been three unexplained but harmless attacks on two NATO aid aircraft and the wounding on Saturday of two British soldiers when their vehicle detonated one of several million land mines strewn across the country.

The Dayton, Ohio, peace accords brought real comfort to families when Bosnian Serb and government armies released prisoners of war, some of whom have been held for two years.

Serb officers said 114 Serbs and 131 troops of the Muslim-led government were freed in a ceremony on a bridge between Serb held Sockovac and government-held Gracanica.

Prisoners from both sides looked tired and nervous as they lined up for release. They did not appear emaciated and were wearing winter clothes supplied by relief agencies. (Copyright 1988 by Reuters Limited.)

The message at midnight mass in Bethlehem was also one of peace. Latin patriarch Michel Sabbah told worshippers: "The beginning of Palestinian freedom is the beginning of reconciliation between Jews and Palestinians." Bethlehem was under Palestinian rule in 1995. Palestinian leader Yasser Arafat, a Muslim, attended the service in the Church of the Nativity with his Christian wife. Throughout Christmas Eve, a carnival atmosphere was reported in Manger Square, with fluttering Palestinian flags, huge pictures of Arafat, and a laser-light dove of peace shown on buildings in the square.

In Chicago at Christmastime, some Chicago police were enforcing an ordinance holding bar owners responsible for rowdy patrons. The problem was that the ordinance had never been passed, only proposed. Ald. Eugene Schulter (47th) accused police officers of harassing departing bar patrons, asking them where they'd had their last drink.

Just before Christmas Gov. Jim Edgar appointed a thirty-four-member commission to suggest a statewide strategy for dealing with street gangs. The panel included police officers, prosecutors, professors, preachers, politicians, and parents.

During the week before Christmas, Chicago agonized over two more cases involving the discovery of children found alone in cold, filthy, dilapidated apartments. The mothers of the eleven children were charged with neglect. At the same time, the Illinois Department of Children and Family Services (DCFS) held its annual Big Holiday Fun party for two hundred children waiting for adoption.

In Santa Monica, California, actor Jimmy Stewart was back home in time for Christmas. The eighty-seven-year-old movie star had tripped over a plant and hit his head on a table leg the Thursday evening before Christmas. He was described as being "in good spirits and in good condition." Stewart, of course, was the star in the Christmas film classic, *It's a Wonderful Life*. The movie itself was forty-nine years old in 1995 and still seemingly omnipresent on the nation's television screens. That was before rights to it were gobbled up by a media company and turned into a once-a-year event.

The Bulls 1995

Michael Jordan was back for the 1995–1996 season, and so were the Bulls. Jordan's 30 points led the Bulls to a 100–86 victory over Utah on Saturday, December 23, 1995. The Bulls sported a record of 23–2, and Jordan was again the NBA scoring leader with an average of 30.0 ppg. The Bulls would win their fourth NBA title of the '90s in the spring of '96.

At the Movies 1995

Toy Story, the first completely computer-generated animated film, was number one at the movie box office. Other movies of the season included Waiting to Exhale, Cutthroat Island, Grumpier Old Men, Sabrina, Tom and Huck, Jumanji, *and* Nixon.

Top Songs 1995

"One Sweet Day" by Mariah Carey and Boyz II Men was atop the music singles chart. Anthology 1, a re-release of the Beatles, was the top album. Aaron Tippin's "That's As Close As I'll Get to Loving You" was the top country tune. "Exhale (Shoop Shoop)" by Whitney Houston was tops in rhythm and blues. "Glycerine" by Bush was number one on the modern rock chart.

Under the Tree 1995

The top toy of 1995 was the Barbie doll. The Special Edition 1995 Happy Holidays Barbie was so popular that many stores were sold out. They had to offer vouchers promising delivery of the doll early in 1996, but too late for Santa Claus.

Under the Tree 1996

Carson Pirie Scott & Co. had fur-trimmed London Fog parkas for $99.99 or $119.99. Comp USA was giving away thirteen-inch color TVs with the purchase of new computers; models included the Compaq 166 MHz Pentium for $1,999.99 (after rebate) and the Toshiba 100 MHz color notebook for $1,399.99 (after rebate).

Sportmart was selling kids' Bladerunner in-line skates for $39.97, men's or women's Rollerblade models were $79.97 to $199.97. Walgreen's last-minute gift suggestions included CD/AM/FM boom-boxes from RCA for $59.99, GE cordless phones for $29.99, or GE answering machines for $24.99.

The Clipper Ship Gallery in LaGrange was advertising prints of Charles Vickery's oil painting, Christmas Tree Ship, for $205,00 unframed.

1996: Christmas on Death Row

The Christmas of 1996 was nearly picture postcard perfect. On Monday, December 23, a quarter inch of snow fell to the ground. On Christmas Eve, there were a few more snow flurries, leaving Chicago with a beautifully white Christmas, although a bit colder than usual with temperatures in the teens. A few days later, the mercury shot into the sixties, and all the snow was gone. The snow came just in time, didn't get too deep, and left promptly.

Also gone, long gone, from the shelves of toy stores that year was the enormously popular Tickle Me Elmo doll. Based on a *Sesame Street* character, the cuddly doll giggled or said something when its side was pressed, and for some reason it set off a craziness that's hard to fathom.

As early as October 15, *USA Today* had identified Elmo as one of 1996's "hot holiday playthings." By December 5, the Associated Press reported a nationwide phenomenon of "blood pressure rising among moms and dads competing for the hottest, hard-to-find Christmas toys, like Tickle Me Elmo dolls and Nintendo 64."

Some people just had to have Elmo for their children. They were willing to do anything. Some lined up way before dawn outside stores that were rumored to have a fresh shipment of the dolls. Others were willing

Shoppers at Water Tower Place

Photo by Terry Wheeler

196

to pay big bucks. The result was a sort of black market for Elmos. As Christmas approached, Chicago newspapers were filled with classified ads offering the dolls for $300, $450, even as much as $1,200! Elmos cost about $30 at the store—if you could find any there.

The craze for Elmos was being compared to the frenzy over Cabbage Patch dolls back in 1983. The phenomenon was even satirized in Arnold Schwarzenegger's timely movie, *Jingle All the Way*.

Adults pushing and shoving and fighting over children's playthings is certainly not what anyone would associate with the true spirit of Christmas. Yet, as the twentieth century drew to a close it was only one symptom of an incipient incivility in society that has had many of America's deepest thinkers concerned. Columnist George Will made the case in a commentary printed in the *Chicago Sun-Times* two days before Christmas, 1996:

> The eclipse of civility is a fact fraught with depressing significance, as explained in the autumn *Wilson Quarterly*, in essays by Richard Bushman, a Columbia historian, and James Morris of the Woodrow Wilson International Center for Scholars. The gravamen of their arguments is: a coarse and slatternly society—boomboxes borne through crowded streets by young men wearing pornographic T-shirts and baseball caps backward; young women using, in what formerly was called polite society, language that formerly caused stevedores to blush—jeopardizes all respect, including self-respect.

Many would identify rap music as one of the forces shaping this incivility because of the violence and degradation of the lyrics of some artists. Their work has tarred the entire genre in many minds. Even the titles of some CDs are turnoffs for many, like *Christmas on Death Row*, released by Death Row Records in time for the holiday of 1996.

Sun-Times columnist Richard Roeper listened carefully to that CD and found redeeming value. Not only did some of the music have a catchy tune, but some of the lyrics carried a 1990s version of the message "Peace on Earth, good will toward men." Like Danny Boy's lyric:

> I'm dreaming of a peaceful Christmas this year
> They'll be puttin' all the guns away...

At the Movies 1996

Movies of the season included Michael Jordan in Space Jam, Disney's 101 Dalmatians, Whitney Houston and Denzel Washington in The Preacher's Wife, Arnold Schwarzenegger in Jingle All the Way, and Jack Lemmon, James Garner, and Dan Akroyd in My Fellow Americans.

On Stage 1996

Charles Dickens's A Christmas Carol was at the Goodman Theatre, the revival Show Boat was at the Auditorium, Joseph and the Amazing Technicolor Dreamcoat was at the Chicago Theatre, and Sunset Boulevard was at the Civic Opera House.

The Bulls 1996

On Christmas Day, 1996, Michael Jordan scored 23 points as the Bulls beat Detroit 95–83. It was the Bulls' eighteenth straight victory over the Pistons. The Bulls were in first place, 25–3.

Or from The Dogg Pound's "I Wish:"

> I done a lot of crazy things in my day
> Please forgive me for sins
> This is the first time in nineteen years that I've prayed
> To be straight up and serious
> I believe in you God, my mom says you work miracles.

"Way to go, kid," wrote Roeper. Perhaps "I Wish" will someday become a Christmas standard.

1998: Toy Story

Friday, Christmas Day, was a partly sunny day in the Chicago area. The temperature climbed into the low thirties. There was no snow on the ground. Nor had there been much of a chance for any. From late November into mid-December, Chicago had experienced a series of unusually mild days, with temperatures getting into the high fifties and even the mid-sixties.

The weather was nice in Chicago at Christmas, but it was miserable in other parts of the country. A wide swath of freezing rain fell from Texas across much of the South, snarling the travel plans of millions. A huge ice storm brought down tree limbs and power lines in Virginia and the Carolinas; thousands of customers were without power for more than a week. In New Jersey, snow may have been a contributing factor in a bus crash that killed eight people. In California, three straight nights of cold killed much of the nation's crop of navel oranges.

Weather of a different sort snarled the travel plans of three adventurer-balloonists. When Chicagoan Steve Fossett, British tycoon Richard Branson, and Swede Per Lindstrand encountered a low pressure system over the Pacific Ocean, it dashed their plans to become the first to fly around the world in a balloon.

On Christmas Day they landed in the waters off Oahu, Hawaii, after having traveled twelve thousand miles since takeoff a week earlier in Marrakech, Morocco. During their voyage, they crossed the Himalaya Mountains and rode jet-stream winds halfway across the Pacific.

The Christmas holiday of 1998 provided a desired respite from all the talk about the Lewinsky scandal in Washington and the military action in Iraq. However, the specter of impeachment hovered over the news of the day like the Ghost of Christmas-Yet-to-Come. On the Saturday before Christmas, following hours of impassioned debate, weeks of speculation, months of

Photo courtesy of JPUSA archives

legal sparring, and years of costly investigation, the U.S. House of Representatives voted to approve two articles of impeachment against President Clinton. He was accused of lying under oath to a grand jury and of obstructing justice. The accusations stemmed not from land dealings he had had while he was governor of Arkansas, which was the original target of the investigation, but from his attempt to cover up sexual encounters between himself and a White House intern, Monica Lewinsky, a woman half his age.

Two days before the U.S. House began its impeachment debate, Mr. Clinton ordered U.S. military forces to strike Iraq. It was an action that had been threatened time and again against Iraqi dictator Saddam Hussein because of his intransigence in allowing United Nations weapons inspectors to search sites in his country for evidence of biological, chemical, and nuclear weapons. The timing of the strike prompted some pro-impeachment Republicans to question whether the real motive behind it was an attempt to delay the impeachment debate.

On the Sunday before Christmas, twenty-seven-year-old Nkem Chukwu, a Nigerian immigrant, gave birth to seven babies at Texas Children's Hospital in Houston. Earlier, on December 8, an eighth baby had been born. "Stunned beyond belief" was the way father Iyke Louis Udobi described his reaction. "I'm still taking it in," he told reporters on Christmas Eve. On Christmas Day, all of the infants were on ventilation and doctors were optimistic. But the smallest of the group would not survive through the weekend.

In Chicago, an anonymous donor had been dropping a gold coin into a Salvation Army kettle since 1982. The publicity generated by that kind gift started a tradition of sorts, causing a stir over both the form and the value of the donation. Every year, somebody—and obviously more than just one person—dropped gold coins into Chicago-area kettles. On Christmas Eve, 1998, Salvation Army spokesman Robert Bonesteel reported that fifty-five gold coins had been collected during the season, including an 1859 double eagle minted in San Francisco. The Salvation Army had already achieved 60 percent of its winter fund-raising goal of $5.9 million.

Under the Tree 1998

Handheld electronic game systems ($129.00) were still popular in 1998, with software titles ranging from $40.00 to $60.00. Barbie dolls were still around, selling for $9.99, even as older versions of Barbie had developed collectors' status and value. The singing group Spice Girls was being immortalized in "dolldom" ($10.77 a set), as were the British TV imports, the Teletubbies ($4.44).

For adults, there was an amazing cornucopia of electronic gear to put under the Christmas tree—and prices were low because of an economic crisis that was sweeping Asia, where much of the stuff was made. There were DVD video systems ($300.00), WebTV Internet browsers ($200.00), even direct TV systems with satellite dishes. A good home computer system could be acquired for around $1,100.00.

On the Table 1998

The Christmas turkey of 1998 could be had for 59¢ a pound at Dominick's. A twenty-four-can case of soda pop was selling for $3.99. A four-pound bag of California navel oranges was 89¢.

At the Movies 1998

Movies of the season included A Bug's Life, Star Trek Insurrection, Jack Frost, You've Got Mail, *and* Prince of Egypt. *Opening Christmas Day would be* Patch Adams, Down in the Delta, *and* The Faculty.

On the Tube 1998

In 1998 the TV had metamorphosed into a global communications tool where one could dial up over 170 stations on the satellite dish. On Christmas Eve, there was a one-hour special that saluted the American Red Cross and honored people who had triumphed over adversity, or HGTV's "Christmas Across America" show, touring holiday celebrations in over two-dozen cities. The erstwhile 1947 movie Miracle on 34th Street *was also playing that evening. And, of course, there was the televised midnight mass from Holy Name Cathedral.*

Polar Express

In the Chicago area there were many special Christmas activities with kids in mind. The annual Christmas Around the World was taking place at the Museum of Science and Industry, Holiday Magic at the Brookfield Zoo, and the special Festival of Lights at the Lincoln Park Zoo. A number of suburban park districts and other organizations reserved special cars on Metra trains to allow children to experience the magic of the story *Polar Express* by Chris Van Allsburg. Amid sugar cookies and hot chocolate, the book is read to children as they ride to a rendezvous with Santa Claus.

On Christmas Eve, 1998, Chicago area-lawyer Ed McNally took the story one step further. According to the *Chicago Sun-Times*, he rented a school bus and took his seventeen nieces and nephews, all clad in pajamas, robes, and slippers—just like in the story—to breakfast, then to a bookstore for a reading of the book, and then on to a toy store in Northbrook where they selected their own presents (within certain limits).

"I'm the brother that's not married and when the kids are with me, all the rules are suspended," McNally told the newspaper. "My sisters think it's Christmas genius. In two hours I'm done shopping with two swipes of a credit card."

It has become somewhat of a tradition that as early as October a certain toy will be declared the hottest of the season. The news media picks up on this and a frenzy is created. There are mad scenes of adults scrambling to purchase the desired toy. A black market for the toy may even develop. In 1998, the "toy of the season" was the Furby, a gremlinlike fuzz ball that spoke its own language. The product was launched with a massive public relations blitz on morning TV shows in October. A bandwagon effect was created, and very soon Furbys were flying off store shelves. The problem was, and is, that children themselves don't decide what "the toy of the season" will be. "The hot toy is just another term for hyped toy," Marianne Szymanski of Marquette University's toy research center told the Associated Press. Furby retailed for about $30. In the classified ads during Christmas week, up to $800 was being asked for black-market Furbys.

According to PNC Bank Corporation of Pittsburgh, the cost in 1998 of all the gifts mentioned in the carol "The Twelve Days of Christmas" (twelve drummers drumming, eleven pipers piping, etc.), if purchased just once, was $14,214.90, or an increase of 6.5 percent over 1997. The cost, if purchases were made repeatedly as the song suggests, would be $58,405.09. The bank's former chief economist had started keeping track of the costs of the gifts back in 1982 as a form of comic relief.

Favorite Holiday Songs

The American Society of Composers, Authors, and Publishers (ASCAP) came out with a list of the most-performed holiday songs written by its members:

1. "White Christmas" by Irving Berlin
2. "Santa Claus Is Coming to Town" by J. Fred Coots and Haven Gillespie
3. "The Christmas Song (Chestnuts Roasting on an Open Fire)" by Mel Torme and Robert Wells
4. "Winter Wonderland" by Felix Bernard and Richard B. Smith
5. "Rudolph the Red-Nosed Reindeer" by Johnny Marks
6. "Sleigh Ride" by Leroy Anderson and Mitchell Parish
7. "Have Yourself a Merry Little Christmas" by Ralph Blane and Hugh Martin
8. "Silver Bells" by Jay Livingston and Ray Evans
9. "Let It Snow! Let It Snow! Let it Snow!" by Sammy Cahn and Jule Styne
10. "Little Drummer Boy" by Katherine K. Davis, Henry V. Onorati and Harry Simeone

Left off the list was "Silent Night," which an Ohio University/Scripps Howard poll found to be Americans' favorite Christmas song, three times more popular than "Jingle Bells," which also was not on the ASCAP list. That's because both were written before there was an ASCAP.

The Ohio University/Scripps Howard poll found that the most disliked holiday song was Dr. Elmo's 1979 release, "Grandma Got Run Over by a Reindeer." Dr. Elmo, really Elmo Shropshire, a California vet-

Top Songs 1998

Topping the pop-music singles chart were "I'm Your Angel" by R. Kelly & Celine Dion, "Nobody's Supposed to Be Here" by Deborah Cox, and "Lately" by Divine. Top albums included Garth Brooks's Double Live, These Are Special Times *by Celine Dion, and* N Sync *by N Sync.*

The Bulls 1998

For many people, a recent tradition had been to watch the Bulls play the Knicks on TV on Christmas Day. It didn't happen in 1998. The players were still locked out in the first labor dispute to disrupt the operation of the National Basketball Association. A women's league, the American Basketball League, had tried to fill the entertainment gap for hoop-starved fans. But it failed, filing for bankruptcy protection three days before Christmas.

erinarian, was out with a new album for the Christmas of 1998. *Entitled Dr. Elmo's Twisted Christmas,* it included the song "Don't Make Me Play That Grandma Song Again."

The Ohio University/Scripps Howard poll concluded that Christmas was America's favorite holiday. Fifty-nine percent of the 1,027 people questioned named it as such. Eighty-three percent said they planned to have a decorated tree in their homes.

A survey by the national pet store chain Pet Supplies Plus found that ninety-five percent of its customers planned to buy gifts for their pets at Christmas, spending about $14 on each animal. Eighty-two percent said they planned to wrap their gifts. Twenty-four percent said they'd spend more on their pets than on their in-laws. The most popular pet gifts included "Edible Holiday Cards" ($3), "The Buster Food Cube" ($20) for dogs and "The Play-n-Treat" ($3) for cats.

Y2K: Predictions for the Next Century

On Sunday, December 23, 1900, there appeared in the feature pages of the *Chicago Sunday Tribune* a long, anonymous essay about what Christmas would be like in the year 2000. The author suggested that relatively few people would be interested in Christmas, that the day would merely be a quiet holiday away from work or school. He wrote that Santa Claus and St. Nicholas would have become myths, and that the practice of gift giving would have long been abandoned because of the frustrations of shopping in crowded stores ("It came to be a season for trampling down a thousand fellow beings in order to give the trophies of the fight

to a dozen.") and the burdens it placed on home budgets. The author thought Christmas trees would be passé, that the practice of denuding northern forests would have ended by about 1925.

He also believed that church creeds would be a thing of the past, replaced by a humanitarian ecumenism ("From every pulpit the fellowship of man had been preached for three score years, and on this broad line, as far as social conditions made it necessary, the day was observed.") and that all human beings would have more than enough of everything they needed, so that "money had ceased to be the end toward which all people moved."

As far as daily life was concerned, the author foresaw quiet, rubber-tired, electrical mass transit moving at eighty miles an hour and expanding the Chicago metropolitan area to suburbs fifty-five miles from downtown. As a result, he wrote, skyscrapers would no longer be necessary. He believed we would achieve perfection in the combustion of coal and the insulation of electric wires.

The author wrote at a time when horseless carriages, electric lights, and local telephones were brand new and amazing innovations. The Wright brothers had not yet flown, the first radio message had not yet been sent across the Atlantic, moving pictures had only been used to record sights and not yet used to tell a story. Imagine what the writer would make of today's air travel, television, and the Internet! Or of the horrors of the world wars and the threat of nuclear annihilation that would unfold in the twentieth century.

What will the Christmas of 2100 be like in Chicago? Predicting so far in the future, especially in times of such rapid technological change, is a riskier proposition today than it was for the writer of 1900.

Who can deny that parents in 2100 will still find delicious warmth in watching their little children's faces light up in joy at the sight of brightly wrapped Christmas presents? Maybe even those toys will include some from today that have passed the tests of time. How about a twenty-second-century Barbie? Or a computerized electric train?

Whatever the toys of 2100, or other Christmas gifts, they are certain to be discussed and advertised in media we haven't even conceived of as yet. The twentieth century brought us radio, TV, and the Internet. Who can guess what the ever-growing media will be like in a hundred years? One thing is certain, however, there will be advertising—that industry is not going to disappear in a hundred years.

But shopping for Christmas gifts will most likely be an electronic affair. Gifts will be bought and sold over whatever generation of the Internet is in place in 2100, and delivered to doorsteps from all over the world.

The Chicago megalopolis has already spread beyond the fifty-five mile radius that that author of long ago predicted. But telecommuting in the twenty-first century will likely reduce the need for a corporate office. Home offices should make for a decentralization of urban areas and less congestion. But I doubt that skyscrapers will be obsolete.

From the pulpits of 2100, ministers will still preach peace and goodwill toward all men. That's because mankind won't have completely achieved it, just as we did not fare very well in the past one hundred years. It seems to be part of the human condition that people will have to work for a universal fellowship and respect for one another. Chicagoans can hope, however, that the next century will find them moving toward a world in which all people will have a voice, a share, and a stake in their future.

What's to come will be answered by and by, but as long as the charity and goodwill of Christmastime remains, there is reason for hope and optimism.

Merry Christmas, everybody!

Photo courtesy of Marshall Field's

Christmas tree at Marshall Field's

Your own Christmas Memories

Your own Christmas Memories

Your own Christmas Memories

Your own Christmas Memories

Your own Christmas Memories

Your own Christmas Memories